BRET HARTE
Argonaut and Exile

BRET HARTE
Argonaut and Exile

Being an *Account* of the *Life* of the *Celebrated
American Humorist*, author of 'THE LUCK
OF ROARING CAMP,' 'CONDENSED NOVELS,'
'THE HEATHEN CHINEE,' 'TALES OF THE
ARGONAUTS,' &c., &c., compiled from new
and original sources

BY

GEORGE R. STEWART, JR.

With Illustrations

KENNIKAT PRESS, INC./PORT WASHINGTON, N. Y.

BRET HARTE IN 1871

THEODOSIAE
QVAE MECVM ADSECVTA EST
CERVVM
QVATTVOR IN
NATIONIBVS

PREFACE

THE investigation upon which this biography is based has extended over a period of eight years. During that time I have visited every place of importance in connection with Harte's life, and have made an honest effort to find all the extant information about him. Although Harte died less than thirty years ago, anyone studying his career is confronted by decided difficulties resulting from the great destruction of records of the early West, from the legend which rapidly developed about him, from his own comparative obscurity before the age of thirty, from his extreme reticence about himself, and from his romantic imagination, which colored what few reminiscences he did leave. In general, I may say that for the earlier half of Harte's life there is a dearth of biographical information, so that except for a complete bibliography of his writings the present volume contains almost all that I have been able to discover about him for that period. For the later half of his life there is much more material, and my problem has been one of selection, so that this less important period of his life should be fairly but not disproportionately presented.

I have passed over very summarily a number of legends (see notes on Chapters VI, VII, and VIII). A biographer is, I believe, pledged to investigate carefully even the most incredible tales, but I see no reason why, having once decided negatively, he should include in his own pages an elaborate refutation of every cock-and-bull story which a credulous or unscrupulous editor may have allowed to appear in print. The burden of proof certainly lies on the other side.

On the whole I have tried to limit myself to the presentation of facts and to avoid much discussion of cause and motive which involves the acceptance of some special theory of psychology. There are, for instance, two outstanding 'problems' in Harte's artistic development — his rapid rise in the late sixties, and his almost equally rapid decline in the middle seventies. Until psychology is much more of an exact science than it is at present, no final solution of either of these will be possible, and I have been content to present all the available facts which seemed to me pertinent to aid the reader in working out for himself any partial solution to which his own personality and training might incline him.

I have devoted but little space to criticism of Harte's work. This has resulted partly from the necessity of keeping the book within a reasonable size, but more from my belief that criticism and biography are essentially different. I have naturally paid much attention to what may be called the biographical aspect of his writings — for instance, to the ways in which they grew out of his own experiences and in which they themselves reacted in turn to influence his life — but I have not in general attempted to expound their significance or to appraise their value as literature.

In the course of my work I have received assistance from so many persons and availed myself of the services of so many libraries, both public and private, that to attempt individual acknowledgment would make this preface resemble the directory of a sizable town. I must therefore be content with a generalized expression of my gratitude. Some specific acknowledgments will be

Preface

found among the notes. I should also like to say that from the scores who have been the objects of my often importunate inquiries I have only in a negligible number of cases received anything except courtesy and active coöperation. A few individuals, however, I cannot without blameworthy ingratitude pass by. Three members of the Harte family have in various ways graciously given their highly valuable assistance — Mrs. Samuel J. Taylor, Miss Ethel Bret Harte, and Mr. Geoffrey Bret Harte. I am also too deeply in debt to fail to mention Mr. Willard S. Morse, Herr Doctor Professor Rembert of Crefeld, and Mrs. Ella Wilson Stewart.

For having read all or part of the book while in manuscript or proof I am grateful to Mr. John McFadzean, Mrs. Leon J. Wiley, and Professor Harold L. Bruce.

I wish also to make acknowledgments with thanks to the following companies and individuals for permission to quote from copyrighted material not elsewhere acknowledged: to Houghton Mifflin Company for general permission to quote from Harte's writings and from others of their copyrighted works; to the Century Company for a quotation from Noah Brooks's *Bret Harte in California* (*Century Magazine*, July, 1899); to Harper and Brothers for several passages from "The Editor's Easy Chair" (*Harper's Magazine*, December, 1903), and from *Mark Twain's Autobiography* (ed. Albert Bigelow Paine); to the Curtis Publishing Company for four stanzas from a poem by Harte appearing in L. A. Lathrop's "Recollections of a Consul" (*Saturday Evening Post*, April 11, 1925); to the *Overland Monthly* and *Out West Magazine* for several brief items by or about Harte specifically acknowledged in the notes; to Charles Scribner's Sons for a passage from the *Life of James*

(ix)

Preface

Anthony Froude by Herbert Paul; to C. Arthur Pearson, Ltd., for several short quotations from T. E. Pemberton's *Bret Harte*; to Miss Margaret E. Murdock for several sentences from *A Backward Glance at Eighty* by her father, the late Charles A. Murdock, published by Paul Elder and Company; to Mr. Geoffrey Bret Harte for an unrestricted permission to quote from the *Letters of Bret Harte*, published by Houghton Mifflin Company.

G. R. S., JR.

BERKELEY, CALIFORNIA
September 8, 1931

ILLUSTRATIONS

CONTENTS

Contents

BRET HARTE
Argonaut and Exile

PART I
1836–1854

BRET HARTE
Argonaut and Exile

•.•

CHAPTER I

THE LIFE-FORCES

In the annals of mankind, the year of our Lord 1836 is not memorable. Uneventful peace brooded over the nations. Science and the arts achieved no major triumphs. The generative powers brought to birth few children destined to fame, and even Death, seemingly grown weary by his harvest of the last few years, struck down few great ones. Britain was settling to comfortable Victorianism, although the young queen was not until the next year to mount the throne. The sovereign people of the United States elected neither a fine colonial aristocrat nor a picturesque backwoodsman, but the urbane and cool Van Buren. No annual circuit of the sun can, however, be entirely without interesting events, and for 1836 the literary historian of the English-speaking peoples may note two occurrences of importance. In England, Dickens began the publication of *Pickwick Papers*, and in America Bret Harte was born.

A drab enough time it was to be born, August 25, 1836, and a drab enough place too, 15 Columbia Street, Albany, New York! Little of romance! Cocked hats and knee-breeches had gone out, and men stalked the streets ungainly apparitions in long trousers and tall

(3)

hats. Railway trains were beginning to run. Everywhere more and more machinery was clacking; a man
named McCormick had even invented a horse-drawn
reaper, and one named Colt a thing called a revolver.
Ocean-going steamships were improving. Arkansas had
just come in as the twenty-fifth State. People went to
church, and there heard authoritatively that slavery
was right because Paul had sent Onesimus back to his
master. Respectable citizens looked upon abolitionists
as perverts. Congress squabbled about the tariff, national banks, and internal improvements.

Yet romance was not altogether dead. Before the
new baby in Albany was a month old, a fine clipper had
dropped anchor in Boston harbor and young Richard
Dana come ashore. He had been off for two years
around Cape Horn to an outlandish place on the other
side of the continent, and there with eyes of wonder had
seen coquettish señoritas and grave señores in a fine big
country called California. In his bag were notes for a
book about it. Also in this same year an outnumbered
band, as at Finnsburg or in Etzel's hall, died fighting, in
the Alamo. By many tricks of fortune the new-born
baby was to become interpreter to the world of the romance of such hard-handed frontiersmen in that distant
California.

If life was on the whole drab in 1836, there was, however, plenty of romance in thought. Byron was but
twelve years dead, Scott but six, and their spirits still
ruled. Cooper, with his courteous Indians and hearty
Jack-tars, was our leading novelist. Our chief essayist
was Irving, one of whose popular sketches maintained
that young ladies frequently died of broken hearts.
Emerson was developing his romantic philosophy of

(4)

transcendentalism. In fact, when one considers it, there was entirely too much romanticism afloat in thought. What else was Henry Clay's spirit of compromise which refused to face issues realistically, hoping that God and the passage of time would right matters? The thirties were sowing in fine phrases what the sixties were to reap in blood. A baby of this year was not so likely to grow up a romantic as one of twenty years earlier, but he had still a good chance of it.

This same decade of the thirties saw the passing of the last prominent men associated with the Revolution and the framing of the Constitution — Madison, Monroe, Lafayette, Freneau, and Marshall. Madison, the last of them, died in 1836. Their deaths marked the end of an era which, in spite of the revaluations of historians and biographers, retains a tinge of heroism. In the same year with the Harte baby the most prominent Americans to be born were Jay Gould and Joseph Cannon. A year older were Marshall Field and Samuel Clemens; a year younger, Andrew Carnegie, William Dean Howells, George Dewey, and Mark Hanna. *Exeunt* the founders of the Republic; enter the chiefs and heroes of the Gilded Age!

But to the shaping of a man more things conspire than the world into which he is born. Already before birth the strange mingling of two life-forces to create one had determined most, perhaps, of what that new life was to be. Lacking omniscience, however, one can actually see in this particular child's ancestry small prediction of literary genius.

In the hour of birth one thinks first of the mother. Elizabeth Rebecca Ostrander had been her maiden name; her father was Henry Philip, and her mother,

Abigail, was born a Truesdale. They were of solid up-state farming stock, English and Dutch, with no tradition of any outstanding personality. Elizabeth Hart herself was a woman of some literary taste, but on the whole seems to have been in character good, amiable, religious, and of ordinary abilities; one can see no special quality which she transmitted to her son.

On the father's side were more traces of the unusual. The grandmother was a certain Catherine Brett. Her paternal ancestors can be traced back through four generations to the times of New Amsterdam when the Hudson Valley was frontier country. In 1663, the Indian raiders carried off from Hurley the wife and the children of Louis Du Bois, who was Catherine Brett's great-great-grandfather. This Du Bois was a French Huguenot, but most of her ancestors were English and Dutch — Bretts, Rombouts, Tellers, and Mattheysens. Among them were some noteworthy individuals. Her great-great-grandfather, Francis Rombout, was an early mayor of New York City. His daughter Catheryna, who married Roger Brett, an English naval officer, personally administered in her widowhood a small principality on the Hudson and was known through two counties as 'Madame Brett.' Her lands covered the whole valley of the Fishkill and the north side of the Wappinger from its mouth to beyond the falls. She came riding once to a wedding in Poughkeepsie with a coach and four, two blacks on the box seat and a third sitting behind to leap down and open the door for her.

From the paternal grandfather the baby derived an even more marked strain of ability. Bernard Hart, born in London of a family of English Jews, came to Canada

as a young boy. In that province he had among many
other kinsmen a certain cousin who, according to tradition, 'left behind him at his death no less than fourteen
families, all established in the world with a good degree
of comfort, and with a sufficient degree of respectability.' If this be not genius, it indicates at least remarkable ability in several directions. But Bernard Hart
himself in 1780, then a youth of sixteen, came from
Canada to New York City. He throve excellently.
The city saw him rapidly become a wealthy and prominent man — quartermaster of a militia regiment,
founder of one club, president of another. It saw him
honorably and devoutly associated with Congregation
Shearith Israel. It saw him in 1806 establish himself
socially by alliance in marriage with one of the oldest
families of the Jewish community, a union blessed by
many and distinguished children. The city saw him,
from 1831 to 1853, secretary of the New York Stock
Exchange. Finally, in 1855, it saw him die at the age of
ninety-one, ripe in years and honors. What the city did
not know was that during the latter half of his life the
estimable man kept a skeleton in the closet.

In 1799, this prominent orthodox Jew had disgraced
himself — he could not have considered it otherwise —
by secret marriage to the gentile Catherine Brett. The
bride's family apparently repudiated her for the mis-
alliance. On February 1, 1800, Henry Hart was born.
About the same time the ill assorted couple separated;
the son remained with the mother and the wealthy
father furnished money for their support.

Inauspiciously born, Henry Hart throughout life felt
ill-luck dogging him. As he grew up, the iron must have
entered his soul. There were the children of the Jewish

(7)

wife pampered and pushed forward while he, the first-born, was thrust aside like a mere by-blow. His father even named a later child Henry, as if to blot out all individuality of that former one. Money, to be sure, the father gave, but as a favor rather than a right — now generously, now grudgingly. The injustice of it! Henry Hart turned to books, refuge of frustrated souls. He gained a knowledge of the classical and romance languages.

In 1817 he entered Union College, a member of the class of 1820. Among his classmates was a William Henry Seward whose later purchase of six hundred thousand square miles of Arctic land occasioned a playful poem by a Western journalist known as 'Bret.' In the preceding class was a certain Andrew Williams who was to be even more closely connected with this same 'Bret.' The fragmentary records of the college give little information about Henry Hart. Catherine Hart supplied the money for his fees. He progressed through the collegiate course of the day and passed his final examinations, but never received his degree. At the last moment he could not find ninety dollars to pay his bill to the college! Bernard Hart may have had excellent reasons, but this seems the act of a Roman rather than of a Hebrew father.

For a man of bookish tastes teaching was the obvious career. Henry Hart went out to teach, lacking the college degree which might have laid open the road to full success in the profession. He is said also to have been a lecturer and a translator, but in what obscure place the works of his pen lie hidden, no one knows. Although brought up in the Dutch Reformed Church, he became a Roman Catholic soon after leaving college. His mo-

ther's family had relented so that he frequently visited
with the Bretts at Kingston. There he met Elizabeth
Ostrander, and in 1830 they were married. Their first
child was a daughter, also Elizabeth. In 1833 Henry
Hart went to Albany as an instructor in the Albany
Female Academy, where in spite of his linguistic training he taught reading, writing, rhetoric, and mathe-
matics. Early in 1835 a new-born son received the
father's name. At about the same time Henry Hart
ventured to strike out for himself and start a private
school at 15 Columbia Street, which was also probably
his own residence. He was still conducting this school
when his second son arrived in the world.

CHAPTER II

FIRST CONSCIOUSNESS

THEY called the baby Francis Brett. It was a name known among the well-to-do Bretts of Kingston who held estates on the Hudson.

A somewhat closer connection with the landed branch of the family would have been welcome, for, as Henry Hart stood and looked into the cradle of his new son in the first few months of life, he must have been doubtful. Times were uncertain; the little school in Albany was a broken reed for the support of five, and before the baby was a year old, it failed altogether. The fault may not have been Henry Hart's, for 1837 was the year of the great panic when wealthier men than he began to wonder how they would feed their families.

In the little near-by town of Hudson he found a position as principal of Hudson Academy, but he was a hired teacher again, no longer the master of his own school. The family moved with him. It was not their first move, and it was far from the last of a weary pilgrimage. New Brunswick, Philadelphia, Providence, Lowell, Boston, and perhaps even other places saw them in the next nine years. The moves tell their own story. The teacher who changes now and then betters himself, but the teacher who shifts yearly shows his inability to get or keep a good place. Now and then the family stayed with Ostrander relatives in New York City, probably little better than as poor relations. Henry Hart, proud and sensitive, not without his own talents, sank deeper beneath the load. Debts piled up. Almost annually, father, mother, and children, bag and baggage, moved on.

The children of a financially pinched family which moves with every recurring summer must live always on the edge of demoralization. A sense of frustration is in the air, of the futility of endeavor and far-planned construction. Some necessity, ugly and not to be understood, snatches away known scenes and playmates, cherished objects, familiar rooms and surroundings. Fresh adjustments are necessary which the children can make only with expenditure of physical and nervous force. A child who looks eagerly out upon the world may thrive upon such a life, and learn to master human beings and new situations, but one who lacks energy to conquer each new environment can only withdraw more into himself and come to rely upon those two pieces of baggage which for least expressage charges afford most pleasure — books and dreams.

Under such conditions little Frank — as they called him — came to consciousness. His first recorded memory dates from about 1840 when the family had for a brief period pitched its tent in Boston; he remembered wandering then on the green slope of the Common and dipping his bare feet into the Frog Pond. The only constant companions of those years were his brother and sisters. With Eliza, five years his senior, he seems to have had little in common. Henry, halfway between Eliza and Frank, was a forward child who read constantly from the age of six onwards, but confined himself mainly to history. He reveled in the pageantry and action of battles, but far from being a mere dreamer showed himself ready to make his dreams the reality on the first occasion. By the advantage of age and more active temperament he kept his younger brother in subjection. For his real companionship the latter thus turned to Margaret, the baby of the family, about two years younger, and upon her lavished his affection.

With the nomadism of his family and the domination of his elder brother, Frank's own weak body conspired to withdraw him from the active life of contact with other children. He developed into a small boy with a large head, round stomach, and short legs — peculiarities which at one period gained him the nickname of 'Tubbs.' The description is suggestive of rickets, and certainly does not bespeak health. He was in fact sickly, and throughout much of his childhood had to be sheltered. Once his condition was so bad that he was sent off to a seaside village in the hope that ocean air might be a restorative. From this convalescence by salt water he remembered a 'legend' about a phantom ship — the fanciful sort of thing which Longfellow might have put into verse. He gained also an affection for sailing ships as things to be sentimental about when viewed from the land, but he did not try to become a sailor. The sickly boy had enough in his dreams.

Cut off from the physical outlets for his nervous energy, he naturally became what is known as a precocious child. At five he could not only read, but his experience in literary taste was so far developed that also, according to family tradition, he recognized the language of a certain primer as unduly primitive, and burlesqued it. At six he raised family laughter by mimicking a schoolboy's recitation of 'My name is Norval.' At the same age he began reading Shakespeare; and thereafter his knowledge of literature widened rapidly.

Another incident occurring when he was about six

First Consciousness

years old shows how much his mind was then under the influence of his reading. One summer when the family was staying with an aunt in New York City, some rankling injustice of childhood spurred him to run away. The idea itself seems to have come to him from reading the 'Ran Away' notices of the newspapers with their intriguing cuts of the pleasantly footloose truant apprentice shouldering stick and bag. So he gathered his childish treasures together, and under straw hat, wearing a bulging gray jacket, plaid trousers, and gaiters buttoned halfway up the calf, the defiant youngster set out to seek his fortune. His imagination burned with thoughts gathered from stories. Robinson Crusoe and Dick Whittington inspired him. He would seek the Isle of France like Paul and Virginia, or the island where Captain Cook was killed. He would go to barter his piece of colored glass with the Indians. With such ideas he was naturally unable to cope with the immediate problem. He met and confided in an elder boy. This rough-and-ready Irish street-gamin, though he knew not Paul and Virginia, knew the ways of practical life; by cajolery followed with threat of force, he soon managed to separate the child from all his cherished possessions. Frank wandered on a little disillusioned. As the stars swing in their courses, he found himself at evening in front of a theater, agape before a billboard announcing the performance of *King John*, probably Gilbert's production at the Bowery in June, 1842. Here he met his only good luck in the form of a lonesome, friendly young man who for the sake of company treated him to the show. The child gained a lurid impression of red-hot irons. Eventually he got back home, and on the strength of his exploit was temporarily able to lord it

(13)

over his brother. The most interesting phase of the child's adventure (as we see it in his reminiscence as a young man) is that he interpreted everything in terms of what he had read.

This early stimulation to reading must have been one strong influence exerted by his father. In spite of their migrations the Hart children do not seem to have suffered for lack of books. In an age, moreover, when all novels and most dramas and poems were banned from the more respectable American homes, Frank was allowed and even encouraged to enjoy the best imaginative literature. Unlike many children of the time, he did not atrophy his own creative powers by continual reading of tracts in which the wooden characters moved clumsily but inevitably toward an end predetermined by the tenets of the author's sect.

In comparison with romantic literature, nothing else counted much in his childhood. He received his religious training, but neither habit nor conviction sank deep. Family conditions were bad for faith. In the background was a Jewish grandfather. In his own family were a Catholic father and an Episcopalian mother who, if they had any convictions at all, must each have entertained serious fears for the damnation of the other. The mother undertook the child's religious care — 'my Puritan training,' he called it — but the father would have had a better chance of success. Catholicism could at least have offered an imaginative pageant fit to cope with his reading, but the bald low-church Episcopalianism of the day had no appeal. He went to Sunday-school and remembered the slogan:

> Always make it a point to have it a rule
> Never to be late at the Sabbath-school.

First Consciousness

He did not, however, have pleasant memories of the institution. He remembered, for instance, a tract given him, called *Conversation between a Converted Heathen and a Missionary*. As he read it, he first came to practice hypocrisy and feel budding skepticism. He did not admit it to his mother or his teacher, but he knew that, deep within, his sympathy was with the heathen unconverted.

Did I dislike that Heathen in his unconverted state? No! Did I not rather rejoice in his tuft of plumes, his martial carriage, his oiled and painted skin? Was not his conduct creditable and romantic compared with that dreadful Missionary who resembled the Sunday-School Teacher, who systematically froze my young blood? What did they offer me instead? Had I any respect for an imbecile black being who grovelled continually, crying, 'Me so happy — bress de lor! send down him salvation berry quick!' in uncouth English? Believed I in his conversion? Did I not rather know, miserable little deceiver that I was, that during this conversation his eyes were resting on the calves of that Missionary's legs with anthropophagous lust and longing?

What chance had any writer of tracts, even Saint Paul himself, to capture a mind already surrendered to Defoe! Note also that word 'romantic' coupled with 'creditable' almost as a synonym, and the dislike for 'uncouth' English. If the young man who wrote that paragraph was properly interpreting his own mind of some fifteen years previous, one sees that the twig was beginning to bend as the tree was to grow.

The only religious experience of childhood which he recalled gladly was one in which romance mingled — a memory most likely of a visit to some Brett or Ostrander at Kingston — when he sat at service in an old yellow-Dutch-brick church with the delicious fragrance of clover blown in at the open windows, out through which he could gaze and see the broken tombstones and the yellow dandelions and the distant Catskills all in one glance. Nevertheless, the mother and the Sunday-school teachers in one way did their work well. They grounded him in the Bible so that throughout his life its phraseology and even whole quotations flowed easily from his pen and from his lips. Almost the last sentence which he wrote echoed a verse from *Ecclesiastes*.

The Catholicism of the boy's father apparently exercised little influence. In an occasional story, such as *A Convert of the Mission*, he was to display some sympathy with the older church, particularly in the ability of its followers to combine piety and gaiety, but this may have been the result of later observation.

His relation to Judaism is more interesting. He was by blood a quarter Hebrew, and certainly knew of his grandfather. Apparently, however, he was not proud of this connection; during his life no one outside of the family seems to have known of the Jewish blood. Jewish characters, moreover, are noticeably lacking in his stories, an absence the more significant since pedlars and storekeepers of that race were everywhere in early California. One can justifiably, however, see the influence of his Jewish strain in the unusually sympathetic way in which his stories present characters of mixed white and Indian blood. These 'breeds' are traditionally the villains in literature, but in Harte's stories they are generally the heroes. The best known of them is also the best loved of all his characters — 'Comanche Jack,' better known as 'Mr. Jack Hamlin.'

For nine years after the birth of his second son, Henry Hart struggled on. Star-crossed in birth and in life, he could not discipline his abilities to overcome his environment. Enthusiasm, a warm heart, and a feeling for literature were not enough in America of the forties. The story of his death illuminates what his life must have been. In the presidential campaign of 1844, Henry Clay, Whig, opposed James Polk, Democrat. The issues involved Texas and Oregon and the usual chicanery in the political balance of North and South — but no great principle. Into this struggle Henry Hart threw himself violently in support of Clay. (Incidentally about this time he began to spell his name Harte to distinguish himself, it is said, from another Henry Hart who was also active in the campaign.) With devoted enthusiasm he temporarily abandoned other employment to electioneer for his candidate, and the Whig defeat was a correspondingly crushing blow. According to family tradition, he never recovered, and his death in the next year was attributed to this disappointment and chagrin.

As to the actual cause one may be cynical after the manner of Rosalind — men have died and worms have eaten them, but not for the defeat of a presidential candidate. The legend of a man's death, however, is often more illuminating than a doctor's autopsy, and the version of Henry Harte's passing shows the romantic environment in which he and his family moved. One can hardly live in an age which produces Irving's essay on *The Broken Heart* without interpreting life after the same fashion.

Although he had offered his children little in a material way, Henry Harte had at least given them an ideal that they might cherish. Years later a genealogist in talking to a famous author mentioned that the latter's children were through their mother connected with a distinguished line including five colonial governors, and he gained as reply:

All that doesn't count with me in comparison with the labor and struggle and thwarted literary ambition of my dear old father who was a schoolteacher at Albany and was barely able to eke out a living. But he was true to his training and inspiration, for he would not give up a vocation which enabled him to cultivate literary graces, even though by so doing he could have earned a little more money. It seems to me that is more worthy of my esteem than the fact that five Governors of Connecticut, including a Secretary of the Treasury, are of blood relation to my own family; I had rather have my family cherish the memory of their grandfather Harte than the traditions associated with five governors of Connecticut.

CHAPTER III

THE SHAPING

THE death of the father put a sudden end to the wanderings of the family, and thenceforth the widow and children lived in New York and Brooklyn. The great city was flourishing in those years; already it was a metropolis of half a million people. Railroads, clipper ships, and steam packet lines were booming. There were some great events in those years when Frank Harte grew from a boy to a young man — the cholera, the Astor Place riots, the departure of the Argonauts. But why go on? To Bernard Hart on the stock exchange, railroads, ships, and great events meant much; to widow Harte and her four children, they were only distant rumblings. Her husband, unlucky and improvident, had left little behind him, and the family lived in cramped circumstances supported by the Ostranders and a dole from Bernard Hart. It was again a bad situation for a sensitive boy, to be living almost upon charity in a family too cramped financially ever quite to assume the position to which birth and breeding entitled it. Such a family must fight jealously to maintain its social self-respect. Here was the infection of snobbery.

Nevertheless, Elizabeth Harte must have settled down in New York with a certain feeling of relief. Now there would be no more yearly moving; one could get settled and send the children to school regularly. The latter fortunately were beginning to grow up. Eliza was almost a young lady, and Henry, only a boy, flew the nest in the year after his father's death. The war with

Mexico in 1846 suddenly gave him a chance of realizing his dreams of martial valor. He was only twelve years old, but he began offering himself to every naval officer about to leave for Southern waters. Finally one took him. With unexpected good luck he romantically suffered shipwreck in the Bahamas. He stood fire at Vera Cruz, and finally got a wound in the face which to his great delight bade fair to leave a visible scar.

At the time of the settling in New York, Frank was nine years old. He was still sickly, and of all the children must have stood in most need of a steady and regular life. During the migratory period he may have gone to school at times, but on account of his weak constitution his training had been irregular; reading and home influences had meant much more than school. He once described himself as having been 'a dreamy lad thirsting for information concerning the world.' This thirst he slaked by general reading rather than by application to a discipline of regular studies.

In New York he went to school until he was thirteen. Obviously this formal education can have meant little to his development, for he could not have progressed much beyond the primary fundamentals. In a passage which probably has autobiographic value he once mentioned: 'a slight knowledge of Latin as a written language, an American schoolboy's acquaintance with chemistry and natural philosophy.' Except for this smattering of Latin there is no likelihood that he gained in school any knowledge of foreign languages. During a convalescence at the age of fourteen he amused himself by studying Greek and learned, it is said, to read well enough to astonish his mother. The facility with Greek necessary to astonish a devoted mother is, however, probably not very great. Like Keats and the outcasts of Poker Flat he read of the 'swift-footed Ash-heels' in translation. There is no evidence, moreover, that this reading in translation affected him deeply or aroused, as with Keats, any great enthusiasm.

The real influence in the boy's mental development was his reading in English, and throughout his life, indeed, he remained a reader rather than a student. Besides the Bible, he read, as the child of a Protestant mother, *Pilgrim's Progress* and Fox's *Martyrs*, but these were not to his taste. His only reference to the *Martyrs* suggests that he knew the lurid illustrations better than the text. *Pilgrim's Progress* he classed with his disliked and despised tracts; he once wrote to a friend that as a boy it affected him

very much in the same way as the converted Africans or Indians who were introduced to me at Sunday School by their missionary showmen, and who talked 'baboon' or 'pigeon' English. I don't think that I, or any other bad boy, was ever convinced by personified Vices or Virtues, or even regarded them as anything but amusing wax figures. I know that I used to roar with laughter over 'Mr. Facing-both-ways' and 'Mr. By-Ends' to the great detriment of my spiritual education. It seemed to me an insult to my intelligence — and you know how sensitive a boy's intelligence is — and how so many good, moral people persistently overlook it, and make their young friends regard them as unbounded liars! — and I would have none of it.

More to his taste were the great old books which the childish imagination could interpret as pure romance. The *Arabian Nights* enthralled him, and the story of that Crusoe who had the consummate luck to be wrecked on a desert island. He read *Gulliver's Travels* as a pure fairy story; even in later life he disliked any

(21)

emphasis on the satire. *Paul and Virginia* stirred him as a tale of a distant land. He followed with equal interest the voyages of Jason and of Cook. Like his brother he loved Froissart's *Chronicles*, in some edition of Lord Berners's translation, quaintly illustrated and equally quaint with its Elizabethan English. In it the child stumbled upon a certain sentence (or else someone pointed it out to him, for it is not unknown to fame) — 'The English go about their pleasures sadly.' This apparent paradox so impressed his imagination that he quoted it four times in his writings, to the end never realizing apparently that 'sadly' in Lord Berners's idiom meant nothing more than 'seriously.'

In 1846 he began to read *Dombey and Son*, then appearing in monthly installments. The art of Dickens, with its mingling of humor, pathos, sentiment, and melodrama, bursting upon him at an impressionable age, became his ideal, and as he read the earlier novels — *Old Curiosity Shop*, *Oliver Twist*, and the others — and in the next few years came to know *David Copperfield* and *Bleak House*, he gave himself up to a whole-souled enduring admiration. At about the same time, perhaps stimulated by his discovery of Dickens, he began to read the eighteenth-century English novelists, and Cervantes. His enthusiasm for Dumas — he once selected *Monte Cristo* as his favorite novel — may also date from boyhood. He liked tales of the sea and read widely of Captain Marryat, Fenimore Cooper, and Professor Ingraham. One evidence of the scope of his reading is an easy and unostentatious reference to Philip Quarles, hero of *The Hermit*, a little-known anonymous romance of the early eighteenth century. His reading of Bayard Taylor's letters as they appeared in print shows that to some extent at least he also kept up with contemporary writings. He seems from an early age to have had a great liking for poetry, but his precise tastes are difficult to determine. From the evidence of his own earliest preserved verses, one would say that the older poets meant little to him, in comparison with Tennyson, Poe, and the Bostonians, with Tom Hood thrown in for a dash of humor. The omissions from the list of his favorite authors are as significant as the entries. Scott and Cooper (except for the latter's sea-stories) seem to have impressed him little. Also — and this is strange — young Frank seems to have escaped much tinge of Byronism.

Perhaps if his earliest verses survived, they would show Byron's mark, for *Autumn Musings*, produced precociously at the age of eleven, is said to have been satirical and misanthropic. The history of this poem is interesting. The child, sickly, sensitive, unduly well-read, wrote some lines expressing in terms of the dying year a mood of dissatisfaction with the world and life, an expression of adolescent pessimism developed abnormally early. He sent it surreptitiously to a cheap little four-page magazine — *The Sunday Morning Atlas*. As he later told his experience, he went out on Sunday morning to the news-stand where the piles of papers were ranged, each held down by a stone. 'With an unmoved face, but a beating heart, I scanned the topmost copy of the "Atlas." To my dying day I shall remember the thrill that came from seeing "Autumn Musings," a poem, on the first page.' The type stared out at him like a three-sheet poster. By slow and cautious stages, ill concealing his pride, he exhibited the paper to the family. Alas, the downfall! Instead of

offering at least lip-praise to what must for a mere infant have been a remarkable production, they laughed
at his calf-philosophy and pointed out the obvious faults
of the verse and solecisms of the language. The hu-
miliated child shrank into himself. The affair may well
have been a determining incident in shaping his character; throughout his life he was always abnormally sensitive and reticent except where he felt himself in wholly
sympathetic company. Years after he expressed himself: 'It was a terrible experience. I sometimes wonder
that I ever wrote another line of verse.'

It was most likely not an accident or wholly the result
of mature observation that the children in Harte's
stories were typically to be secretive, suppressed, highly
imaginative, and misunderstood by their elders. Clarence Brant, Johnny Medliker, Sarah Walker, and the
rest, although in widely differing environments, probably reflect to some degree their author's own childhood.
Memories of his own early years may also have made
him so sympathetic — in life as in his writings — with
children, and so quick to realize their tragedies. Although what little we know positively points to a good
relationship between Frank and his mother, there is a
decided absence in Bret Harte's stories of the mother
motif. He was often sentimental, but not about mothers. The explanation is probably that Elizabeth
Harte, with the best good will and maternal devotion,
was for some reason unable to inspire confidence and
real love in her son. Perhaps in an evil moment she
joined in the scoffing at *Autumn Musings*.

Fortunately the shock of that Sunday morning was
not quite severe enough to make Frank give up writing.
There is no record that he published anything else in

the next few years, but he at least wrote one long poem, called *The Hudson River*. In its revision his mother appears in a good light; she helped him in studying his work and even wrote out her criticisms.

We should not, however, think of Frank as an abnormal youth, wholly interested in reading and writing. His life, only a step removed from poverty, threw him even too closely into contact with the world. At thirteen he went to work in a lawyer's office, and a year later in a merchant's counting-room. From the age of sixteen he supported himself — good enough evidence of a capacity for practical life. Although at some time he had an attack of smallpox which left him pitted for life, his health and vigor improved as he left childhood behind. This increased physical strength, along with his continued contact with life as a working boy in New York City, tended to make him less of a dreamer and more of a practical youth.

The family was, moreover, not so badly off as to prevent his knowing some normal social life and amusements. He attended lectures, and seems to have heard Emerson, Sumner, Wendell Phillips, and Everett. He certainly heard Bayard Taylor, who, fresh from his travels abroad, delighted him and seemed 'a living Robinson Crusoe, or a reincarnated Sinbad.' Frank cherished also a healthy interest in girls. He once declared that even in his school-days he was reduced to silent rapture by a 'peerless creature' with round red cheeks and long black braids of hair. A love of fine clothes even beyond his purse also developed in him early.

One of his few reminiscences of youth recalls January 1, 1852, when after the custom of his city he went out to pay his New Year's calls. He was fifteen years old, gawky, of course, of medium height, slender now that his childish tubbiness was left behind, not bad-looking with his fine forehead and wavy black hair. It was a great day, for now at last he seemed come into man's estate, and as he tried to stalk along in dignified fashion, his thoughts were largely upon his first skirted coat and patent-leathers. The streets were full of other callers passing to and fro, and in every house the parlor blazed with light. He entered one and paid his respects to the hostess, a little self-conscious of his new manhood. To sustain it and his self-confidence he drank the offered wine and also certain 'hot-stuff,' which half-strangled him. Almost overcome with feeling, he approached the house where lived that one whom he designated 'Psyche-my-soul.' He entered with heart thumping almost to his distraction. But the hostess assisted; he approached Psyche, and (note some ability for a practical life) was able so far to collect himself as to claim the privilege of the day — a New Year's kiss.

CHAPTER IV

CALIFORNIA, HO!

IN January, 1848, when Frank Harte was twelve years old and still a schoolboy, James Marshall picked up some gold nuggets on the South Fork of the American River. He tried to keep the secret, but the news leapt abroad — to the workmen at Coloma, to Sutter's Fort and all California, to Oregon and Mexico, to the ends of the earth. A year later, and throughout the foothills and along the streets of tent-built San Francisco, men of all nations were thronging. The gold-rush of '49 was on!

New York City sent its quota. When the news came in, the exchange, the streets, and the drawing-rooms buzzed of it. Thousands left the city and thousands more came pouring in from up-state and from New England to ship for the voyage round the Horn:

The people all were crazy then, they didn't know what to do.
They sold their farms for just enough to pay their passage thro':
They bid their friends a long farewell: said, 'Dear wife, don't you
cry,
I'll send you home the yellow lumps a piano for to buy.'

By hook and crook men raised passage-money and a stake:

> When I left the States for gold,
> Everything I had I sold,
> A stove and bed, a fat old sow,
> Sixteen chickens and a cow.

So the ships dropped away below the Battery with the men shouting and singing. They were going 'to see the elephant' in California about which young Dana had written a book, but which was still as intriguingly distant as even the Isle of France, or the island where Captain Cook was killed.

Frank Harte must have seen them go. Did he dream of going with them? There lay the ships at dock; a boy might slip aboard as a stowaway, go where he could shake gold from the grass-roots, and come back in a few months singing:

> I took my shovel, pick and pan,
> And went to mining like a man;
> I picked up chunks that weighed a pound,
> That lay like lemons on the ground.

Those lists of ships sailing for California! Their very names should have stirred a romantic boy — splendid and favorite packet-ship *Orpheus*, the fast-sailing new brig *Sarah McFarland*, the *Falcon*, the *Crescent City*, the *Christobal Colon*, the *Henrico*, the *Josephine*, the *Griffin*, the fine ship *Tarolinta* and the good ship *Tahmaroo*, the new fast sailing copper and copper-fastened clipper-built schooner *Sea Witch*, the first-class newly coppered, strong and heavy white-oak timbered packet-ship *Apollo*. Oh, how could anyone at all have resisted shipping for California! Through December, '48, and on into the zero weather of a bleak January, the mania ran. Already people were talking of the new Argonauts.

But at twelve a boy does not run away so quickly as at six. He has seen the difficulties, and realized the hardness of the world. Frank was perhaps a keen enough reader to notice that along with the glowing reports from California were sinister ones of scurvy afloat and disease in the mines, of dangers and disturbances. To a studious and quiet boy New York must have seemed well enough. He could get three meals there and plenty of good reading which gave him a chance for fireside adventure, a very satisfactory kind involving a minimum of labor and peril with a sufficient amount of excitement. So the ships and the brigs and the barques faded away below the Battery, and excitement fell off somewhat.

Gold really came back, however, millions of it to confound the scoffers. People still talked of California, and ships still kept taking them there. Among others who heard the call was the elder brother, Henry, who had come back from the wars, a wounded veteran at fourteen. Grown restless on city streets, he shipped for California, landed in San Francisco in 1850, and remained.

In the next year Eliza married. The family was coming of age and breaking up rapidly. The mother had been a widow some seven or eight years, and there was a new figure appearing on the scene — a certain Colonel Andrew Williams. He had been a college friend of Henry Hart's; since, he had lived in Wisconsin and then in California. Women whom one married were still rare on the Coast in the early fifties. When Mrs. Harte left New York for California late in 1853, she was already engaged. She and Colonel Williams were married in a hotel in San Francisco on the day of her arrival.

She had left the two younger children behind in New York with Eliza, now Mrs. Knaufft, probably because she wished Margaret to finish a school term. The boy of seventeen and the girl of fifteen were, moreover, scarcely children any longer, and could be trusted well enough to make the journey to California, which by that time followed well-established, generally safe routes.

On February 20, 1854, with the two aboard, the

steamer *Star of the West* cast off from Pier No. 2, North
River. She met heavy weather, and had to lie at anchor
off Staten Island until the next day. Gales pounded her
all the way down past Hatteras and farther, but at
length she made port at Greytown on the Mosquito
Coast. As she lay at anchor, queer vessels, mere mud
scows with stern-wheels, backed up alongside and the
passengers, among them Frank and Margaret, crowded
aboard. The voyage of one hundred and twenty miles
up the San Juan River began. They found themselves
among the marvels of a tropical forest. Yellow water
gurgled alongside, dense green walls rose on either side,
tangled with vines and spotted with bright flowers.
Alligators dozed on logs, and endured a harmless bom-
bardment of pistol-bullets. Monkeys skylarked among
the trees; gaudy parrots flew to and fro. Sand-bars and
islands variegated the scene. Now and again the boat
tied up, and stark Indians clad only in breech-clouts
carried firewood aboard. The rapids of Machuca interrupted the voyage, and the passengers floundered
around a muddy portage, buying luscious fruits from
the natives and rejoicing to be again on land.

They spent a night on the river in the midst of mysterious jungle noises. Next day they transferred again,
this time to a steamer on Lake Nicaragua. As they
neared Virgin Bay and saw the heavy breakers, a chill
must have fallen on their spirits, for ugly news had met
them. Four days before, the launch carrying off passengers to the lake steamer had been swamped and in
the ensuing panic nineteen people had drowned. The
surf ran equally high on the day when Frank and Maggie
disembarked, but there was fortunately no accident.
Once ashore the passengers scrambled for places on

mule-wagons or for donkeys to take them the twelve miles over the divide. Again they saw the tropical forest, close at hand now, as the road climbed and plunged among cliffs and abysses. And then the quickening of all spirits as they saw at last the far stretch of the blue Pacific!

San Juan del Sur received them, a huddle of huts brooded over by buzzards. Among the huts rose a few barn-like buildings complimentarily referred to as hotels, in which the voyagers might feed on beans and hardtack. Presently the steamer *Brother Johnathan*, Captain Bodfish, took them aboard for San Francisco, eleven hundred strong, all, except two hundred, male. They sailed on the night of March 8, and adventure kept pace. Heavy gales banged them in the Gulf of Tehuantepec. Two days out from San Juan a boiler failed. The ship rolled heavily at anchor for six hours until the crew had patched up the damage, and then limped into Acapulco. They lay in port two days for more repairs. Ashore was much excitement, for a revolution was in progress, and Alvarez, 'the southern panther,' was busy fortifying the city. The *Brother Johnathan* got away from Acapulco, but a few days later one of the flues burst with much noise and a flood of steam throughout the vessel. It caused a panic among the passengers, whose nerves by this time were justifiably on edge. (Had they known that their good vessel was destined eventually to sink with a loss of two hundred lives, they might have been even more nervous.) But slowly, with only one paddle-wheel working, the laboring engines took them northward. They saw land to starboard, a mysterious skyline showing the serrated edge of mountains, or the low dome-like hills of Baja

Bret Harte

California, 'yellow and treeless as sand-dunes.' Frank came to know the fine roll of the Spanish place-names — Los Lobos Island, Cape San Eugenio, Rosario, Ballenos Bay. They passed Santa Catalina Island, mountainous and inhabited only by goats, fit kingdom for a Crusoe. Then came the bold heights of the wooded Santa Lucias. Finally, on the pleasant afternoon of March 26, eighteen days from San Juan and long overdue, the *Brother Johnathan* raised the headlands of the Golden Gate.

To Frank Harte at an impressionable age, on his first long journey, had been granted what most boys vainly dream for. He had known storm at sea, and twice seen a ship close to disaster. He had been on the edge of revolution. He had seen strange lands and peoples, and heard unknown languages. He already teemed with literary ambitions, and one might well expect that this voyage would have been a treasure of experience from which he might draw later. On the contrary, one searches almost in vain for allusion to it in his published writings, letters, and recorded conversations. *A Man of No Account* may be a generalized reminiscence, but scarcely a specific one. The only reference which seems definite is in *The Crusade of the Excelsior*. That story begins on August 4, 1854, upon the barque *Excelsior* off Cape Corrientes. Dawn is breaking over a heavy sea; far off the passengers see the faint outline of the Mexican coast with the peak of Colima showing white and ghost-like. There is reference to a peculiar 'pinkish opal color' of the sea at sunrise. The seamen mention the names of some points along the coast with fair geographical accuracy. That is all, for the story immediately becomes a highly unreal tale ostensibly in Lower California, but really in a fanciful land made up for the oc-

California, Ho!

casion. For the very reconstruction of his voyage we must in fact rely upon the luckily full newspaper accounts.

One forgets the unpleasant things, many believe, by forcing them below the level of consciousness. The long voyage for some reason — sickness, perhaps — may have become to the young man a mere nightmare. His failure to refer to it, however, is matched by his almost equal reticence about the whole period of his childhood and youth. One forgets the unpleasant things.

Bearing this reticent, sensitive-faced young man, halfway between seventeen and eighteen, and already proud of a tiny silken mustache, the lame *Brother Johnathan* labored in through the Gate. The passengers gazed at the green hills, and fidgeted to be ashore.

PART II
1854–1860

CHAPTER V

OAKLAND

THE steamer from the Isthmus was of vital importance to San Francisco, and every interference with its regularity struck close home to the life of every citizen. As the *Brother Johnathan* neared the dock, the passengers saw a dense throng blocking all passage about the Jackson Street wharf. The newly established telegraph had announced the ship as sighted, and one of the largest crowds ever seen in the city had gathered to learn what accident caused the delay. One who is minded mystically could, however, see in this gathering a prophetic welcome to the youth who more than any other person was to make famous the name of California and the deeds of the Argonauts. The newspapers, not being so gifted, made no comment upon his arrival except to list him among the cabin passengers.

The ferry-boat for Contra Costa pushed out across the Bay; advertisement described her as the splendid new steamer *Clinton* which three times a day made the passage (fare recently reduced to fifty cents) between San Francisco and Oakland. Frank and Maggie Harte, looking ahead, saw only a rolling plain scattered with fine live-oaks; in the background were grass-grown hills. The ferry-boat entered a narrow estuary, but still was no sign of houses. Finally it slid in at a landing, and at last the town came into view. Back from the water ran an unpaved, unkempt street, ridiculously wide in comparison with the feeble row of low wooden buildings on either side. Oakland was less than four years old, but already decay was evident in the unpainted redwood houses and the flimsy one-rail fences. Broadway ran for only little more than a block, and there was not much besides. The two young people, fresh from the metropolis of the continent, came ashore in their new home.

They found their stepfather an agreeable enough person. He was a man of some property and of standing in the community, facts plainly reflected in his courtesy-title of Colonel. He served as vestryman in Saint John's Episcopal Church. He dabbled in local politics, which offered the excitement of vigorous struggles over ownership of the water-front and manipulation of ferry-lines. In 1855 he served as councilman, and two years later became Oakland's fourth mayor. He was cultivated, kindly, generous, courtly in manners, doubtless a little pompous.

Pomposity certainly showed in his oratory. One day, for instance, he addressed a communication to the city council regarding certain tolls which restrained the trade of the village. His words ran:

Another incubus on the prosperity of this city is the toll-bridge to Brooklyn across the northern arm of the San Antonio Creek. The importance to us of an untrammeled intercommunication with the surrounding country is incalculable.

His next sentence totalled a hundred and fifty-four words. Throw in an 'er' or two to indicate the manner of delivery, and you have a distinct suggestion of Colonel Starbottle. The resemblance in fact does not end there. Colonel Williams was not indeed a Southerner, and did not indulge habitually in duels and cultivate the company of flashy actresses. But Starbottle

(38)

'THE STEAMER HAS ARRIVED'

MINERS AT WORK

This illustrates almost every variety of mining mentioned in Harte's stories. It shows the use of pan, cradle, long-tom, sluice, tunnel, flume, and shaft.

and Williams were both apparently colonels by courtesy, they were both 'gentlemen of the old school' and
political 'warhorses.' And above all there was that
style of oratory. Frank Harte, who had burlesqued his
primer at the age of five, could scarcely have lived in his
stepfather's house for many months without realizing
the possibilities offered by that gentleman's style of
speech-making. In later years Starbottlean periods
must have flowed easily from the pen.

Into this stagnant village Frank's life descended.
The events of this period are almost entirely lost; we do
not even know how long he stayed in Oakland. A little
girl named Mary Tingley came in those days to visit at
the house next to Colonel Williams's and she later rec-
ollected Frank as a lad of no particular importance who,
as far as she could remember, did not even have any
regular work. He did work, however, at some time, in
the apothecary-shop of a certain Mr. Sanford, and from
this experience a little survived so that he was able
occasionally to throw some pharmaceutical gibberish
into his writing.

Evidence from other sources shows us plainly, however, what life in Oakland was in '54, and what experiences must have been thrown in Frank Harte's way.
The 'city' (it had been so incorporated on the day before
he landed in San Francisco) had only a few hundred inhabitants. In the election of March 25, the court had
reported three hundred and sixty-eight votes cast, but,
as the county historian sadly adds, 'votes, then, were
no indication of the number of settlers, and it is certain
that there was no such large number of legal voters in
the town.' Oakland was the county seat and boasted a
newspaper, a fire department, three or four little

churches, and the Oakland College School. The population was not increasing rapidly, and the general tone of life was dull. Cows and goats wandered in the streets.

The village itself could supply little provocative to a romantic imagination, but the back-country was more stimulating. In the cattle ranges the old life of Mexican days still lingered. Dark-skinned, mustached rancheros — bright serapes, flaring trousers, silver-mounted bridles — came clinking into town on springy half-wild mustangs. Dark, beknifed vaqueros rode by with riatas at their saddle-bows. They looked like bandits; one could imagine them riding with Joaquin Murrieta, whose band the rangers had scattered less than a year before. They drank at the bars and wrangled in the streets with Americans scarcely less primitive than they.

On holidays Oakland saw enough of roystering and debauchery, but the real center was at the little Mexican town straggled around Mission San José thirty miles to the south. There on Sundays the less respectable Americans joined with the Mexicans, and word came back to the county seat of riotous gambling, fandangos, and drinking, and of combats in which wild range bulls fought with grizzlies. There on Good Friday they still held high festival at the hanging of Judas in effigy.

Other tales were in the air too. California had not yet settled down — not by any means. In those years, before the Second Vigilance Committee, criminals still ran wild in San Francisco itself. In the mines life was primitive; the San Francisco papers on the day of Harte's arrival told of the lynching of a horse-thief at Jackson, and stated that miners in Sierra County were making fifteen dollars a day 'as a regular thing.' Close to Oakland there is plenty of record that the law of tooth and nail still ruled in 1854. Vaqueros, overhauling in the hills a man suspected of cattle-stealing, took the shortest way with him. On September 21, two puffs of smoke rose among the oak trees and the town learned later that a citizen had departed *via* the field of honor. Six weeks later a noted Southern Colonel similarly departed; he had, like Colonel Starbottle, previously indulged in many such meetings, and at the time of his passing already carried three bullets in various parts of his body. Even when ferry-boats ran but three times a day, the East Bay was not without subjects for conversation.

All in all, however, Frank's life in Oakland must have been comparatively barren. *Chu Chu* and *The Devotion of Henriquez* enshrine some personal reminiscences of the period. The stories are told in the first person by an American youth whom his Spanish friend calls Pancho, that is, Frank. The scene of the stories is a village called Encinal, a Spanish rendering of Oakland, and the description of the surroundings is fitting. At some distance is a small Mexican town called San Antonio, where, as actually at Mission San José, there were bull-fights in the Plaza del Toros. The description of the bull-fight is sufficiently vivid and circumstantial to make one believe that its author had once been an eye-witness.

Stories and poems dealing with the old Spanish and Mexican days in California were to be common in Harte's writings. He must have worked up most of the atmosphere from books, for the life of the pastoral days had almost vanished before 1854. Nevertheless, at Oakland he would have had some chance to form an idea of what the old times were. He may have had as friend a young grandee like Henriquez, have adored a Spanish girl like Consuelo, and have ridden a broncho like Chu

Bret Harte

Chu. At Mission San José he could still have had a glimpse of an old Spanish mission settlement far gone in decay. According to one account he made friends with a priest and became his pupil, presumably in Spanish.

Frank seems to have cherished little affection for Oakland. About ten years later he was to be a rising journalist in San Francisco when an earthquake severely damaged that city and left Oakland unharmed. There was naturally some discussion of the matter and 'Bret' contributed an opinion on Oakland's invulnerability:

Schwappelfurt, the celebrated German geologist, has endeavored to explain this singular fact by suggesting that there are some things the earth cannot swallow, — a statement that should be received with some caution, as exceeding the latitude of ordinary geological speculation.

CHAPTER VI

GREENHORN

FOR three years following his arrival in California, almost nothing can with absolute certainty be determined about Harte's life. Between March 26, 1854, and March 1, 1857, there is only one date determined by a contemporary document. Moreover, in this period the legendists and the counter-legendists have long made free. The former have declared Harte the two-gun hero of a Western epic; the latter have called him an effeminate young 'squirt' who never even entered the mining country. This merry game has continued for many years until in attempting to get at the truth one seems to be following a trail across ground trampled by a herd of horses and other animals. The darkest years are those before 1856, but even for this period some evidence is available. The earliest accounts of Harte's life, written before the legend had developed very far, are of some weight. A few of his own writings can be accepted as at least partially autobiographic, although these, like his oral reminiscences, show the effects of a romantic imagination. There are also a few traditions, especially those surviving in his own family, which seem trustworthy. None of these sources by itself supplies conclusive evidence, but when the account built up from more than one of them fits into a consistent chronology, we may believe that the result, if not absolutely sure, is at least worthy of some confidence.

The earliest, and so probably most authentic, accounts of Harte's life represented his first occupation in

California as school-teaching. There is nothing incredible in this, for his youth and own comparative lack of formal education would have been no bar to his taking the desk in a frontier schoolhouse. In those years the State Superintendent of Public Instruction frequently complained that children were subjected to teachers who should themselves be in school. Harte himself declared that he had spent some time at teaching, and to place this period shortly after his arrival is consistent with other evidence. Since he came to California toward the end of a school year, Frank probably lingered in Oakland at least until the autumn. If he then went out as a teacher at the opening of the term, where did he go? In *How I Went to the Mines*, a sketch of some autobiographic value, he mentioned Madroño Valley, apparently a fictitious name. In a late interview he was reported as saying 'near Sonora,' but this was the chief town of a large district and Harte speaking in London might have meant by 'near Sonora' any place in the southern mines.

Evidence gathered from his own writings suggests a more definite location. In *M'liss* the schoolmaster is a principal figure, and because of the careful details most writers on Harte's life have agreed that in this story he made some use of his own experiences. Its testimony is the more trustworthy because of its early date, 1860, a time when no legends about his early life had yet developed and when his own memories were fresh. The action of *M'liss* takes place at Smith's Pocket. The name is probably fictitious, but in the story the settlement is located just where a Sierran river debouches from the foothills and entering upon the plain ceases to be a mountain torrent. Surveying the possibilities in

Greenhorn

the southern district one lights upon La Grange, located just at the proper spot on the Tuolumne. Other evidence as well points to La Grange. In the first place, it had a school in 1854, something which cannot be said of all California towns by any means. Moreover, the original title of *M'liss* was *The Work on Red Mountain*, and near that landmark Smith's Pocket was located. An actual Red Mountain is only a few miles above La Grange. Finally there are many occurrences of the name in Harte's stories. This would mean nothing if it were a startling bit of Californian nomenclature like Red Dog or Fiddletown; but although actually called after an early French settler, La Grange carries only bucolic suggestions. It is not what one would call a 'Bret Harte name,' so that a personal familiarity best explains its occurrence. The characteristics of La Grange and 'Smith's Pocket,' moreover, are similar. Both were mining towns. In 1854 and 1855 La Grange was running full tilt. 'Smith's Pocket,' indeed, is stated to have been in decadence, but the activity of its bar-rooms and its life in general rather indicate a still vigorous prime. If the hypothesis of La Grange be correct, young Harte must have spent some months in a typical mining town of the middle fifties.

M'liss, *Cressy*, and *The Tale of Three Truants* doubtless enshrine some of Harte's own experiences in this period as a teacher and reflect his character at the time. In general atmosphere these stories show a love for children and more sympathy with pupils than with their parents. In two of them the story turns upon the relation of the young, unmarried man, who is the teacher, and the adolescent girl, who is the pupil. Like all youthful teachers, Harte must have faced this pro-

blem, and, since he was a highly susceptible youth, some
M'liss or Cressy, enticing in spite of her frontier crude-
ness, probably caused him plenty of trouble.

Accounts agree in making Harte's attempt at school-
teaching unsuccessful. Most likely, *How I Went to the
Mines* reports correctly that the removal from the district of some of the more prolific families left the school
without a sufficient number of students. In any case
Harte was out of work and without immediate prospects. At this point the action of *How I Went to the
Mines* begins.

This sketch was written more than forty years later.
It lays no claim to biographical accuracy, and certain
improbable incidents were doubtlessly elaborated for
the sake of giving point to the narrative. The story,
however, employs the first person — with Harte usually
a sign of autobiographic tendency. Harte's sisters accepted it as essentially accurate; so did his devoted
friend, Pemberton. The narrative, moreover, has the
ring of authenticity; the intimate experiences and petty
difficulties of the boy walking to the mines are hardly
ones which an elderly gentleman would be able to imagine in London. In general it harmonizes nicely with
the evidence of *M'liss*, the only discrepancy being that
'Madroño Valley' is represented as not a mining town,
but forty miles from the nearest diggings. This may,
however, have been a fictitious element introduced for
the obvious literary value of giving the hero a sudden
and dramatic entry into the gold country. As a matter
of fact the nearest mining town is also the one where the
hero's friend was living, an unlikely coincidence which
lends strength to the suspicion that the location of
'Madroño Valley' may be a mere literary device.

Greenhorn

So the young school-teacher was left jobless. The
month, according to *How I Went to the Mines*, was May;
the year, from other evidence, was almost certainly
1855. The sketch declares him nearly 'broke,' as the
result of having lately spent too much on fine apparel, in
this case 'boiled shirts.' This is a consistent touch, for
he was throughout most of his life improvident and was
always a lover of good clothes. Let his own account
continue. His family was far away, and even in Oakland
he had no sure employment. Naturally he decided to
try his luck in the mines. To signalize his 'abandonment
of a peaceful vocation for one of greed and adventure,'
he went out and spent five of his seven dollars for a
second-hand revolver. In a certain mining district he
had a friend, or acquaintance rather, whom he decided
to find.

The story describes the two-day journey with vivid
touches which stand out sharply against the vagueness
of most of Harte's later writing. There were the patent-
leather shoes, the blistered feet, the red dust, the incongruous morocco dressing-case, the revolver which
insisted on working around and dangling, embarrassing
and unromantic, right in front. He spent the night in
the open, and, like the greenhorn that he was, forgot to
camp near water. The second day was harder. The
shoes hurt him so much that he finally took them off,
and walked barefoot in the dust. To avoid being seen in
such a state of demoralization, he left the main road
whenever possible and followed the trails. Dead tired
toward sunset, he came to 'an unfathomable abyss' and
looking across saw on the other side his hoped-for mining camp.

Arrived at the settlement he entered the bar to inquire for his friend, and merely to keep up appearances ordered a whiskey which he did not really want. While he was drinking, a gun-fight suddenly began in the bar-room. The dazed ex-schoolmaster, who was in the line of fire, not knowing what he was supposed to do and fearing to do something which would display his green-ness, did nothing and remained standing. A bullet smashed his glass. When the shooting was over, the youngster achieved fame by coolly asking the barkeeper for another drink of whiskey because it was not his fault that the first one had been spilled. This scene is prob-ably fiction. But *quien sabe?* Gun-fights happened in bar-rooms of 1855, and from what we know of Frank Harte, his desire for correctness of behavior was a dom-inating impulse.

After he had finished the whiskey, he found, not his friend, but his friend's former partners, who sensing his plight took him in on shares. In the morning he awoke in a regular miners' cabin with bunks around the walls. His new partners were elated to find him a greenhorn at mining, for this meant luck. They sent him out on his own. He got color in the first pan, and soon found a nugget worth twelve dollars. This incident even more likely than that of the broken glass is fiction, for in it the writer is obviously playing up to an old California tra-dition.

A few sentences at the end of the sketch, however, have more than mere probability to make them acceptable:

Then we worked at the claim daily, dutifully, and regularly for three weeks. We sometimes got 'the color,' we sometimes didn't, but we nearly always got enough for our daily 'grub.' We laughed, joked, told stories, 'spouted poetry,' and en-joyed ourselves as in a perpetual picnic.

Greenhorn

One reason why this seems accurate is that it fits so exactly to Harte himself. He was not strong enough to have gone at mining seriously, but this 'perpetual picnic' was exactly what he would have liked and exactly what any mining party of which he was a member would probably have become. The other reason for accepting the 'picnic' version is that in the *Treasure of the Redwoods* and *Captain Jim's Friend* Harte presented just the same picture of a few youthful and congenial friends engaging for a season in amateurish mining. The evidence in the last story is particularly strong because it was published a decade before either of the others, was written in the first person, and contains several incidents suggesting an autobiographic background. These versions mutually support one another, and all together gain support from their consistency with Harte's character and from their own unheroic nature. This was scarcely a sort of experience which one would take the trouble to invent once, much less to invent and then repeat twice after ten years and claim as one's own.

As to the location of Harte's experience in the mines, strong evidence points toward the Stanislaus River near Robinson's Ferry, which is now called Melones. This district is (with the slight exception of that around La Grange) the only one in the foothills with which Harte in his writings displayed any evidence of personal familiarity. Generally his geography as checked by place-names is so ridiculous that it is obviously fictitious. For instance, he once routed a character from Fiddletown to San Francisco by way of Hangtown, Dutch Flat, and Sacramento, an itinerary not only as circuitous as that by Robin Hood's barn, but also cut by almost impassable canyons and without established stage-routes. Along the Stanislaus, however, Harte displayed himself familiar with a large number of names and even with their geographical relations. The Stanislaus itself is mentioned probably twenty times to one for any other river; Calaveras holds almost equally the lead among counties, and when it yields place Tuolumne is usually the substitute. The Calaveras River, however, which flows through a more northerly part of the county, is not mentioned. The conclusion from the place-names is that Harte had some personal knowledge of the country centering about Robinson's Ferry and lying on both sides of the Stanislaus, here the boundary between Calaveras and Tuolumne. His horizon on the north seems to have been at Angel's and Murphy's and on the south at the picturesque landmark of Table Mountain.

To the evidence of the place-names *How I Went to the Mines* adds two striking confirmatory details. In that sketch the distance travelled is given as forty miles, the actual distance separating La Grange and the district on the Stanislaus. Moreover, at the end of the second day the young schoolmaster came to an 'unfathomable abyss' and across it saw the camp for which he was making. Again the geography checks, for if Harte was walking from La Grange, the abyss would have been the canyon of the Stanislaus, and the mining camp just beyond, Robinson's Ferry itself or some near-by settlement to the north of the river.

Two other bits of evidence go to prove that Harte knew the Sierran foothills in the fifties. In a little essay of 1860, when listing various churches which he had known, he mentioned:

Greenhorn

that log-built 'meetin-us' up at Nigger Bar with the sepul-
chral spicery of the pine-logs about it, and the tapping of the
woodpecker overhead.

The very unpretentiousness of this reference in pre-
legendary days is almost final proof of a personal experience. Another of Harte's reminiscences seems to
embody an incident which he actually witnessed on the
Stanislaus. Some enterprising clothes-dealer had apparently sold to the miners a large number of white
duck sailors' jumpers and pants. These soon became red
from contact with slumgullion, but whether in white or
red, the miners so dressed made a picturesque scene on
the river-bars. The memory remained vividly with
Harte. He wrote it in one of his introductions; he nar-
rated it in full to an interviewer in 1894; in a letter of
1890 he defended this costume for miners with the bel-
ligerency of a man supporting a belief based upon personal experience.

If Harte in the middle fifties spent some time on the
Stanislaus, he would have had a good chance to observe
mining life of the sort pictured in his stories. 'The year
1855 was prolific of exciting events,' notes the historian
of Tuolumne County, and thereupon glibly narrates
six murders, a lynching, a double execution, and a street
shooting affray. Calaveras had an even worse reputation than its neighbor. By 1855, however, the production of many of the southern mines was beginning to fall
off and the towns to decay. This suits well with the
pictures displayed in most of Harte's work. The great
popularity of a few of his best stories has obscured the
fact that he was really the writer, not of California in
'49 and '50, but of California in the middle fifties and
even later. The flavor of decay hangs about his mining

towns; they are just the places which he might have seen in Calaveras in 1855. On the other hand, they are not entirely ruined; they are not the same towns as Mark Twain described them ten years later, or as Harte might have seen them had he merely gone into the mining country in the later sixties as a professional writer 'working up' a background for stories.

In *How I Went to the Mines* the partners worked the 'Greenhorn Claim' for three weeks; they may then have moved on to another. In *The Treasure of the Redwoods* the work had been going on for three months before the opening of the story. In *Captain Jim's Friend* the idyllic life continued until the winter rains brought it to a sudden and bedraggled end. These are not actually contradictory, but the details of the last fit in best with the next piece of evidence.

On Jackass Hill, just above the Stanislaus, was the cabin of the Gillis boys, who have since become famous as Mark Twain's friends. The last survivor was William Gillis, a man of intelligence and, there is reason to believe, of veracity. The story which he told was this. In December, 1855, his brother Jim was at the cabin when a very dead-beat young man came limping up. He was in city clothes, and wore patent-leather shoes which were punishing his feet. The young fellow gave his name as Harte and told a hard-luck story. He had tried his hand at mining somewhere to the north; he had looked for a position at school-teaching; now he was nearly 'broke' and was trying to get back to the Bay. Gillis offered him the ready hospitality of the mountains, and Harte stayed for a night or two. He told his host of his literary aspirations, but said that so far he had been able to dispose of only a few stories and poems. Once back in civilization he intended to try again. When he went on, Gillis gave him twenty dollars to see him through.

This is a good story, but it cannot therefore be dismissed as untrue. The Gillises may have indulged in practical jokes and told tall tales, but there is nothing to indicate that they were deliberate liars. So far as it can be tested, the story holds water. Even if the patent-leathers have been borrowed from *How I Went to the Mines*, the date checks; so do Harte's story and his character. The geography offers a slight difficulty, for the direct route from Calaveras County to the Bay lay westward through Valley Springs, not southward by Jackass Hill. But a man who is 'broke' and 'bumming' his way must follow lines of least resistance, not direct routes; Harte may have been making for Sonora as the likeliest place from which he could work his way to Oakland. The greatest argument in favor of Bill Gillis's story lies in his consistency in telling it. I have heard the story from his own lips, and I have read it as he wrote it down and as others have reported him. These different versions cover a period of more than ten years. Now a man who is unscrupulous and imaginative enough to invent a story is almost certain to improve and elaborate it with re-tellings, especially over a long period. But Gillis's versions differ only in small, unessential details.

In any case, by the end of 1855 Harte had in all probability already experienced everything which he was to know at first-hand of early Californian mining life. After this date the record of his life is never again so obscure.

CHAPTER VII

EXPRESSMAN–POET

A LARGE part of 1856 Frank spent in Oakland. In that year his stepfather built a new house at the corner of Fifth and Clay Streets, then the residence district. A square little wooden building it was, differing in external appearance but slightly from many old-fashioned bungalows still standing in the city. Its only second story was one of those small projections at the top, called a 'cupola.' This enclosed a square room little larger than a big box; like a proper box it had a lid in the form of a skylight which lifted to allow the entrance of air. An observer described it as 'a cozy nook and well-enough lighted, but all that the eye could feast on was the fleckless, fathomless blue of the stark California sky.' This was Frank's room.

There he settled down, and, as he had told Gillis he intended, set out to write. He was still under twenty, and doubtless dramatized himself a little as the future great author. The tiny room under the roof gave him a good opportunity. He did not allow his mother to enter there lest she disturb his books and important papers. Besides writing he read voraciously. He found a bookseller from whom he could buy volumes of Dickens on instalment at ten cents a week. The bookseller finally became interested in him, and advanced him the whole set. He built a shelf for these and his other books, and read till the pages began to fall out. Then he allowed his mother to sew them in again.

Putnam's and *Knickerbocker*, according to family tradition, printed some of the verses and prose sketches which he sent in at this time. It is likely enough, for the latter especially was hospitable to Western writers. Contributions to these magazines were, however, generally unsigned, and since in addition Harte's style was as yet unformed, no contributions can be identified as his. He probably had some more remunerative work also, so as not to remain a mere dead weight upon the family. This as likely as 1854 may be the period when he worked in Sanford's drug-store. About the end of September, however, he went off on another venture.

Abner Bryan had a cattle-ranch in Sycamore Valley near Alamo, some twenty miles across the hills from Oakland. He had also four young sons, and not caring to have them grow up like range-cattle he decided to hire a tutor. In some way he lighted on Frank Harte. If on leaving Oakland Frank had any ideas about going to a spacious hacienda in vast plains over which colorful vaqueros galloped, his illusion was soon dispersed, for Abner Bryan, as his name suggests, was not perpetuating the old Spanish traditions. His ranch lay on the southern spurs of Mount Diablo; the house was set in a deep canyon, 'a mere shanty,' Frank declared, 'that might be a hunter's cabin in the wilderness.' There was in a way more flavor of the frontier about Contra Costa County than about Calaveras.

Like many in the second wave of frontiersmen, Abner Bryan was full of the old-time religion. Frank had scarcely unpacked his bags before he was taken off to attend a camp-meeting. His impressions of this event were vivid and lasting. One of his few definitely dated stories is *An Apostle of the Tules*, a tale of Contra Costa which begins on October 10, 1856, at a camp-meeting in

(55)

Tassajara Valley. The date, remembered after nearly thirty years, is wrong by only a few days. At the meeting he was impressed by the unhealthy emotionalism and general sordidness of the frontier religion, but with a young man's eye he noted that the homely garb of the girls seemed to make the ugly ones uglier and the pretty ones prettier.

Soon after returning from the meeting, he wrote to Maggie. This letter of October 8, 1856, the earliest known extant piece of Harte's writing, is a remarkable bit of work. It shows evidence of careful composition with obvious attempts at literary effect. There is a suggestion of the romantic novelists — Sir Walter or 'Solitary Horseman' James:

As Mr. Bryan (father of the boys I am teaching) is not a farmer but a drover, there is nothing of the rural character of a farm, saving the corral at the bottom of the field and the haystack at the top, and the whole place is as wild as the God of nature made it.

The word 'drover' has a particularly Waverleyan flavor; Mr. Bryan might have answered to 'cattleman' or 'cattle-rancher,' but never to 'drover' — not in Contra Costa. The characterization of the boys is another fine set-piece:

The four boys are named respectively George, Wise, Tom, and Johnathan. They are tractable and docile. George has religion; Wise is a mighty hunter; Tom, mischievous and rides a colt as wild as himself; Johnathan, a natural mathematician.

It was raining while he wrote, and he confessed himself depressed — quick reaction to weather is common in young poets; but he concluded the letter with a few lines of verse 'wherein,' as a commentator has expressed it, 'a tear was borne with the flowing water to testify to his tender regard for his "peerless sister."'

Expressman-Poet

Of other events we know nothing definite. The description of the view from the summit in *A Legend of Monte del Diablo* may indicate that he once climbed the mountain. His experiences in Contra Costa must have helped form the ideas of rural life in California which determine the atmosphere of such stories as *Cressy* and *The Convalescence of Jack Hamlin*. It is notable that even in the fine farce of the latter he had no romantic conceptions of the charms of country life.

His engagement with the Bryans proved, however, to be temporary, and before the end of the year he was again out of work. He was also, as he confessed himself incidentally, in love; but this affair like the tutorship was transitory and not even the lady's name is preserved.

At the beginning of 1857 occurred the incident which of all Harte's experiences has most stirred people's imagination. Unfortunately almost nothing definite is known about it. On the last day of 1857 Harte in reviewing the year wrote that he had 'played the expressman for a brief delightful hour.' Thirty-seven years later he was quoted as saying:

It was conceived that I would answer for a Wells Fargo messenger. A Wells Fargo messenger was a person who sat beside the driver.... Stage robbers were plentiful. My predecessor in the position had been shot through the arm, and my successor was killed. I held the post for some months, and then gave it up to become the schoolmaster near Sonora.

This latter quotation is from an interview which elsewhere shows itself as inaccurate as interviews are likely to be. Even the last sentence does not check with other information. According to his diary he was unemployed at the beginning of the year and by other evidence he

(57)

was in San Francisco before April 5, probably before March 1. In the interim he obviously could not have been express-messenger 'for some months' and school-master besides.

A highly inaccurate interview based upon conversation with an elderly man who, as can be demonstrated in other cases, was letting his legend color his reminiscences — this is not sufficient basis for a belief that Frank Harte, a tenderfoot from the East, a slight, scarcely strong youth, a lover of verse-making, ever rode on the box-seat armed to the teeth as a gun-guard upon bandit-haunted roads. It fails, moreover, to be consistent with what can be discovered from other sources. According to Bancroft's *History of California*, stage robbery did not really begin in California until 1859. This is the evidence also of what Harte himself wrote before the legend infected him. We read, for instance, in *A Lonely Ride*, 'The road from Wingdam to Slumgullion [that is, in the heart of the mining country] knew no other banditti than the regularly licensed hotel-keepers.' The only really good evidence is the single sentence in the diary. Its strongest emphasis is upon the brevity; the period was so short that he could imagine himself merely to have played. This would mean probably a few weeks at most. 'Delightful' scarcely implies 'dangerous,' but it does imply something more than mere office employment. 'Expressman' does not carry the full implication of 'gun-guard,' or 'treasure-messenger,' words which in later years Harte and others used.

If, however, Frank Harte's experience was nothing more than to ride some bucolic stage-route for a few weeks, he probably gained much from it. The stage was always a center of interest, and among those who came crowding about for the latest news he must have come to know the Western types. Stage-drivers, moreover, were generally colorful personalities, and as many have suggested, Harte's driver may have been Yuba Bill.

But *what* would Yuba Bill have said, had he known that his companion on the box-seat was writing some 'po'try' about a valentine! One is appalled to consider the cataclysm of irony which this knowledge would have loosed. At least Bill would probably have so exhausted himself as to have little left to remark some weeks later on learning that the delinquent had gone on to publish some *Lines Written in a Prayer Book*. This was, however, the sad decline of Frank Harte. He had apparently grown tired of trying to write for Eastern magazines, and begun sending poems to the *Golden Era* of San Francisco. His first, *The Valentine*, appeared on March 1, 1857, and is the earliest of his published writings to be preserved. This poem and the half-dozen which followed were signed 'Bret.' Slight, sentimental or mildly satiric, they gave no indication of real ability. From this time on, Harte's bibliography always supplies some record of his life; he never stopped writing until he died.

The *Golden Era* yields also a biographical note. On April 5 appeared in the column *To Our Correspondents* the humorously brief comment: 'Bret — San Francisco — no room for Love and Physic this week.' One hastens to explain that *Love and Physic* was a poem which did appear in the following issue. More interesting is the fact that Harte was in San Francisco. That he remained there is shown by a similar note on June 28. Harte then was giving his address as San Francisco from the early spring until the summer of 1857. Of what he was doing except writing verses there is no record.

The likeliest suggestion is that he was again working with an apothecary. Readers have frequently seen him in 'the junior partner of the firm of Sparlow & Kane, Druggists and Apothecaries, of San Francisco,' that young man who plays his part in the story *How Reuben Allen "Saw Life" in San Francisco*. Young Kane had certainly much in common with young Harte; he had made 'one or two previous light-hearted essays at other occupations, for which he was singularly unfitted' and was now embarked 'on his present venture, still less suited to his temperament.' Like Harte, he had little education and no special training as a pharmacist, and realized his own inefficiency. His extreme caution may reflect Harte's own, for the latter confessed that he once made a blunder in a prescription, nearly killed an invalid, got into much trouble, and thereafter became highly cautious.

The incidents of the story in themselves give no suggestion of autobiography except perhaps at the opening in which Kane looks out between the red and green lights, and slightly bored with life takes a piece of licorice from a jar on the shelf and sets out to chew it. The shop is circumstantially located, and the accurate description of the view and the arrangement of streets suggests strongly a personal memory. The city directory for the year shows several drug-stores located closely enough to the proper spot, but no firm with names anything like those of Sparlow and Kane. The name of F. B. Harte also fails to appear; by the time when the directory was compiled, that migratory youngster had already moved on.

CHAPTER VIII

CONSECRATION

In the little town of Union, California, the steamer from San Francisco one day in the early summer of 1857 landed a stranger. He was a young man of twenty-one, medium in height and slight of figure, with an aquiline nose, bright eyes, and silken Dundreary mustaches. The inhabitants of Union further noted that he was gentlemanly, courteous, and reserved in manner; his pleasant voice he did not employ in talking about himself. Something about him suggested the aristocrat, although with this mingled something of the dilettante. His clothes doubtless accounted for much of this impression. He was dressed fashionably, but not so well as to hide from the keener eyes an obvious need of money.

As a novelist of that day might have put it, 'The reader will probably already have surmised that the newcomer was none other than our hero, Frank Harte.' The description, based upon that of one who knew him at the time, shows Harte as he appeared, when at the end of three obscure years in California he emerged into full light. There is, one will notice, nothing to suggest either a miner or a gun-guard.

Harte has not, conversely, left his impressions of the town and its inhabitants; the impressions could not have been extremely favorable. The settlement, numbering about five hundred inhabitants, was called indiscriminately Union or Uniontown, although both names were soon to yield to Arcata. It stood at the northern end

Bret Harte

of Humboldt Bay, and in 1857 — only seven years removed from the wilderness — consisted of one building
of brick, and of perhaps as many as a hundred of wood.
Most of them were one-storied; some were only log
cabins. Rail fences were much in evidence. There were
the usual unkempt streets, a church or two, a flagpole,
stores and saloons, and a long pier running out across
the tide-flats. A few tall redwoods stood in the out-
skirts, and some great stumps — ten and twelve feet in
diameter — studded the town. To the south were the
mud-flats and the Bay. On the other sides there was a
narrow fringe of cleared land and beyond that one of the
most magnificent forests in the world — unbroken miles
of gigantic redwoods.

There was some logging, farming, and cattle-raising
in the vicinity, but the town really existed as a point of
reshipment. Its citizens unloaded goods from the
steamers, and forwarded them by pack-train to the pop-
ulous mining district on Trinity River. This traffic,
however, was already declining, and the town was
threatened with ruin because shippers had discovered a
cheaper route *via* Red Bluff, the head of navigation on
the Sacramento River.

The Uniontowners themselves were a mixed lot.
Indians lounged about, peaceful and dirty, demoralized
by the sudden disruption of their primeval life. Rough
cattlemen and mule-packers caroused in the saloons.
Miners passed through on their way to the diggings, or
came down to spend their bags of dust on a spree.
There were also more stable and respectable people —
the saving remnant of a frontier settlement — who
carried on the business and professional life, went to
church, sent their children to school, attended the

SONORA IN 1853

Such scenery explains Harte's inability for many years to grow romantic about mining life

Consecration

Lyceum debates, and according to their lights worked toward the foundation of a civilized community. With these last Frank Harte naturally associated.

Family connections, which had originally taken him to California, had now brought him to Union. Maggie at eighteen had married B. H. Wyman, a purser on one of the coastwise steamers, and gone to live in the little northern town. Whether Harte in following her had any definite prospects is not certain. For several months there is no record of him except the dribble of contributions continuing in the *Era*. These naturally showed the coloring of his new environment, but the only one worth special mention is *A Trip up the Coast* of October 11, which, as far as is known, was Harte's first published prose. He continued this in two other instalments which gave impressions of his voyage and of the Humboldt district, and are of some interest. These prose pieces resembled his letter from Alamo; they were often a little too pretentious for the subject-matter, and in attempting a fine literary polish sometimes became merely windy and wordy.

On October 19 he settled down for a while to more serious employment as tutor to Captain Liscom's two boys, who lived a mile or more north of town near Mad River. The boys were Charles, aged fourteen, and Frank, a year younger. Their tutor instructed them in Reading and Spelling, Geography, Writing and Journalism, and Arithmetic. He received board and room, and twenty-five dollars a month.

The day of his beginning the new work was doubly important, for on that day he also began a diary — the only one which he is known to have kept. As diaries go, it is not much. Its most revealing quality is its lack of

Bret Harte

revelation. But although its comparative objectivity emphasizes our impression of Harte's natural reticence, nevertheless in it he spoke out more clearly than he ever did in letters or conversation, and through it we are able for the first time, and for one of the few times, to have some idea of what the man was really feeling and thinking behind that careful mask which he presented to the world.

He kept the diary in a thin large volume about eight by fourteen inches, originally intended for some kind of tradesman's day-book rather than for a diarist. The lines allotted to each day permitted the writing of about a hundred words, and he rarely exceeded the space. Besides a diary the volume was also a teacher's record-book; this may in fact have been the primary reason for its existence, for Frank regularly noted his pupils' work before he went on to his own doings.

The diary reveals fully the daily routine of his life. On the mornings he was busy with his pupils. On the afternoons he often went duck-shooting on some of the near-by marshes or else walked to town to see various friends, including some young ladies. For evenings the common notation was 'read and wrote.'

Although he went duck-shooting so often, he was apparently a poor shot, for he generally came home with only one or two birds, sometimes empty-handed. One entry shows that he did not have a gun at the time of going to Union, and was apparently not very familiar with the use of firearms. After one rough, wet expedition, he was thoroughly exhausted and entered the comment, surprising in a youth of twenty-one, 'the thing *didn't pay*' — another good evidence that he was physically incapable of many of the experiences credited to him.

(64)

Consecration

He mingled in the better class of social activity which the settlement offered. A certain *gaucherie*, however, springing probably from his natural sensitivity and reticence kept him sometimes from enjoying himself. On November 26 he noted: 'Went to town and took a Thanksgiving dinner with B. H. W.... In the evening went to a dancing party — saw everybody — tried to dance and couldn't — very much annoyed, came home incontinently — went to bed and spent a restless night.' The same tendency threw him also into occasional fits of melancholy.

Also he fell in love again. 'My charmer' as he called her was apparently one Lizzie Bull. She, it must have been, who, poetically transmuted into 'Elise,' inspired him to some lines which he did not later include in his collected poems:

> A Rose thrown on the drifting tide
>   That laughs along the tinkling brook,
> Though here and there it idly glide,
>   Finds rest within some sheltered nook.
>
> And thus some heart tossed on the stream
>   Of time — impelled by passion's breeze,
> And folly's breath — may find a dream
>   Of Hope — upon thy breast — Elise!

(One may defend the pun in the fifth line by the example of the best Elizabethans.) Miss Bull was the daughter of one of the local hotel-keepers, but whether she could resist this expression of passion, we unfortunately do not know. Like the earlier affair, however, this one seems to have been a youthful fancy, and we may say, following his own lead, that he escaped heart-free.

Sunday entries show that the diarist usually went to

(65)

church. Like a refusal to go hunting on Sunday as 'a matter of conscience,' this attendance at church seems a mere survival of early training. Actually he displayed no feeling for religion. The sermons he usually thought poor, and he characterized them as such in round, even disrespectful, terms. He may already have been developing that antipathy for ministers which he so strikingly displayed in his writings. M'Snagley, Belcher, Staples, Windibrook — Harte had sketched the back-slapping and the hypocritical reverend American gentleman years before Sinclair Lewis was born. By his gospel a prostitute or a gambler might have saving graces, a Protestant minister scarcely.

The diary reveals also the young man's intellectual development. As hobbies he botanized and sketched. He read constantly — of fiction — *The Daltons, Sparrowgrass Papers, Charles O'Malley, Tom Cringle's Log, Genevieve, Shirley, St. Giles and St. James.* The last he admired greatly. In addition to fiction his listings included Irving's *Life of Washington, Dr. Kane's Voyage* (noted as an interesting book), and *The Conquest of Peru.* This was only a part of his reading for a period of less than five months in a frontier village where there was no public library and where books must have been difficult to obtain. It is an impressive record both in amount and in quality. He was not satisfied, however, and once noted impatiently in his diary, 'mean to give up novel reading.'

During these last months of 1857 only his two prose contributions *Up the Coast* appeared in the *Era*, but he was constantly writing. The diary shows that he had already a critical faculty sufficiently developed to reject, or at least consider rejecting, some of his own work.

Consecration

The most remarkable literary revelation, however, regards the poem *Dolores*. This romantic verse-tale with a wholly imagined Spanish atmosphere extended to forty-nine lines. The youthful poet began it on October 29, finished it two days later, and on November 1, noted that he read the poem to Maggie, made alterations, and sent it off to *Knickerbocker*. In spite of this rapid composition the poem was accepted and appeared in the issue of January, 1858.

There are other interesting notes in the diary. One reference shows that he had already become a smoker. His interest in clothes appears: 'Mrs. L. gave me through Frank a vest, an acceptable present.' Another note shows the proximity to the wilderness: 'In the morning Mrs. Liscom thought she saw a *bear* about 1/2 mile from the house, from the description should judge she was correct.'

The great revealing passage in the diary is, however, that written on New Year's Eve. On Christmas Day he had fallen into a fit of melancholy and with a touch of adolescent Byronism had written: 'What the d——l am I to do with myself! — the simplest pleasures fail to please me.'

A week later he wrote a full page of the large day-book. At the beginning there is Byronism.

New Year's Eve [he began]. All by myself. I might have spent the evening in town — but for certain reasons, I have preferred staying by myself. — I have hardly got over my Christmas fears and forebodings. — Memo. — tomorrow will commence my good practices for the future year. Before I close this journal containing but a small portion of last year's doings let me indulge in a retrospect. I am — at the commencement of this year — a tutor at a salary of $25 per mo. — last year at this time I was unemployed, last year I

Bret Harte

thought I was in love — this year I think the same though the object is a different one. I have taught school, played the Expressman for a brief delightful hour and have travelled some. I have added to my slight stock of experiences, and have suffered considerable. Ah! well did the cynical Walpole say that life is a comedy to those who think — a tragedy to those who feel. I both think and feel. My life is a mixture of broad carication [?] and farce when I think of others, it is a melodrama when I feel for myself.

The pose seemed to fall away as he wrote on:

In these 365 days I have again put forth a feeble essay toward fame and perhaps fortune — I have tried literature albeit in a humble way — successfully — I have written some poetry: passable and some prose (good) which have been published. The conclusion forced upon me by observation and not by vain enthusiasm that I am fit for nothing else — must impel me to seek distinction and fortune in literature.

These are not the words of one who had put stage-robbers to flight and quelled turbulent miners.

He went on with his consecration to literature:

Perhaps I may succeed — if not I can at least make the trial. Therefore I consecrate this year or as much as God may grant for my service to honest heartfelt sincere labor and devotion to this occupation — God help me — may I succeed.

This consecration of himself he continued steadfastly to fulfill — and to expiate — throughout all his years.

CHAPTER IX

ON DEDLOW MARSH

ALTHOUGH December 31 marked the climax, the diarist continued for two months longer. Some of the later entries throw illuminating flashes, that of January 29, for instance:

came out again with the Col. had a quiet little chat drank whiskey ad lib. and lay at Col. Boutelle's all night.

On February 2 Maggie was nineteen, and had a birthday party — in more ways than one it proved:

Sky-larking and nonsense. Lizzie sang and I had a short passage at arms with some of the gentlemen? who interrupted her. I was called out by Miss Bull who told me Maggie was sick and wanted Mrs. Martin. went to Mrs. Martin's and did not get her. went to Mrs. Wyman's and got that lady to come with me. At 1/4 of 11 *I became the uncle of a little girl.*

The note for February 19 may have been the seed of his story *High Water Mark:*

This P.M. Mr. Lincoln and wife came to Capt. L's having been driven out of their house by the rapid rise of Mad River.

February 21 outlined a typical Sunday:

Went to town A.M., saw Lizzie Bull — went to church, heard Burton preach — a damd poor sermon — took dinner at Capt. Bull's, in the afternoon. Mrs. B. H. W. and Lizzie sung and played. Cassie Martin called. took supper at Capt. Bulls and called on Judge Wyman in the evening — return early lay at M. H. W's.

On March 3 the diary contained the unexpected information that its writer was considering a position at keeping store. The next day he closed the bargain. He was to take charge of a drug-store for two weeks in the absence of the proprietor at fourteen dollars a week and board. He put up a prescription to demonstrate his proficiency.

This entry was the diarist's last. One regrets greatly that he did not continue somewhat longer, for just at this time Indian troubles became acute. Union was only one of several settlements around the Bay; in addition there was a military post, so that the whites had no need to fear serious reverses. Moreover, a few years of contact with the whites had well tamed the tribes living close to the Bay. They followed peaceful pursuits, earned money and spent it in the stores. The townspeople regarded them in friendly fashion as paying customers. Farther away, however, the wilder members of both races were in constant broil. The frontiersmen were ready to shoot an Indian for any or no reason; the mountain Indians, moreover, were belligerent, and quick to retaliate by stealing the white man's cattle, burning his barn, or, if chance offered, putting an arrow into his back. Troubles ranged all the way from individual vendetta to petty warfare.

On September 26, the excitement culminated. Peaceful Indians reported that a war-party from the mountains had attacked their village, and was close at hand. The townspeople were momentarily in a panic, and after the old frontier tradition of rallying on the block-house at once gathered the women and children into the brick store-building. (Harte's little niece, Floy Wyman, was one of the babies carried to shelter.)

The breaking-off of the diary has left us without record of Harte's experiences at this time. In such an emergency, however, all the able-bodied men would constitute a garrison, and he may even have been a member of some informal military organization and have gone on scouting expeditions, enough to account for the later stories that he had served in Indian campaigns. But the scare soon passed, and there is no likelihood that he ever burned powder. From what we learn later, we can be sure that he would by preference have burned his powder against the white ruffians whose brutalities goaded the tribes into war. He would not have gone Indian-hunting except from necessity.

At this time in Humboldt, however, he came to know the Indians — their characters, customs, even a few words of their language. The numerous Indians of his stories show the results; they are always sympathetically but seldom romantically presented. After living at close contacts with the 'Diggers,' he could scarcely become one who could propagate the idea of the noble Redman.

During this threatening of blood and fire Harte had been variously employed. His original engagement with the drug-store had been only for two weeks, and he was throughout most of the year without any steady work. Maggie must have worried about him. He had many lovable traits, to be sure; he was fond of the baby and of his puppy 'Bones,' but there was no denying that he had not accomplished much since coming West. In those four years he had been scarcely more than a drifter, seldom able to hold a place more than a few months. He never had any money ahead. He seemed content to spend all he made in clothes and to be really interested in little except writing and an occasional girl. To people in general, once they got over his fine clothes

Bret Harte

and aristocratic bearing, he was not very impressive. Leon Chevret, keeper of the Hotel Français, epitomized young Harte's two phases — 'He have the Napoleonic nose, the nose of genius; also... his debts trouble him very little.' Charles Murdock was a friend, but the best that he could write of Harte at this period was:

He was willing to do anything, but with little ability to help himself. He was simply untrained for doing anything that needed doing in that community.

And again:

He seemed clever rather than forcible, and presented a pathetic figure as of one who had gained no foothold on success.

Frank himself probably sensed his own low state at this time. He seems in later life to have spoken even less about his years in Union than about his early experiences in general. Dedlow Marsh, the name which he most often used to describe the district, may be a punning reference to his own state.

One of the odd jobs at which he worked was putting up a fence. He labored bravely at the post-holes, but the final result was crooked. A more ambitious undertaking was his organization, after his father's example, of a private school. It consisted only of a few children of the better families gathered into a rude one-room building on a hill near the edge of town. He had a good touch with children, and his pupils liked him. Instruction, of course, was rudimentary; so was the equipment. The schoolmaster could not afford window-glass, and so, to keep out the wind and to keep in his pupils' wandering glances, he tacked unbleached muslin over the windows. All went well until one day a gale blew in from the Bay.

(72)

On Dedlow Marsh

The muslin ripped out, books and papers blew across the room, the frightened children shrieked, and the school — to use words which might have suggested themselves to its literary master — broke up with most admired disorder. This petty disaster was the signal for the parents of one child to withdraw their daughter, and whether because of it or other reasons the school soon died out.

Socially, Harte continued to enjoy himself and get along well. Only with the rougher part of the population was he unpopular. The diary shows that he relished social whiskey in a friend's house, but he did not patronize the saloons and stand treat with every cattleman and packer. As a result these came to sneer at his fine clothes, and look on him as an outsider, a snob. Among the soberer young men he made a few good friends such as Murdock and Brizard. Comrades gathered sometimes in Harte's room for the long evenings of talk dear to young men just discovering the glories of the world and of their own minds. But an incident of some of their meetings serves to bring Harte's poverty into relief, for Brizard at times brought not only a congenial mind, but also an armful of cordwood to fortify the empty fireplace against the Bay fogs.

In mixed company also Harte was popular. He liked a game of whist. He soon established a reputation as a wit and a conversationalist. People noticed his trick of saying things neatly. He displayed a keen sense of humor, and was never serious in company, although he might be moody or depressed. Often he was sarcastic, but usually in a genial way. He liked to tease, however, and could even be mischievous. There was a certain Englishman born within sound of Bow Bells, who happened just to have married the local schoolmistress. To the intense confusion of his wife and the amusement of the company in general, Harte once ensnared this Cockney into quoting a line which he rendered: 'The 'orn of the 'unter is 'eard on the 'ill.' Harte and Murdock once out walking passed a new house wholly lacking in design or ornament and apparently modeled after a packing-box. 'That,' said Harte, 'must be of the *Iowan* order of architecture' — a remark which at least is interesting as showing that poor jokes about Iowa passed current in California at a very early period.

During 1858, Harte was apparently not even progressing as a writer; except for *Dolores* and the last instalment of *Up the Coast*, both written in 1857, his publications for the year were only two small poems in the *Era*. This does not mean, however, that he was not writing; his success with *Dolores* had probably led him to neglect the West and attempt to establish himself in Eastern journals. One of his poems in the *Era* of this year is interesting as his first trial of dialect; and at the same time as a curious evidence of his callowness. The dialect is not Western or any other which he actually knew, but as bad a scrap of bastard Scots as one can find:

> The Bailie o' Perth was a blithesome mon,
> And a blithesome mon was he,
> And his gude wife lov'd him well and true,
> And the bailie he lov'd she.

The year 1858 was in short a thoroughly discouraging one; just at the end, however, came a new job and expectations.

CHAPTER X

THE NORTHERN CALIFORNIAN

In 1858 the leading citizens of Union began to view-with-alarm their town's decline and the advance of its rival eight miles to the south. Two years before, Eureka had captured the county seat; now the county's only newspaper followed. The Uniontowners decided that they needed some sort of journal to offset this lost *Humboldt Times*, for even a small weekly would bolster their town's prestige, and give publicity to the project of a wagon-road to Trinity River, which might restore to Union the reshipment trade. The actual founders of the newspaper were Colonel S. G. Whipple and Major A. H. Murdock, father of Harte's friend Charles.

Colonel Whipple himself was to be editor. He engaged a printer, but one other hand was needed — a boy or low-priced man to assist the printer and be generally useful. Charles Murdock was anxious for the place, which seemed to offer an opening toward a career in journalism. At the same time, however, Frank Harte applied for the job, a pathetic figure desperately in need of work and pitifully anxious for some connection, however tenuous, with literature. Because of his father's interest in the paper, Murdock could of course have had the place, but he recognized Harte's much greater need, and withdrew in favor of his friend. So Harte at twenty-two assumed the neither very lucrative nor very honorable post of printer's devil, and Charles Murdock took over a tin-shop.

On Wednesday, December 15, 1858, the citizens of

(75)

Union received the first issue of the *Northern Californian*. It was the usual little four-page country weekly differing in no essential way from some dozens of others then published in the State.

Frank's work was at first entirely mechanical. On two days he helped the printer with the type-setting. On a third day he stood behind the desk rolling the forms and getting professionally black while the printer ran off the 'outside' on a hand-press. On the other three working days he distributed type and helped the printer with the 'inside.' From the very beginning he seems to have thriven. In his previous life in California he had been a good example of a man unsuccessful because in the wrong work. His self-appraisal in the diary was correct; the moment he established even a slight connection in literature his interest focused and he became successful.

Almost from the first he began to help with the editorial work. As early as the issue of February 9 one begins to find squibs and brief essays through which peep characteristic gleams of a satiric humor. Less than four months after the first issue, Colonel Whipple went off to San Francisco and left Harte in charge for three weeks to issue the paper on his own responsibility. These numbers were not noticeably better or worse than the others. On his return Whipple wrote an editorial acknowledgment:

We are under obligations to our friend Mr. Frank B. Harte for Editorial assistance during our recent absence of three weeks in San Francisco. Mr. Harte has frequently contributed to our columns, and is a graceful and easy writer.

From this time on, he was really an associate editor, and there are several references to him as the 'Junior.'

The Northern Californian

In June and again in October he was in charge. At the same time he continued with the mechanical work. He got along well with this, too, and even became a passable type-setter. On the whole the Colonel must have thought his Junior a real jewel; he could do anything from rolling the forms to writing the editorials.

From the tone of his contributions to the *Northern Californian*, Harte too must have been happy. There was an exuberance about them which showed that his self-respect was prospering again. During this whole period he did not contribute to the *Era*, good evidence that he had sufficient scope for his creative forces. Only one of his contributions to the *Northern Californian* is signed, but many others can be identified by internal evidence, and the issues appearing while he was in charge can probably be credited almost entirely to him. Very likely also with such an eager and capable assistant at hand Colonel Whipple was only too glad to let him do as much writing as he wanted for all the issues.

This opportunity seems to have been the best thing that could have happened. His writings previous to this time had shown almost no promise; they had been in fact about as bad as they could be. The great trouble had been that aside from a desire for expression he had had no real reason for writing at all; he had had nothing to write about and no one to write it to. Accordingly he had merely tried to sound literary and important. As soon as he started to write for the *Northern Californian*, all this changed. He had definite subject-matter and a known public. He had to tell of the new road or the last Lyceum debate in such a way that Colonel Boutelle, Mrs. Martin, and the rest would know what it was all about. Moreover, if he wrote too much, few would read it or there might not be space to print it. If he wrote in too high-falutin' a style, people would be quick to make fun of him. Accordingly his worst faults disappeared at once. He learned to try to express what had to be expressed in the fewest and most accurate words. When he had done this, he had mastered a fundamental of literary art. Look, for instance, at a sentence with which he concluded a humorous editorial telling of the absence of his chief in San Francisco:

The one half of a broken pair of scissors, the Derringer he left with us, which wont imitate his example and go off, a challenge, two quarrels, a few letters written in an indignant female hand, and our debilitated self await his return.

This is by no means a model of how to write an English sentence; it shows too plainly the influence of that Western humorous style which the brilliant amateur journalist 'John Phœnix' had just popularized in the San Diego *Herald*. Nevertheless, in comparison with the sentences of the letter from Alamo this is a great improvement. It is quick and to the point; it is not splattered with adjectives; it does not disdain the colloquialism of 'wont.'

Fortunately again, he had to write mainly in prose. Frank had begun his literary career apparently with the ideal of becoming a romantic poet. Now he had a gift with words, but when it came to writing a real lyric he was as badly off almost as a blind man painting a picture or a deaf man playing the violin. A reticence too deeply ingrained for him ever to master, or perhaps even to realize, simply prevented him from speaking out. So instead of giving vivid expression to his own feelings, his

The Northern Californian

poetry echoed what others had already expressed. There was, however, satiric verse for which he was better equipped.

The *Northern Californian* had little enough space for poetry. The Uniontowners would not have been interested in the outpourings of the Junior's ego, and would probably have made fun of them, but even the frontiersmen could appreciate humorous verse. Only two poems in the file can be definitely ascribed to Harte. Both were humorous. One, *To Bary Add*, purported to be some verses written to Mary Ann by a lover with a cold in the head; the other, *Why She Didn't Dance*, signed Frank 'Bret,' like the later lines *To the Pliocene Skull*, echoed the meter and the manner of Dr. Holmes's *De Sauty*:

> Tell me, brown-eyed maiden, O, gazelle-eyed houri,
> Draped in gorgeous raiment, circumscribed in gingham,
> Round thy neck a coral, and from each auricular
> Pendulous an earring.

The last stanza, the Pike maiden's reply, showed that in a year Harte had advanced enough to have abandoned Scots dialect known at second-hand for Western, which he had actually heard:

> I've jest sot and sot — till I'm nearly rooted,
> Waiting for the fellers, dern their lazy picters,
> Stranger, I'll trot with ye, ef you'll wait a minit,
> Till I've chawed my rawzum.

This was Harte's first essay at the dialect which he was to make famous.

The Junior also had his chances at journalistic repartee. The *Northern Californian* and its rival down the Bay fought bitterly over official advertising, and clashed on various policies. Matters finally became personal.

Bret Harte

When the *Humboldt Times* ran a pompous article on the glories of Eureka, Harte printed a parody in mock-heroic vein. The *Times* replied *ad hominem*, and, taking a suggestion from *Why She Didn't Dance*, referred pointedly to a mill which ground out poetry. Harte countered in kind. Then the editor of the *Times* tried some bating:

Large Raddish [*sic*]. — Some friend has laid a very large and peculiar shaped raddish on our table. We intend sending it to the *Northern Californian* as a present to the junior editor.

The retort came promptly and neatly:

If the peculiar shape of the radish be owing to its being so very badly spelt, we would remark that we have already had too many such specimens from that editor's table.

At this point the controversy ended, honors resting with the upper end of the Bay.

The varied experiences of this time were to be of great value. The backgrounds of the Humboldt district itself frequently served as the setting of stories — the fog-haunted marshes, and the great redwood forests. But aside from this, many of the incidents and characters which Harte later transferred to the more romantic Sierran setting must have come to him in the North. *The Boom in the Calaveras Clarion* offers a striking example of this procedure. In many ways Union had as much the atmosphere of a mining camp as if it had actually been one. Note for instance a paragraph, almost certainly the Junior's own work:

On Sunday evening an affray occurred between two ex-members of the 'Roll of Honor' — an American and a Spaniard — at the Drummond House. Both parties being 'titely slight' at the time, the origin of the difficulty is not

The Northern Californian

VOL. 1.   UNION, HUMBOLDT COUNTY, WEDNESDAY, NOVEMBER 30, 1859.   **NO. 51.**

Poetry and Miscellany.

Why She Didn't Ran.

(verse illegible)

A Hit in the Cloud.

PART OF A PAGE OF THE NORTHERN CALIFORNIAN

Note the uncollected poem by Harte and the advertisement of the American House inserted by John C. Bull, Lizzie's father

known. It appears that the Spaniard opened the ball, by sending one from a revolver at the American's head. Ajax's shield was nowhere in comparison with the head it struck; the ball raked all around the skull and then glanced off — considerably damaged. The American retaliated — in the old fashion of indictments — with divers guns, bullets, knives, hands and feet, and considerable blood was spilled; but the injuries of either party are not serious. We are not aware of any arrests being made, as neither party gave themselves up.

Another and longer account described the drunken brawl between the District Judge and the editor of the *Humboldt Times,* him of the 'raddish.'

The Junior must also have had plenty of chance to read exchanges and so in the papers from the mining towns or the quotations from them in the San Francisco dailies pick up many fine details. One clipping from the *Trinity Journal,* reprinted in the *Northern Californian,* is of interest. It tells how two miners were caught in a snowstorm and found later, like the outcasts of Poker Flat, lying dead, 'about twelve feet apart, having evidently become exhausted and laid down to die.'

The Junior kept on with his varied work all through 1859. In the first column of the third page, which seems to have been his special charge, he ran occasionally a brief editorial essay, but most of the space he devoted to local news — the weather, the depredations of a mountain lion, the large vegetables brought in by 'agricultural subscribers,' the mishap of his friend Colonel Boutelle who was stabbed by a jealous husband, the debates of the Lyceum on such questions as, 'Which is the strongest passion — Love, or Anger?' and, 'Is intemperance in the use of intoxicating drinks a greater evil than War?' His own name never appeared among the debaters. In fact its only appearance in the column was among the list of subscribers to the Mount Vernon fund to which 'F. B. Harte' with a characteristic prodigality gave five dollars, a sum exceeded by only one contributor. Things were going well; his friends must have been much encouraged about him. In a few years he might expect to be an editor in his own right, marry, settle down as a small-town worthy, and be known as Mr. Frank Harte until he attained the age and dignity to be called Colonel or Judge.

ANNA GRISWOLD HARTE

CHAPTER XI

THE OUTCAST OF UNIONTOWN

COLONEL WHIPPLE left for San Francisco again at the end of February, 1860. If he had decided to wait for the next steamer, there might never have been a Bret Harte. All unconscious of being an agent of Fate, however, the Colonel embarked, leaving his efficient Junior in charge as usual. There had been disturbing news from Eureka on Sunday, and on Monday the Colonel touching there *en route* sent back a report for the benefit of the news columns. He did not think it necessary to return; quite possibly he blessed his luck that he had already decided upon his visit to San Francisco.

What had happened was not unprecedented in frontier annals. Indian troubles had continued to smoulder and occasionally to blaze in Humboldt County. The storekeepers and the soberer townsfolk remained on good terms with the peaceful seacoast Indians, but back in the forests and hill-country both whites and reds were growing more bitter in feeling and more violent in action. The sight of an occasional murdered settler gave the cattlemen and the general riffraff of the frontier ample excuse in their own minds for shooting Indian bucks indiscriminately. The handful of troops could do little to keep order. The worst of it was that under such conditions the partisans of violence inevitably became dominant so that Humboldt County presented the not uncommon picture of a frontier community controlled by its lowest elements. A communication to the San Francisco *Bulletin* about this time declared that the sheriff

(83)

and the editor of the *Humboldt Times* were the chief backers of this policy of Indian-killing.

Giving a sort of philosophical support to this procedure was the popular doctrine of 'Manifest Destiny'; that is, that the Anglo-Saxons (whoever *they* might be) inevitably and therefore rightfully, after the manner of chosen peoples, would and should kill the original inhabitants and possess the land. A resolution passed at a public meeting illustrates the prevailing temper of the community:

Resolved, That as it is the white man who pays and supports Government, their lives and property should be the first to receive protection from that Government. But as white men and human beings of a superior race — from principles of humanity — we are sensible that the Indians should have protection also.

The resolution continued with the cool and high-handed but customary suggestion that the white men be given the Indians' lands, or, as worded, that the latter be segregated on reservations. It was the inevitable, ever-recurring problem of the frontier, old as the first English settlements.

About this time certain members of the superior race tired of waiting for the government, and decided to display their superiority — at least in craft and initiative. The coastal tribes, it is true, seemed harmless, but probably they were in secret league with the murdering mountain tribes; at any rate, an Indian was an Indian. There was a large 'rancheria' of peaceful Indians on an island separated from the town of Eureka by only a narrow channel. At the end of February the inhabitants of the island celebrated a religious festival which demanded a three-day feast and a dance. Thirty of their

The Outcast of Uniontown

kinsfolk from Mad River, also 'peacefuls,' joined them for the celebration. At the end of the ordeal the simple savages lay down to sleep off the effects. A small band of the superior race had been awaiting this moment. These four or five armed themselves with knives and axes in addition to their customary firearms. They did not care to use the latter, for they wished to work silently. Noise might bring out witnesses, and even in praiseworthy actions one sometimes prefers to be unrecognized. There was no need of firearms anyway; these bold champions of the race of just King Alfred, the Venerable Bede, and that gentle Edward the Confessor, knew that — apparently for religious reasons — most of the bucks had left the island so that the tribe was stripped of what poor fighting-men it possessed.

About four in the morning the white men landed silently. Their work, as became members of a superior race, was rapid and efficient. They killed about sixty Indians, mostly women and children, either sleeping or attempting to escape. A few managed to hide themselves. The attackers found the axes and knives sufficient; they had to fire only a few shots. On account of haste and darkness they failed to dispatch all the wounded, and missed a few babies. On the whole, however, their Sunday morning's work seems to have been all that one could expect.

In a letter to the San Francisco *Bulletin*, 'Eye-Witness,' under careful cover of a pseudonym, described the scene at daybreak:

A short time after, the writer was upon the ground with feet treading in human blood, horrified with the awful and sickening sights which met the eye wherever it turned. Here was a mother fatally wounded hugging the mutilated carcass of her dying infant to her bosom; there a poor child of two years old, with its ear and scalp torn from the side of its little head. Here a father frantic with grief over the bloody corpses of his four little children and wife; there a brother and sister bitterly weeping, and trying to soothe with cold water the pallid face of a dying relative. There an aged female still living and sitting up, though covered with ghastly wounds, and dyed in her own blood; there a living infant by its dead mother desirous of drawing some nourishment from a source that had ceased to flow.

The wounded, dead, and dying were found all around, and in every lodge the skulls and frames of women and children cleft with axes and hatchets, and stabbed with knives, and the brains of an infant oozing from its broken head to the ground.

This was the famous massacre of February 26, 1860, reports of which found their way as far as to the metropolitan dailies of New York City.

When Colonel Whipple sent back his report and continued on to San Francisco, he, wittingly or not, placed Harte in a desperate situation. Of the latter's own feelings there can never have been any doubt. He did not visit the island, but he probably saw the mangled corpses unloaded from canoes as the remnant of the Mad River Indians passed through Union bearing home their dead. He was a sensitive youth, reared with high ideals. One needs little imagination to feel the sickening and revulsion with which he saw the brutally mutilated bodies, the smouldering anger which, the worse for being impotent, gnawed at him as he thought of the cowardly ruffians of his own race.

But to publish what he felt — that was a different matter! Would he have the courage? The massacre was on Sunday; the paper must appear on Wednesday.

The Outcast of Uniontown

Harte knew the situation. From the better class of townspeople he might expect sympathy, but hardly armed support. But the others — the rough cattlemen, packers, loggers — frontiersmen, good enough at heart some of them, but just now exasperated past reasoning about Indians! In town was the even more dangerous rabble of saloons and gambling-houses, the professional rowdies. They already disliked him, he knew, for his fine clothes and snobbish manners. Men fresh from the blood of women and children would not hesitate over lynching or shooting down an impudent cub of an editor who dared oppose them. A less upright man would have equivocated; a less courageous one would have flinched; but to the credit of Harte's often assailed character, let it be known that in his youth he met squarely — and we must believe with eyes open — as severe a test as can be imagined.

On February 29 the *Northern Californian* left no doubt of what the temporary editor thought of the massacre and its perpetrators. In as large type as the paper's usage allowed, he headed the news column boldly:

INDISCRIMINATE MASSACRE OF INDIANS
WOMEN and CHILDREN BUTCHERED

The account was circumstantial and declared the killing done 'by parties unknown'; but the words used left no doubt of the editor's indignation:

Little children and old women were mercilessly stabbed and their skulls crushed with axes. When the bodies were landed at Union, a more shocking and revolting spectacle never was exhibited to the eyes of a Christian and civilized people. Old women, wrinkled and decrepit, lay weltering in blood, their

Bret Harte

brains dashed out and dabbled with their long gray hair.
Infants scarce a span long, with their faces cloven with
hatchets and their bodies ghastly with wounds.... No resistance was made, it is said, to the butchers who did the work,
but as they ran or huddled together for protection like sheep,
they were struck down with hatchets.

Harte might justifiably in the absence of his chief
have declined to comment editorially on an unprecedented situation, but his indignation was too great.
He granted the difficulty of the Indian situation. 'But,'
he continued, 'we can conceive of no palliation for
woman and child slaughter. We can conceive of no
wrong that a babe's blood can atone for.'

Within a month Harte left Uniontown. There can be
little doubt that he departed by request. Even before
he left, Whipple had withdrawn considerably from the
Northern Californian's original editorial position on
'Indian massacres.' Various traditions — not from the
best sources — attempt to fill in the details of the incident. By one of them Harte was made to sit with two
pistols awaiting the coming of a lynching mob, and was
only saved by the timely arrival of a detachment of
troops. Murdock, the best authority on Harte's life at
Uniontown, noted merely, 'he was seriously threatened
and in no little danger.' One cannot help thinking of the
morning in Poker Flat when Mr. John Oakhurst suddenly sensed that a committee was waiting upon him
with an order to leave town; the vivid quality of the
scene may not be the result entirely of a dramatic imagination. The old Californian custom could serve to
rid a community of bad characters and also of others
who by most standards were too good. Whether Harte's
notice was formal or merely implied, whether he had the

customary twenty-four hours or until the next boat, we do not know.

The steamer churned up the muddy waters of Humboldt Bay. Harte was aboard for San Francisco. As it happened, he was not the only fugitive on that voyage. The *Columbia* carried also one Henry McKay, under-sheriff of Humboldt, departing with seven hundred dollars belonging to that county. With the cool effrontery so dear to the West he hailed the unsuspecting pilot as the latter left the ship, and entrusted to him the key of the jail to return to the sheriff in Eureka.

As he left the Bay, Harte was little if any richer in money than when he had entered it three years before; in experience he had gained much, but he had not yet discovered how to put this experience to use. The events of the last four weeks had inspired in him a never-ending hatred of frontier lawlessness and brutality. This made him condemn the execution of even so evil a desperado as Tennessee; the critics who have blamed this 'sentimental weakness' in Harte have probably, however, never felt themselves in danger of being informally hanged. The memory of those last days in Uniontown haunted Harte's imagination. They made him more sensitive than ever to the wrongs of the weak creatures of the earth — animals, children, and oppressed races. Sometimes his feelings were to spoil his art by making him picture these creatures *too* pathetically.

There were to be definite reminiscences also in his stories. Princess Bob is the survivor of a massacred tribe. *Three Vagabonds of Trinidad*, one of his last writings, is almost a document on the case. The setting is the Humboldt country. A ruffianly Mr. Skinner talks

at length on "Manifest Destiny." The three vagabonds
are a dog, a young Indian, and a Chinese boy. All three
perish in conflict with the 'superior' race. But as the
lighthouse fell away behind, all this must have been
only an inchoate mingling of indignation, anger, and
fear within Frank Harte.

On March 28, Colonel Whipple gave him a good paragraph of farewell:

Mr. F. B. Harte — This young gentleman, who has been
engaged in this office from the commencement of the paper,
left for San Francisco a few days since, where he intends to
reside in the future. In addition to being a printer, Mr.
Harte is a good writer. He has often contributed to the columns of this paper, and at different times when we have been
absent, has performed the editorial labors. He is a warm-
hearted, genial companion, and a gentleman in every sense of
the word. We wish our friend the success to which his talents
entitle him, and cordially commend him to the fraternity of
the Bay City.

With what seems little better than irony the *Humboldt
Times* reprinted all of this except the last sentence.
Doubtless the editor thought the incident of the 'rad-
dish' sufficiently avenged.

In Humboldt County matters grew worse for a while.
The Junior was not the only one to feel the threat of the
mob and to leave. But that story is not part of his
biography.

PART III
1860–1871

CHAPTER XII

WANTED — A PRINTER

AT one-thirty on the afternoon of March 27, 1860, the little steamer *Columbia* from Umpqua and Humboldt Bay was reported ten miles off Point Lobos. As the afternoon waned she ploughed in between the green hills lining the Golden Gate. She rounded North Point; the docks of San Francisco came into view; the passengers with baggage ready for landing gathered on the deck.

Among them was a quiet-mannered, retiring young man of twenty-three, whose name was down on the list of passengers as F. Harte. He was not a man whom you would meet in a crowd and remember — merely a young fellow of medium height, slender, not very robust-looking. Fine, wavy, dark hair, worn a little long for a suggestion of the poetic temperament, set off a handsome, sensitive face. His dress was fastidious, with a touch of dandyism. He was no hand-shaker or back-slapper, not the sort to indulge in effusive farewells with his fellow passengers or to jostle for first place at the gangway, not the sort, you would say, to forge ahead in the great city of the West, fierce, restless San Francisco, which even now was coming into view off the starboard bow.

Fifteen massive docks stretching into the Bay, great warehouses, the tall chimneys of factories — these one noticed first and close at hand. Then one looked farther and saw streets in defiance of topography audaciously breasting the heights, and rows of buildings clear to the

tops of great hills. Church-spires, the towers of engine-
houses, five-story brick buildings with flags atop! For
this was no longer that miraculous city of the Argonauts
whose tents and shanties, burned one day, sprang up
again the next. Where the brigs had ridden at anchor,
were now paved streets. On the Plaza the old adobe
from which the Vigilantes hanged Jenkins, had disappeared along with that great gambling saloon, the
Parker House. On the site of the latter stood the city
hall, new built of Australian free-stone. Gone were the
flannel shirts, the knee-boots, the revolver-belts; they
had yielded to top hats and broadcloth. Three-card
monte had given place to the Stock Exchange. Vice had
somewhat retired to cover, for property value had become a watchword. No longer did the newspapers wag-
gishly, in scarcely veiled language, announce the arrival of shiploads of *filles de joie*. Instead, they reported
gravely that Officer Baker, disguised as a countryman,
had detected three booksellers trafficking in obscene
literature. Eighty thousand people the city claimed,
and was to be marvellously put out when the new census
gave credit for only fifty-six. In short it was now an up-
to-date commercial city with enough of the pioneer
tradition remaining to impart a touch of color and rest-
lessness to its life — less frank and free-handed than the
city of the forty-niners, less brutal, perhaps not less
cruel.

But as the passengers gazed, the *Columbia* gained its
dock; hackmen and hotel-runners shouted in rivalry;
Harte descended the gangway, and all unknown came
into his kingdom. Although he had had some previous
acquaintance with San Francisco, his real residence in
the city began thus in 1860 and was to continue for

eleven years. In these years he made himself. He entered as an unheralded and insignificant youth; when he left, newspapers ran columns upon the event. But young Harte probably did not even stop to dream of all this on that fine spring afternoon when he came ashore at the foot of Folsom Street. More likely he gave a sigh of relief that he was well out of a bad business there in the North. That he should have come to seek his fortune in the great city hardly needs explanation; that has been what ambitious American lads have always done, and he was not only ambitious, but had already dedicated himself to literature, an art which flourishes only in cities.

There is an amusing parallel between Harte's arrival in San Francisco and Franklin's in Philadelphia. Both were young and printers by trade. Both were in a sense fugitives. Both were to make names for themselves in literature. Franklin arrived with a Dutch dollar and some coppers. Harte had probably little more, for there is tradition of an unpaid board-bill left behind in Union, and besides he was chronically, in the miner's phrase, 'cleaned out.' But aside from these superficialities, there is little resemblance between the rational, shrewd young Franklin and the improvident, sensitive young Harte. Of one thing we can be sure. Harte did not stroll up Market Street, San Francisco, as his predecessor had Market Street, Philadelphia, munching a large puffy roll; to have made that awkward, ridiculous appearance would have haunted his thoughts for years.

Harte was in addition more fortunate than Franklin in having connections in the new city, so that he ran no risk of actual destitution. His mother was still in Oakland, and Maggie with her husband and baby, who had left Union before him, were living in San Francisco. There was also a distant cousin who kept a fashionable, if hardly respectable, restaurant on Commercial Street. There Harte found lodgings, as befitted a literary aspirant, in a small room at the top of the house.

In *Bohemian Days in San Francisco*, Harte has recorded some impressions of these first weeks. Written forty years after the events, this sketch is like most of his reminiscences a curious mixture of what he actually saw and of what he might have seen. The ship-hotel *Niantic*, for instance, which he glibly described, was in reality burned in the great fire of May 4, 1851, three years before he landed in California. On the contrary, the *San Francisco Directory* for 1860 confirms his statement that he lived close beside the Branch Mint, and his reference to the excitement caused by rumor that gold was escaping through its chimney is also based upon fact. Whether he won several hundred dollars on one spin of the roulette wheel only to lose them on the next, whether he saw a malefactor submitted to barbarous punishment in a Chinatown dive, whether he said good-morning to a gambler going out to be killed in a duel at Mission Dolores — these are matters which one may believe, or which one may at will put down as the romancings of an old man, not under oath, who was writing a good story for a magazine. Like Harte's other sketches of similar type, moreover, *Bohemian Days* is mainly an objective description of the city and so has little biographical value. The young man, its narrator, moves through it as the shadowiest of protagonists. The only impressions which we get of him are those of 'a very lanky, open-mouthed youth'; an unimportant hanger-on at his cousin's restaurant, eagerly interested in the strange life around him, listlessly inquiring for employment.

In 1860, Harte would probably have been ready to accept almost any kind of work; in the last few years he had been a Jack-of-all-trades — apothecary's clerk, tutor, expressman, schoolmaster, and finally printer. This last accomplishment was now in demand, and within a week or two he was at work in the composing-room of the *Golden Era*.

First issued on December 19, 1852, the *Golden Era* continued for thirty years — a very unusual period for an early Western magazine. In 1860, it was appearing weekly in the ordinary format of a newspaper, but in the nature of its contents more closely resembled a magazine. According to its announcement it was devoted to literature, agriculture, the mining interests, local and foreign news, commerce, education and the fine arts — a considerable load indeed for its eight pages. It was distinctly a Californian, not a San Franciscan, journal, and the large circulation in the mining districts did much to determine the tone of its contents. The editors were J. Macdonald Foard and Joe Lawrence, the latter described as 'the very pattern of paternal patronage' and such an inveterate pipe-smoker that he was a pillar of cloud as he sat in the editorial chair. The magazine accepted verse, but did not pay for it; a dollar a column was the regular rate for prose. The *Era* still practiced some of the amenities of frontier journalism, witness such a reply to a correspondent as: 'P. D. D. — Chinese Camp — Your last is a nice specimen of chirography, truly! You must have used a crowbar instead of a pen, and liquified asphaltum as a substitute for ink. Sacrificed!' Harte's employers had no high opinion of his ability; for one of them later mentioned him as 'not much of a compositor.' Of others who knew him at the time one referred to him as 'learning to set type' and another as 'nothing but a poor hanger-on.' His own opinion of the trade is succinctly set forth in the little sketch, *Wanted — a printer:*

'Wanted — a printer,' says a contemporary. Wanted, a mechanical curiosity, with brain and fingers — a thing that will set so many type in a day — a machine that will think and act, but still a machine — a being who undertakes the most systematic and monotonous drudgery, yet one the ingenuity of man has never supplanted mechanically — that's a printer.

Two years had passed since he had contributed to the *Era.* In the interval, however, he had written much and now that a mechanical employment had brought him to the editor's door he immediately began to hand in material. As Mr. Foard told of it:

Occasionally he gave me a little sketch or poem to help out, which I put in unknown to the rest of the management. After a while they would say, 'That's rather a nice little thing. Whose is it?' And I would say, 'Oh, I got it out of the box.'

The first of these contributions which can be identified appeared on April 29, barely a month after its writer had landed in San Francisco. It was signed *Bret Harte*, the first use of this famous signature. Since he was at the time always known as Frank, he was able to make use of this modified spelling of his middle name as a kind of pseudonym. After two contributions so signed, however, he still further followed the popular fashion for concealment by dropping his last name and appearing, as he had done when writing from Arcata, merely as

Bret. From these modest beginnings the clipped form became more and more important until it finally displaced his first name in private as well as in literary life.

Nothing in this early work of the young printer strongly suggests his future development into a famous writer. The first contribution was called *My Metamorphosis*, and ranks as Harte's first published story. It is the tale of a young man who, surprised while bathing in a fountain, concealed himself by lying half submerged among the statuary. It shows the schoolboy's inability to make a story out of a situation. Others followed — *Boggs on the Horse*, a sorry attempt at humor; *A Story of the Revolution*, *A Child's Ghost Story* — poor strivings after the charm of Irving and Dickens. The *Era* paid a dollar a column for such contributions, and yet the editor has not been ranked among the great philanthropists. There is a strong tradition that Harte set many of these sketches directly into type without having written them previously. For any evidence of literary finish which they display, one would be ready to believe in addition that he set the type while standing on his head. The story, however, could easily have developed out of the memory that Harte had been at once type-setter and writer. In view of his extreme care and slowness in composition only a few years later, one must be skeptical about attributing to him such unusual facility in 1860.

The only promise in the writings of this time rested in their variety. In his first half-year with the *Era* he contributed five poems and more than a score of prose items. Among the latter are short tales of several types, humorous and satiric sketches, and essays upon local themes. He even undertook a regular column called

Bret Harte

Town and Table Talk which offered comment upon the various phases of San Franciscan life as they appeared to the writer.

In this column Harte figured himself as 'The Bohemian.' With the Bohemian on his mild local adventures moved some shadowy figures — Jefferson Brick, Alexis Puffer, and J. Keyser. Harte probably conceived them merely as projections of his own personality, and now and then used their names as his own pseudonyms. A fifth character, 'Constantina, the peerless,' represented more likely some actual young lady whom Harte escorted to the fair, and once to the fashionable 'Church of St. Crœsus.'

In life 'Constantina, the peerless,' may have been Miss Augusta Atwill in whose album on September 16, 1860, over the neat signature Frank Bret Harte appeared two stanzas called *Lines by an Ex-Schoolmaster*. Whimsical, carefree, happy in bad puns and conventional lover's vows, they show that the hated 'Click! Click!' of type was not unduly depressing.

All in all the slavery to typesetting had compensations. There was for instance the regular pay, a luxury which he had not always known. When to this he had added what he picked up by writing, he was probably able to live in comfort as a bachelor and to have a half-dollar left to spend in squiring Constantina. From his room at 148 Commercial Street he could step out into the center of the colorful thronging city, in itself a delight to one who had spent the greater part of six years on the frontier. He used to breakfast regularly, it is said, at a cheap German restaurant. He ate by himself and had a regular order — rolls, Westphalia ham, and coffee at twenty-five cents. In the evenings after work he went often to plays and operas to which his association with the press may have given him passes. Contemporary plays were largely melodramas, and Harte soon fell under the spell of Dion Boucicault, an influence which dominated his dramatic taste throughout life. He also enjoyed the operas and saw many — among them *Trovatore*, *Puritani*, *Lurline*, *Lucia*, and *Ernani*. A parody of *Manahatta* in a time when Whitman was almost unknown shows that he must have devoted some of his evenings to contemporary literature. On Sundays — he had outgrown his conscientious qualms of three years previous — he enjoyed visiting the city's pleasure-resorts. He expressed a liking for the lager beer of Russ Garden and Hayes Valley.

A second-rate type-setter writing sketches so commonplace as to suggest that he did not even know how commonplace they were! A man of twenty-four enjoying himself complacently among the theaters and beer-gardens of a provincial city! Here was little to suggest a brilliant future, and yet at this very time, Fortune, as so often in the form of a goddess, was just ready to appear before him.

CHAPTER XIII

THE LUCK OF FRANK HARTE

CERTAINLY no one in California was better fitted for the rôle of goddess than was Jessie Benton Frémont. Daughter of a great senator and wife of a popular hero, she was remarkable also for her own charms of personality, her intellect, vivacity, taste, and literary ability. Even by 1860 'Care and sorrow and childbirth pain' — the pathetic words which she inscribed in the family Bible — had dimmed her beauty, but at the age of thirty-seven she still remained a woman before whom one might bow down.

Her husband, the great Pathfinder, owned a vast estate in Mariposa County, and thither he had taken his family. But the Sierran foothills bake out in the summer, and when the children began the pastime of cooking eggs in the dust of the roadside, Madame Jessie took them and fled. Her sleek team with its Indian driver could usually make Stockton in two days, but the heat told on horseflesh too, and the second night found the party forced in spite of fears to stop at the disreputable Ten-Mile House. There the ruffianly Missourian innkeeper refused to take them in, and was attempting to drive them away, when accidentally learning that, besides being a Black Republican's wife, she was old Tom Benton's daughter, he became at once all affability. Next day on the river boat, Mrs. Frémont found a copy of the *Golden Era* and in it a passage describing a man similar to the one whom she had just encountered. The coincidence, more than the literary art, perhaps, aroused her interest. Later in San Francisco while talking to her acquaintance, the editor of the magazine, she inquired the author, and learned that he was a young type-setter.

There was small literary life in San Francisco, and doubtless Mrs. Frémont, herself literary, had ambitions for a salon. The young compositor was shy, but the goddess insisted. When he arrived, she must have thought him a poor capture. But although a goddess, she was also a mother, and she saw before her a poor, lonely, sensitive, yet withal appealing, lad. The upshot was that Harte began dining with the Frémonts every Sunday.

Six days of slavery to the type-stick, of meals in cheap restaurants, of lonely hours of reading and writing in the garret room — and on the seventh a glimpse of the greater world. Colonel Frémont, that Ulyssean wanderer, had at last given his wife a home. Standing high on Black Point it commanded a vista which stretched from the Pacific over all the busy waters of the Golden Gate to the islands of the Bay and the high hills beyond. Close below was the Fort, so close that when salutes were fired the very glass of the windows was in danger from the concussions of the great Columbiads. Here a struggling young author could be sure of many things. The friendly welcome itself made him feel that he was not altogether unappreciated. Then there was the dinner; at twenty-four one does not despise flesh-pots. But more than the dinner were those whom one met at it — 'the Colonel' himself, or Mr. Baker just elected senator for Oregon, or the even more enthralling Reverend Mr. Starr King, the Unitarian minister who was rapidly gaining his reputation as the greatest orator of the city. Free-soilers all, even Abolitionists, they must have spent many a Sunday hammer and tongs at it over politics — reminiscences of the Colonel's campaign for the Presidency in '56, bloody Kansas, that promising candidate from Illinois named Lincoln, the prospects for the election and afterwards.

On October 26, Senator Baker made a campaign speech for Lincoln before a great audience. The incident which followed was probably planned in advance; one feels in it Jessie Frémont's dramatic instinct. For just as the speech finished, a young man suddenly leapt upon the platform, and frantically waving an American flag, inaugurated a quarter-hour of cheering, the greatest demonstration of the campaign in San Francisco. The young man was unknown to the audience; his name was Frank Harte.

But even in the autumn of '60 the talk at the Sunday dinners was not all political. Jessie Frémont might develop the conversation out of her own rich experiences — of Andy Jackson, who had held her as a child on his knee, of Queen Victoria's court, or society in Washington, London, and Paris. Here he might be content to listen and learn, the lad unknowing in the ways of the great world, with the stain of printer's ink still on his fingers. He learned much, but he did not always listen. For Harte, if not formally educated, was well read and in certain ways not inexperienced, and when once the warmth of an assured friendly atmosphere had thawed through his reserve, few surpassed him as a table companion. Years after, Elizabeth Frémont, in 1860 a girl of eighteen, remembered him as 'brilliantly clever' even in those days when as a gawky lad he had come to dinners at Black Point.

The Luck of Frank Harte

His real chance came, however, when Mrs. Frémont, Elizabeth, and sometimes Mr. King, drew aside with him. Then he could take a manuscript from a bulging pocket, and read. At last he faced discriminating critics — Starr King, representative of the best New England culture, and Jessie Frémont since childhood a keen reader of the world's best literature, herself the collaborator in a vividly written book which had stirred the whole country. Here banalities and puerilities could not pass. The criticisms were kindly but keen; sometimes they caused him to bridle up, more often to draw back into himself and sulk. But generally he had to admit their force. Sometimes, too, as he read, he saw that his words were finding the mark, and had the heady pleasure of seeing these great people of the world moved toward tears or laughter by his own creation.

Having become self-critical, he began to develop. The sketches in the *Era* improved — not strikingly, but at least noticeably. He cast off the grammatical crudities of the frontier, which had not bothered him when writing for the *Northern Californian*, and began to perfect himself in the use of that highly correct English which was to distinguish him from many of his Western contemporaries. Less frequently do we find this young provincial attempting the pseudo-cosmopolitan air of:

One day, I found myself loitering, pencil and sketch book in hand in one of the pleasantest midland counties of England.

There was instead a drift toward realism. On October 7, 1860, appeared *A Man of No Account*. This character-sketch — of no great account itself — was his first attempt in prose to utilize the Californian background, and is interesting as the earliest writing which he included in his collected works. In the next month came *Ran Away* and *Ships*, which were to some extent based upon his own life as a child. It began to look as if those critics in the Frémont drawing-room had been giving some old advice about writing from experience instead of books. In the same month also appeared *A Night at Wingdam*, not without merit as a bit of atmosphere, and introducing Wingdam, capital of the Bret Harte country, a place as vaguely pictured as many-towered Camelot, and as difficult to locate on any map.

A more ambitious effort followed with the publication in two instalments, December 9 and 16, of *The Work on Red Mountain*. With a new title this story some ten years later emerged as if from the grave, and became one of the most popular tales of its generation. It was the basis of three plays which were presented hundreds of times; a Royal Academician painted an imaginary portrait of its heroine. Our own contemporaries have produced *M'liss* three times on the screen, once with Mary Pickford in the lead, and once under the title *The Girl Who Ran Wild*.

Between October, 1860, and the next May every issue of the *Era* except one contained one or more items which can be identified as Harte's. These comprise fifty prose items, many of them extending over more than a column, but only four poems. The *Era*, one remembers, did not pay for verse. That he snubbed the Muse partly at least for financial reasons seems the more likely because two of the poems which he did publish helped pad out a prose column. The greater number of the contributions were local sketches. *Town and Table Talk* ran until February 3, and then, without altering its contents greatly, continued as *Bohemian Feuilleton*. He did not always maintain the improvement which had begun under Mrs. Frémont's patronage. Two items of early 1861, however, marked the forward path. The vividly written *High Water Mark* was based upon experiences in Humboldt County; and *The Mysteries of the Two Metropolises* was a first attempt at a burlesque novel.

Although he still wrote much trash, Harte had by the spring of 1861 advanced a long way. He had opened up a rich vein by beginning to write of the Californian mining camps. He had shown aptitude for portrayal of character and for the utilization of atmosphere and picturesque incident. He had actually written a story which many critics have ranked with his best work. Yet, after this promising start he turned aside and spent seven years in experimenting to find his proper medium. Perhaps the time was not ripe for *The Luck of Roaring Camp*, but one wonders whether, had Harte been allowed a normal development, he might not have made his strike in 1861.

But it was no time to talk of normal development; already the Valkyries were mounting. State by state the Southern commonwealths drew off; Beauregard raised his batteries against Fort Sumter; rumor of secessionist plots swept through San Francisco. Frank Harte was still setting type. The bookstores sold Hardee's *Tactics*, and *The Work on Red Mountain* lay forgotten in the *Golden Era*. Mrs. Frémont prepared to go East. Harte must have been discouraged. A year in the city, and he still just supported himself by setting type and contributing to a dollar-a-column magazine! From somewhere the offer came for the joint-editorship of a newspaper in Oregon. He agreed. So this was the end!

Bret Harte

A year in the city; failure; back to the frontier! He went to Mrs. Frémont with his new plan. Then spoke the goddess.

The daughter of Tom Benton was schooled in the ways of party politics and patronage. Had not the Colonel's party swept into power? New Republican officers were arriving in San Francisco; among them a Mr. Beale with Lincoln's appointment as Surveyor-General. Mrs. Frémont said a word, and Frank Harte received a place as clerk in the Surveyor-General's office. It was not much, but there was a possibility of more beyond. The newspaper in Oregon had to make other arrangements.

She sailed for the East. (In the epic the *dea certa* appears to the hero only at critical junctures and for brief moments.) Harte apparently never saw her again, but she had already influenced the whole course of his life. She had given both criticism and sympathy, the most definite forms of what is called inspiration. She had made for him powerful friends, especially Starr King. She had obtained for him an occupation less deadening and more profitable than type-setting. Without the governmental appointments which he held for eight years in San Francisco, Harte would probably never have been able to develop as a writer.

He himself once wrote to Mrs. Frémont:

If I were to be cast away on a desert island, I should expect a savage to come forward with a three-cornered note from you to tell me that, at your request, I had been appointed governor of the island at a salary of two thousand four hundred dollars.

CHAPTER XIV

POET-OF-THE-DAY

IN February, 1854, the steamer *Star of the West* had carried Harte on his journey to California. In January, 1861, the *Star of the West* put into Charleston Harbor bearing supplies for Fort Sumter. With a puff of smoke from a shore-battery a Confederate shot passed across her bows. Three months later the guns opened in earnest.

The telegraph sent the word west to the Missouri. There the pony-riders took it. Up the Platte, through the passes, and across the long desert reaches they plied quirt and spur. Ten days old the news came to San Francisco. For the moment men were hysterical with vague fears of a Southern *coup d'état*, but in a few days the national flag flying everywhere declared the city's staunch loyalty. As Harte years later described it:

From every public building and hotel, from the roofs of private houses, and even the windows of lonely dwellings, flapped and waved the striped and starry banner. The steady breath of the sea carried it out from masts and yards of ships at their wharves, from the battlements of the forts, Alcatraz and Yerba Buena.

How one of these flags came into existence we know, for Frank and Maggie labored over it all one night, she sewing, he cutting out the stars.

With all this enthusiasm one wonders why Harte, young and unmarried, Northern by birth and Republican by association, did not enlist. One must remember, however, that enlistment in a California regiment meant only humdrum garrison duty or police work on the plains. To get into real fighting, a Californian had to pay his own way to the East, and there join some state regiment. Harte had been a sickly child, moreover, and was never a robust man. One should remember the wet hunting expedition which he had decided 'didn't pay.' Such a constitution would not have lasted long at campaigning, even if it could have passed the army physical examination. Nevertheless Harte's failure in some way to get into the fight constitutes one of the best refutations to those who have attempted to make of him in his younger days a devil-may-care frontier ruffler and gunman.

In any case he continued upon no more warlike a staff than that of the Surveyor-General in the office at Montgomery and California Streets. Among the employees of that bureau Harte did not hold an important position; he was entitled merely 'clerk,' and in the list his name appeared next to the last. The regular pay for a clerk was one hundred dollars a month. His work probably consisted of copying and recording documents concerning public lands, and its only lasting influence upon him may be seen in the frequent mention of frauds and disputes over land-tenure in California, as in *Gabriel Conroy* and *Susy*. Most of these troubles involved the grants of Mexican governors, and in *The Story of a Mine* one of the characters actually bears a name, de Haro, associated with a famous case of which Harte must have known. This work may also have stimulated him to study Spanish. There is no evidence that he ever had much facility with that language, but an industrious student has compiled a list of one hundred and fifty-five Spanish words and phrases occurring in Harte's stories.

At about the time when he entered the Surveyor-General's office, Harte ceased to write for the *Era*, and there is no record that after May 12, 1861, he published anything for more than a year. This abrupt cessation may indicate that his leaving his post as type-setter to take a new job occasioned a quarrel. When he recommenced publication, he was still a clerk, but as a writer was in a new rôle.

Of the men who helped rally California in Lincoln's support none was more prominent than the diminutive clergyman, Thomas Starr King. Many have considered him responsible for holding the State firm, and in commemoration his statue stands in the National Hall of Fame and his name identifies the peak which overlooks Yosemite Valley. This bantam-weight of the First Unitarian Church in those early days of the Civil War ranged California like a comet, dazzling audiences by the brilliancy of his eloquence and leaving a trail flaming with denunciations of secession. When the State's allegiance had been assured, he turned his attention to procuring a toll of California's gold for the Sanitary Fund and other alleviating agencies. On August 13, 1861, for instance, he called at his church a meeting of former residents of New York to raise money for the families of volunteers from that State fallen in the war. Two hundred attended, and on the committee appointed to carry on the work was 'F. B. Hart.' (The humble clerk seems to be rising in importance.)

In those simple days before house-to-house canvasses had been conceived, the approved method of raising money was to gather people into a hall and there play upon their emotions by oratory. In this art Starr King was a master. He needed auxiliaries, however, particularly a poet to supply a few gracefully turned lines, and in this part Frank Harte found himself thrust forward. Among the first of these poems was *Reveille*, which was probably read at some patriotic meeting in the first year of the war. Although it soon became popular, its original reception was unfavorable; perhaps Harte himself was the reader, a rôle in which he was never very effective. On July 20, 1862, *A Volunteer Stocking*, also a war poem, marked the return of *Bret* to the *Era*. In September he wrote *Our Privilege* in support of the Sanitary Fund, a highly successful piece which was reprinted in various papers. King forwarded it to the *Boston Transcript*, where it appeared along with the sponsor's letter containing the first public prediction of fame for its author: 'Mr. Frank Bret Harte, who will yet be known more widely in our literature.'

Just before this pleasing success, Harte had taken a decisive step. He had always been susceptible; the objects of his youthful affections had been many — the red-cheeked schoolgirl, 'Psyche-my-soul,' the nameless lady of '56, Lizzie Bull, 'Constantina, the Peerless,' and now Anna Griswold. Harte's admiration for Starr King had led him to attend the Unitarian Church. Before long a stronger motive than friendship helped sustain this religious zeal, and his eyes sought the choir-loft as well as the pulpit. The quartet which led the singing in King's church was largely a family affair. Mr. and Mrs. Leach carried the tenor and soprano, and the latter's sister, Miss Griswold, a tall brunette, sang contralto.

She was the daughter of Daniel S. Griswold, of New York City, and genealogists can trace the line back to a distinguished colonial ancestry. The family was noted for musical talent. She was somewhat older than her admirer in the congregation — in the later twenties, then an age when a woman began to feel that marriage had passed her by. It was not a very acceptable match. Harte's family, especially his mother, objected that the lady was too old for him. On her side friends thought that she — a fine musician — was throwing herself away upon a penniless and uncertain clerk and scribbler. But Harte was not without a mind of his own, and Miss Griswold was of a determined, even dominating, character. In the Methodist Church at San Rafael, on August 11, 1862, they were married.

Harte left his sister's home where he had been staying for more than a year, and the new couple began living at 524 Sutter Street. The husband's salary was small for two, and the war was sending prices up. Almost immediately they felt the pinch. They had counted probably on some income from her singing, but she was soon in delicate health. A baby was expected. The new wife spoke bitterly to friends of the hardships of poverty which she had to undergo.

The reappearance of Harte's signature in the *Era* coincided with his marriage, and was the result probably of need for money. Whether the preceding twelvemonth had been a period of constant literary practice or of quiet mental development, he returned to the *Era* a more finished writer than he had left it. From this time on, he contributed much less frequently and the quality of his work showed corresponding improvement. Of the fifty or more contributions of the earlier period he included only five in his collected works. Out of thirty-three published in the year following July, 1862, he considered thirteen worthy of preservation. Two of his first contributions in 1862 were *Fantine* and *La Femme*,

Bret Harte

burlesque novels purporting to be translated from the French. The only narratives of this period were the two Californian sketches — *Notes by Flood and Field* and *A Lonely Ride*. Most of his prose consisted of a series of essays begun with *Melons* on October 5, 1862, and appearing under the general title *Bohemian Papers*. Altogether they totaled a dozen, but only a few were included under that title in the collected works. Nevertheless they marked a great advance over *Bohemian Feuilleton* which had been wholly local and ephemeral. He was now emulating, not without charm, the English essay in its best tradition. About half the contributions of this period were poems, a renascence of verse which must be credited to the fame attributed to Harte as poet-of-the-day. *The Goddess*, for instance, was signed in full, and after the title was the note:

Recited by the Rev. T. Starr King at the benefit given by the Ladies Patriotic Fund to the families of the California Volunteers.

By his work as *Bret* in the *Era*, and even more by the publicity which King gave to his poems, Harte was by the spring of 1863 rapidly becoming known as a promising local writer. At the same time, however, he remained a low-paid clerk with a complaining wife, worrying about how he could support a child as well. After hours he labored at writing to get a few dollars ahead. Then — Mrs. Frémont was indirectly responsible — the clouds broke.

CHAPTER XV

A DOMESTIC BOHEMIAN

MRS. FRÉMONT had introduced her protégé to Starr King, and Harte had cemented the friendship. By his war poems he had come to deserve well, not only of the orator, but also of the city as a whole. On May 2, 1863, Robert B. Swain, one of King's prominent parishioners and Harte's near neighbor on Sutter Street, assumed the office of Superintendent of the United States Branch Mint in San Francisco, and Harte's appointment as Clerk to the Superintendent followed shortly. Mr. Swain admitted that he had installed Harte so that the latter might have a better opportunity for writing. The duties in fact were not arduous, and the pay was good. In 1863 he received one hundred and eighty dollars a month, which even with allowance for war-prices was a comfortable income. In following years Harte's often needy journalistic friends sometimes wrote good-natured squibs on his luck — 'he occupies a high, responsible and lucrative position in the Mint... with very little to do.'

In addition to the financial establishment the same summer saw public acknowledgment of Harte's literary standing. For the Fourth of July, 1863, while the fate of Gettysburg and Vicksburg still hung in the balance, the Union leaders in San Francisco planned a great demonstration. The organization of the parade filled half a column in the papers, from the four mounted police, and the First Light Dragoons in the advance, to the rear of the Fifth Division, composed of the Laborers' Pro-

Bret Harte

tective Association, and the contingents of two breweries. The First Division was assigned to a brigade of militia. In the Second Division, thus properly heralded, came the Grand Marshal himself in yellow and gold; behind him the Assistant Marshals in red and silver; next, two carriages — in the first the President and the Orator-of-the-Day, wearing blue, white, and silver; in the second, similarly arrayed, the Chaplain, the Reader, and the Poet-of-the-Day. Alas, by 1863 people had grown a little tired of parading, and the reality fell far short of what had been planned. Many companies walked with depleted ranks, and the Poet-of-the-Day, Mr. Frank Bret Harte, never wore his blue, white, and silver trappings. The papers reported that he was ill; one suspects that he lay 'crafty-sick,' too diffident to display himself before the many-headed multitude.

His poem, however, did service for him. The meeting was in fact much more successful than the parade. In five minutes after the opening of the doors, the Metropolitan Theater was jammed. First came prayer, music, and the reading of the Declaration. The Band played, and then the Reader got through the Emancipation Proclamation — not without hissing from various parts of the house. As the report in the *Bulletin* continued:

Another patriotic ode by the Euterpeans — The *War Cry of Freedom* — and then the Poem of the Day, written by Frank Brett Harte, was read by the Rev. Thomas Starr King. The Poem was gracefully written, and contained several very happy thoughts. Commencing with the early and storied battles of the revolution, a very brief recitation brought the verses down to the present:

The twig our fathers planted then, has grown a spreading tree,
Whose branches sift their blossoms white, to-day, on either sea.

A Domestic Bohemian

In allusion to the golden blessings wherewith the hand of nature has crowned our section of the country, the poet says:

> Shall *we* turn away when our brothers appeal
> To the youngest of all, who, like Benjamin, found
> The silver cup hid in his measure of meal?

And the poet lets his sword flash up in the sunlight when even a thought of invasion or a boiling over of the copper kettle seething in our midst occurs:

> Let the foe tempt our youth in his treacherous haste,
> Our blades shall defend the bright colors we bear,
> As the cactus protects in the desolate waste
> The one tint of Eden that God has left there!

'The poem,' commented the *Golden Era*, 'elicited appreciative demonstration from all parts of the house.' After these preliminaries the Reverend Thomas Starr King delivered the oration with his usual success.

Although there is an undeniable anticlimax in being an absentee poet-of-the-day, the celebration of that Fourth of July had served to put Harte's name publicly before the city. At twenty-seven he thus ceased almost suddenly to be a struggling clerk, and found himself an established man with a family, a local reputation, and a good income.

It is amusing that at this time, when his readers knew him as the Bohemian and might naturally have imagined him a gay blade, Harte was in reality a steady-going employee, husband, and father. His respectability seems in fact to have been a good joke among the roystering, free-lance journalists with whom he was professionally associated. In the *Golden Era* of November 22, 1863, Harte's good friend, Webb, obviously writing ironically, declared that all the contributors to the magazine were staid and sober family men with the one unfortunate exception of Bret, and in the next issue he continued the friendly satire with charges of drunkenness and fast life. Another friend has stated directly that Harte was not a Bohemian in the common acceptation of the term.

From incidental references in various sketches we may make out a fairly clear composite picture of Harte's life at this time and a very simple, bourgeois life it appears. In the morning with fine disdain of those riding in omnibuses he went on foot to the office, an exercise which from one of his residences consumed an hour. He walked with a graceful and easy carriage, but some people said he minced. His clothes were his distinguishing feature; he had the ability of dressing even beyond the height of fashion, and yet appearing in good taste. He liked to set off his whole costume by just the proper cravat; it was usually of a solid color and glowed like some rich jewel of crimson, indigo, or orange. After business hours he returned home, and in the evenings always planned to devote two hours to writing; but domestic complications frequently intruded. The baby — named Griswold but called Wodie — sometimes disturbed the arrangements of his study. Mrs. Harte suggested strongly that some hours spent in papering and painting the house would repay more than the same time spent in writing. Obediently the author tried, but like most literary men made a botch of manual labor and had finally to call a professional to aid with the gummy strips. The watering of the garden — known after the Irish cook's malapropism as the 'scrubbery' — was another duty of the *pater familias;* so engaged he speculated, as other Californians have done, why, no matter what seed was planted, the result was always hollyhocks. Amusements

A Domestic Bohemian

also were simple. After dinner he walked in the garden smoking a cigar. He went to plays, and with his music-loving wife to the opera. He read much, mostly in current fiction and poetry. Frequently he browsed in the Mercantile Library, but wondered why any man with a home to go to should prefer deliberately to sit down in the reading-room.

Nevertheless, for all his domesticity Harte was beginning to form some close associations with individual members of the Bohemian group, friendships which meant much more for his literary development than did his home life. Of these new friends the most important for the time being was Charles Henry Webb. He was two years older than Harte, and had had an even more adventurous career. At seventeen, after reading the newly published *Moby Dick*, he had impulsively shipped aboard a whaler and spent four years in the South Seas and the Arctic. Returned, he became inevitably, and remained a journalist.

For [as he wrote in a characteristic paragraph] never shall it be said of me that I put my hand to the plow and turned back. For that matter never shall it be said of me that I put hand to a plow at all, unless a plow should chase me upstairs and into the privacy of my bedroom, and then I should only put hand to it for the purpose of throwing it out of the window.

He went to the front as a war correspondent and at Manassas his memoirs indicate that he, like Bardolph, ran when he saw others run. In 1863 he left New York City and came to San Francisco as literary editor of the *Bulletin*, bearing with him the whiff of metropolitanism. He wrote breezily in both verse and prose, and soon began contributing to the *Era* as 'Inigo.' In conversation

(119)

he was delightful, for a not unpleasant impediment in speech served to make his puns the more excruciating. He and Harte in a few months became friends and allies.

In the same year Harte came to know Charles Warren Stoddard. 'Charley' was seven years younger — only a youth of twenty in 1863. He had led a more sheltered life than Webb, and had developed more in the gentlemanly tradition of letters. In 1855, as a lad of twelve he had been brought to California. He was scarcely more than a boy when as 'Pip Pepperpod' he began writing verses for the *Era*. He soon became Harte's most intimate friend, and even addressed a poem *To Bret* in the *Era*, beginning a little fulsomely —

> Oh, Bret, sweet rhymer and most pleasant friend.

His youth and easy-going disposition made him naturally a follower and supporter rather than a leader where Harte was concerned.

At this same time also, Ina Coolbrith was becoming known in the city. She was only nineteen, a year younger even than Stoddard. In 1850 she had been brought across the plains in an emigrant party which Indians had attacked and almost captured. The famous pioneer Jim Beckworth had carried the child of six through Beckworth Pass in his arms. At twelve she had published a poem. In San Francisco she had since 1862 been writing verse for the *Bulletin* and the *Era*, brief lyrics which, although slight, often displayed the authentic touch. She was extremely beautiful, with a face which in rare fashion combined power with its beauty.

For the ten years since 'John Phœnix' and 'Shirley' had written for the *Pioneer*, San Franciscan writers had

produced little of note. Now there was a stirring. Webb
was teeming with projects; Harte was developing skill
as well as facility; Stoddard and Miss Coolbrith were
promising followers. In this same year of 1863 three
enlivening visitors shook journalistic California out of
its dullness.

Ada Clare, 'Queen of Bohemia,' fresh from Pfaff's in
New York, descended upon San Francisco to the great
fluttering of literary dovecots. 'The Showman,' Artemus Ward, passed through. Harte met him, contributed
an essay on him to the *Era*, and received a letter of
thanks. In future years their names were often, although with little real reason, to be coupled.

In August the flamboyant Adah Menken — one of
the most amazing characters of her generation — burst
upon San Francisco. She is remembered as an actress
for her rôle of Mazeppa, in which she allowed her magnificent body to be stripped almost naked and tied to a
horse's back. She rivaled the Wife of Bath by having
four husbands, and therewith much other company in
youth, and later. Like the Wife also she was no mere
creature of sex; intellectual men delighted in her conversation; she wrote poetry more genuine than much
which has received higher praise. Her volume of verses,
Infelicia, bespeaks that, as with the Wife, much knowledge of the old dance had not brought happiness. In
her weeks in San Francisco she played Mazeppa for a
gaping male audience; Webb concluded: 'She is best in
her line — but it isn't a clothes-line.' She also wrote
for the *Era*, and held a kind of literary salon for the
Bohemians. They remembered her. Years later — long
after she had died miserably in poverty — Harte
sketched her faintly in the *Crusade of the Excelsior* as

Bret Harte

Mrs. Hurlstone, that woman of many husbands described as 'Such a figure in tights!' and as writing poetry 'on the liberation of women — from — er — I may say certain domestic shackles.'

In this tense half-year, when the strange names Chickamauga and Chattanooga filled the papers, Harte was promoted from clerk to Secretary to the Superintendent and continued writing for the *Era*. He had not forgotten that he was dedicated to literature and was striving for fame as well as for money. Even in 1862 he had stated in *Melons*: 'I was engaged in filling a void in the literature of the Pacific Coast.' The description of his method of work which he included in the same sketch indicated that he was already the careful, slow, and even hesitant writer, whom his San Franciscan friends described as filling the waste-baskets with discarded manuscript and even writing an informal note to a friend three or four times over.

Two items of this half-year are of interest. In October he won an isolated success in the East when the *Legend of Monte del Diablo* filled eight pages in the *Atlantic Monthly*. This graceful sketch was as good as many others in the magazine, but not remarkable enough to win the author any national standing. In form and content it directly followed Irving, whose influence was still strong in American literature. As Irving had endowed the Hudson and the Catskills with pleasant myth, so Harte sought to do for the suggestively named and picturesque double-peaked mountain of Contra Costa, which San Franciscans can occasionally make out, looming mysteriously up beyond the Berkeley Hills. The Spanish in California, indeed, occupied a position closely comparable to that of the

Dutch in New York, and for several years Harte, doubtless encouraged by his initial success, continued his attempt to create far-western counterparts of *Rip Van Winkle* and the *Legend of Sleepy Hollow*. The resulting score of poems and sketches are, however, marrowless. The best of them, *The Right Eye of the Commander*, has vitality in that it contains a dash of Harte's own style, a parody which satirizes the romance.

In the *Story of M'liss*, Harte experimented again with a narrative of the mining country. On September 20, the first chapter appeared under an especially decorated title-plate, and received an editorial puff which declared 'this splendid novel' to be 'by one of the best writers of Romance in America.' The expansion of the brief tale of three years earlier proved, however, to be difficult, and Harte languished in the attempt at sustained narrative. After missing installments in several issues, he 'wound it up in disgust.' He always published the shorter version in his collected stories until a squabble over copyright made the inclusion of the longer one seem advisable.

This unfortunate serial was among Harte's last contributions to the *Era*. His signature 'Bret' was now known and appreciated in the city and throughout the State. A journalist, who on departing for the East at this time wrote a farewell article in the *Era*, praised him as an outstanding writer and declared him fit for a national public. The moment was ripe for a change. Webb had an idea.

CHAPTER XVI

THE CALIFORNIAN

As early as November, 1863, Inigo and Bret had been exchanging pleasantries in the columns of the *Era* about the new magazine which they were going to found. The former, addressing a letter to a fellow contributor, had sportively announced, 'Bret is to write all the clever things for it, I am to get the credit of them, and you are to furnish the money.' Apparently the rising young writers felt themselves cramped by being connected with a periodical of which they were neither editors nor proprietors. The disappearance of Bret's signature from the *Era* after January 4, 1864, was therefore not surprising. Preparations, however, were not yet complete, and for several months Harte's only publications were a few poems in the *Bulletin*.

While hopes were high for the new venture, an unexpected event still further cut Harte off from the past. On March 4 the flags in San Francisco flew at half-mast; courts adjourned; the Mint closed; the *Bulletin* ran an editorial lined in black. For Starr King was dead.

Of several poems occasioned by his passing the most noteworthy was Harte's *Relieving Guard*. The friendship between the two had been sincere and warm; in the younger man's development it had meant much. But Harte was now ready to make his own way; King, even had he lived, would probably have ceased to exert much influence. Beloved though he was, the great preacher was really a link to a dying past; he stood for

The Californian

the Unitarianism of New England, for Webster's spread-eagle oratory, and for Longfellow's pretty poetry. All these amenities and fine phrases were only walking ghosts in that year when Grant marched into the Wilderness and 'Uncle Billy' flung his army against Kenesaw Mountain just to teach his men that he was not afraid of killing a few of them. Although the ghosts of old New England continued to haunt him in future years, Harte developed his own special talent only as he escaped from them to walk with the flesh and blood of his own generation.

On Saturday, May 28, 1864, the *Californian* finally burst upon the not very expectant world. Webb had raised enough money to found the magazine, and he was at once proprietor and editor. With its sixteen folio pages, the *Californian* was double the size of the rival *Era*, and was in paper, type, and general appearance greatly superior. Upon a decorated scroll it carried for motto Job's words, 'Surely there is a vein for the silver and a place for gold where they fine it.' The reference of the gold was of course Californian; that of silver a compliment to the territory eastward at a time when almost everyone in San Francisco was speculating in Nevadan silver mines. It was distinctly the best magazine which had yet appeared on the Pacific Coast, and its staff was with reason proud of it. Webb, Harte, Stoddard, Ina Coolbrith, a now unremembered Emily Lawson, and later Mark Twain were the chief contributors. As was customary at the time, the *Californian* filled its gaps with translations and reprints from contemporaries, but the greater part of its reading-matter consisted of original articles, stories, poems, and reviews.

Bret Harte

In comparison with the *Era* there was about the *Californian* an urban and cosmopolitan air, and a lack of interest in local themes unless humorously treated. The name was thus in a sense a misnomer.

Webb always zealously maintained that he, not Harte, was the founder. The latter's original connection with the *Californian* was that of star contributor. *Neighborhoods I Have Moved From* and the *Ballad of the Emeu* on the front page of the first issue were both his. On the editorial page on September 10, however, stood out in small capitals the name F. B. Harte. Webb had already announced in the preceding issue that in the new editor readers would recognize 'one whose graceful contributions to this and other journals have already made his name a household word on this coast.' Harte's first venture in the editorial chair continued for only a few weeks; he seems, indeed, to have been merely a substitute for his friend during the latter's trip into the mining country. He naturally made no changes of policy; the only important result of his editorship was the enlistment of a new contributor.

In 1864, Sam Clemens was reporting for the *Call*, and rather bored with life in San Francisco after the excitements of Virginia City. As it happened, the *Call* and the offices of the Mint shared the same building. A friend introduced Clemens and Harte, and from the meeting the latter carried away the impression of a striking head, dominant, eagle-like eyes and nose, a careless dress and manner, and a drawl which was slow, satirical, and irresistible. The two soon became friends, and the propinquity of their offices allowed them to be much together.

Harte recognized Clemens's ability, embryonic as it

The Californian

was, and on becoming editor engaged him to write an article a week for fifty dollars monthly. The *Era* paid as much as that, but as Clemens wrote at the time: 'I quit the "Era" long ago. It wasn't high-toned enough. The "Californian" circulates among the highest class of the community.'

His first contribution was *A Notable Conundrum* on October 1, signed with his usual Mark Twain. As editor and friend Harte labored over Clemens's writing, showed him his obvious crudities, and helped him correct them.

Webb resumed the editorship on November 26, and for about four months subsequent Harte did not contribute. There is no indication, however, that this was the result of any disagreement. On April 1, 1865, Harte recommenced writing, and the rest of that year was the period of his greatest activity for the magazine.

In general, his writings for the *Californian* were of the same nature as his work for the *Era* in '62 and '63; the collected *Bohemian Papers* indeed include contributions to both magazines. The *Californian's* paradoxical lack of interest in California kept him from any further attempts at stories of the mining country. His most promising development at this time was as a humorist in both verse and prose. Much of his humor was the more appreciated for being local and satiric. The *Ballad of the Emeu* — that 'Emeusing' ballad, Inigo called it — was suggested by the bird kept on exhibition at a resort on the edge of the city; a series of parodies in verse offered humorous pictures of urban life; the *Petroleum Fiend* satirized the first oil boom, and the *Devil and the Broker* the excitement of wild-cat mining speculation. The most notable contributions were, however, thirteen of the 'condensed novels,' which laid the foundation of his reputation as a humorist.

Throughout December, 1865, Harte was again editor, just at the time, it happened, when he became involved in one of the most amazing incidents of his career.

CHAPTER XVII

TEMPEST IN A TEAPOT

ONE can imagine scarcely any literary activity which could at the present time create less disturbance than would the collection and publication of a diminutive anthology of verses by Californian writers. The intensity of the local commotion aroused by the appearance of Harte's little volume, *Outcroppings*, is thus of curious interest.

Since the ships of the Argonauts had poked their noses into the Bay to the tune of *Susannah*, versewriting had flourished in California. There was scarcely a rural weekly that did not run its occasional poem. Helen of Troy and Petrarch's Laura were hardly more berhymed than were the Golden Gate and the Yosemite. As Harte once commented, 'A beautiful bird known as the California Canary appeared to have been shot at and winged by every poet from Portland to San Diego.' In a community so self-conscious as early California it was inevitable that someone should attempt to preserve the best of these fugitive pieces, and at the beginning of the Civil War a precocious young lady, Miss Mary Tingley — she who as a girl had visited at the house next to Colonel Williams's in Oakland — had first showed to Starr King and then offered to a local publisher a large folder of clippings in verse and prose collected from the periodicals. The publisher, Mr. Roman, had considered the moment unpropitious, but had retained the folder with an indefinite suggestion of publication after the war.

Bret Harte

This Anton Roman was to influence Harte's life profoundly. As a young man he had come to San Francisco
in 1850, and headed directly for the mines about Mount
Shasta. A year later, having struck it rich on Scott's
Bar, he was back in the city laden with a hundred
ounces of gold-dust. He was fond of reading, and
dropped into a bookstore, where a suave salesman per-
suaded him to invest all his hundred ounces in books.
It looks like the old game of bamboozling the yokel out
of his cash, but young Roman turned the trick for himself. From camp to camp among the miners, he peddled
the books with such success that he bought more of
them and quit gold-digging. After various experiences
he set up in San Francisco in 1860 as a bookseller and
publisher, and maintained for many years the flourishing house of A. Roman and Company. No writer himself, he stood ready to gamble on writers by financing a
book or a magazine. He represented literature's necessary alliance with business.

Miss Tingley's folder cluttered Roman's shelves for
several years. Finally Lee surrendered, and the publisher judged the time ripe for the appearance of California's Parnassus. For editor, however, he approached,
not Miss Tingley, but Harte, whose local reputation as
a poet and man of letters was well established. Roman
offered Miss Tingley's collection as a starting-point.
Harte accepted with the stipulation, probably because
he already was contemplating publication of a volume
of his own work, that none of his own verses should appear in the anthology.

My First Book, written in 1894, was Harte's version
of the course of events. It was on the whole less imaginative than most of his reminiscences, and was true at

least to the spirit of the action even though it travestied Roman's personality, made him speak 'Pike' dialect, and in the end, to balance the last paragraph, actually consigned him to an early grave in spite of the fact that he outlived Harte himself. From this retrospect of thirty years Harte wrote:

We settled to our work with fatuous self-complacency, and no suspicion of the trouble in store for us, or the storm that was to presently hurtle around our devoted heads. I winnowed the poems, and he exploited a preliminary announcement to an eager and waiting press, and we moved together unwittingly to our doom.

From the large acquisition of material sent in voluntarily, from Miss Tingley's folder, and from his own sources Harte made his selections, and in time for the Christmas trade in 1865 *Outcroppings* made its appearance.

It was a small, thin volume, modestly and attractively bound. It bore the imprints both of Roman and of the New York house which had actually done the printing, and was incorrectly dated 1866. In addition to the imprints and a small decoration the title-page read only: *Outcroppings, Being Selections of California Verse.* The editor's name appeared neither there nor in connection with the short preface which contained an acknowledgment to Miss Tingley, an apology for the limitations of California verse, and a sop to the feelings of those whose poems had been omitted. The volume contained only forty-two short pieces, by nineteen writers.

Copies [wrote Harte] were liberally supplied to the press, and authors and publisher self-complacently awaited the result. To the latter this should have been satisfactory; the book sold readily from his well-known counters to purchasers who seemed to be drawn by a singular curiosity, unaccompanied, however, by any critical comment. People would lounge in to the shop, turn over the leaves of other volumes, say carelessly, 'Got a new book of California poetry out, haven't you?' purchase it, and quietly depart. There were as yet no notices from the press; the big dailies were silent; there was something ominous in this calm.

The calm must have been only a matter of hours, for Harte, if he did not like Byron awake one day to find himself famous, at least awoke to find himself the most belabored man in print and conversation upon the Pacific Coast. His attempt at editorial anonymity had been of no avail. The local world fell into three camps. The first was that of Roman, Harte, and the sixteen still surviving poets whose verses were included; the second, of the poets whose work had been excluded, and they were legion. In the third were the inhabitants of California who did not write poetry or have a poet in the family — one has the impression that they were only a handful; these aided the general commotion by crying 'Fight dog! Fight cat!' Among the last was the editor of the *News Letter*, who satirically summarized the situation in his issue of December 9, 1865, under the heading 'A Commotion on Parnassus':

Mr. Frank Bret Harte's long-promised and much talked of book of the California poets has at last arrived in this city. Within two hours after it was known to be in town, a mob of poets, consisting of 1100 persons of various ages and colors, and of both sexes, besieged Roman's bookstore, all eager to ascertain whether they had been immortalized by Harte. Mr. Bell, the poet of the *Elevator*, was the first who succeeded in securing a copy. But on issuing from the store, with his prize, seventeen *Flag*-poets, including eleven males and six females (four of the former being gentlemen of color) pounced upon the unfortunate contraband editor, and captured the

Tempest in a Teapot

volume. Meantime, an *Alta* poet, having discovered that he was left out in the cold, rushed down to Meiggs Wharf to drown himself, but upon observing the disagreeable temperature of the water, changed his mind, and concluded to abuse the heartless Harte in the newspapers instead. On Tuesday the book arrived in San Francisco; on Thursday the news had been circulated throughout the State, and the 'country poets' were in a state of fearful excitement. Yesterday it was rumored that a delegation of three or four hundred of these were coming down on the Sacramento boat, in a 'fine phrensy,' and swearing dire vengeance against Harte. That gentleman by the advice of his friends, immediately repaired to the Station House, to be locked up for protection.

On the same day Inigo in the *Californian*, with thoughts of Thanksgiving still in mind, commented: 'I am thankful today that I... am not the editor of Outcroppings.'

Harte, as if he had not done enough already, gave more ammunition to the enemy by the silly mistake of publishing in the *Californian* immediately under his own name as editor a review of *Outcroppings*, which assumed ignorance of the identity of its compiler and even implied that he was to be sought among the contributors; the reviewer added his sophistical opinion that he could not 'help thinking this volume premature.' Whether or not Harte actually was the author of this review, its appearance in his editorial column made him responsible and laid him wide open to attack.

On the heels of the original excitement followed the reviews, and the poor editor found himself pummeled from all angles. He was found guilty of such a catalogue of offenses as might have appalled the Devil himself. He had omitted poets who should have been included, notably a certain Frank Soulé, who, to judge by the reviewers' references, was a veritable Californian Homer.

(133)

But the editor's omissions were not more heinous than his commissions. Had he not chosen unduly from the verses of his friends the contributors to the *Californian* — Coolbrith, Lawson, Stoddard, and Webb? The comment in the *American Flag* expressed the extreme point of view:

Outcroppings is a Bohemian advertizing medium for Webb, Harte, and Co. As a collection of California poetry it is beneath contempt.

The reviewers also noticed the preface as an ungraceful apology for Western poetry amounting to an actual slur even upon the verses published in the volume. The notice in the *Californian* was called disingenuous, or even dishonest. The editor's omission of his own poems brought forth the inquiry whether he considered them too good or too poor for the anthology, and the invariable answer that it must have been the former, and that he was too proud of his verses to include them after a derogatory preface. In pursuit of the man and the compiler, the reviewers were in fact so eager that they sometimes fell to complimenting Harte as a poet, declaring that the best way to have improved the volume would have been to include some of his own work. Even in the columns of his own magazine the editor was not safe from the fun-makers and could not maintain his anonymity, for in the very midst of the tumult *Inigo* roguishly declared:

I notice that the editor put none of his own compositions in the volume... making a feint of modesty. May we not say to him, 'feint, Harte, never won fair lady'?

The longest and most vigorous review appeared in the *Territorial Enterprise* of Virginia City, the journal for which Mark Twain had formerly reported. Throughout the length of several columns the unfortunate editor and his work were subjected to piecemeal vivisection. Webb's verses were characterized as 'trash.' Of the notice in the *Californian* the comment ran: 'to say it is silly is not enough — it is most intolerable snobbery.' Another Nevadan paper, the *Gold Hill News*, called the whole collection effeminate, unworthy of the virile West, and epitomized it as 'purp-stuff,' an epithet which thirty years later still stuck in Harte's memory.

Gossip went even further than the reviews. Rumor had it, Harte, making sure of Parnassus by even the most despised route, had, by surreptitiously using a signature H. C. B., actually inserted one of his own poems. Tradition of this still lingers among book-collectors and has appeared in print, although there is the strongest direct evidence to the contrary. To cap the whole, Miss Tingley's friends charged Harte with unethical practice in using her material and downright dishonesty in breaking the seals of her folder and scattering her papers. They even threatened prosecution.

On the other side Harte and his friends struck back. Mark Twain in a brief article declared Harte to have shown 'rare good taste and ability in all respects save one — he has not put in a single line of his own poetry,' but added, 'He will catch it from all the water-and-milk and thunder-and-earthquake poets.' Harte himself countered by printing in the *Californian* two satiric reviews of an imagined *Tailings, Being Rejections of California Verse*, supposed to have been compiled by the editors of the Nevadan papers, in which he paid back vigorously the scalpings which *Outcroppings* had received in their columns.

(135)

Bret Harte

So great was the popular interest that on the one hand H. H. Bancroft, Roman's rival publisher, took occasion to announce the undertaking of a bigger-and-better collection to be called *Poetry of the Pacific*, and on the other hand some enterprising advertisers issued a little blue pamphlet entitled *Outcroppings*, containing parodies, and announcing the virtues of Ward's Shirts and Le Count's Bookstore.

Like this last little volume, one cannot help feeling that much of the hullabaloo about *Outcroppings* was less in bile than in laughter, that Gargantuan laughter of the West. Harte himself thought so thirty years later, and, although time had perhaps caused him to forget the rankling of reviewers' darts, still the very fact that he cared to recall the matter at all shows that he did not consider it too deeply. It is always easier and more amusing to 'scalp' a book than to praise it, and, the fashion once set, every succeeding reviewer set out to make the chorus fuller. Fine ethical points of a preface or personally written review were not likely so seriously to bother Western editors who could still remember when navy pistols and bowie-knives were standard office-equipment.

In Harte's career the whole affair was a minor interlude. *Outcroppings* itself has collected dust these many years, and most modern readers who stumble upon it will be inclined, I am afraid, to have some sympathy with the opinions of the Nevadan reviewers. But this was not Harte's fault, for he could only choose from verse which was available; that he chose as well as could be expected is indicated by *Poetry of the Pacific*, which is much worse, that is at least, there is five times as much of it.

Tempest in a Teapot

On the whole, however, the incident showed Harte unpleasantly; for the first time he made public display of certain unadmirable qualities. His preface was ungracious to the poets whose work he used, and suggested that the editor was apologizing for his connection with the volume. The omission of his own poems also was suggestive of egotism. In respect to the *Californian* notice, he was culpable, not only for disingenuousness, but also for childish silliness in supposing that his identity as anthologist could ever be concealed in the small gossipy San Francisco of those days.

The most serious charge against Harte was that of dishonesty with respect to Miss Tingley. At that time she worked in the Mint and saw him daily, but she did not know that he was using her material until the book appeared; this certainly suggests double-dealing. On the other hand, much can be said for Harte. The result showed that he depended but little upon her collection, for most of the poems in *Outcroppings* had appeared in magazines during the three years while her selections had been in Roman's possession, and others were well known to all readers of Western verse. Nevertheless, Harte in the preface honestly acknowledged a debt to her. The real responsibility, moreover, was Roman's; the collection had been entrusted to him; without his initiative Harte could scarcely have had access to it or even have known of it, and he may well have supposed that the publisher had acquired rights to the material. This is confirmed by Harte's statement in a letter to Roman:

I understand that Miss Tingley disavows your right to use her selections. I trust you have written to her before this, and relieved me of responsibility in the matter.

Bret Harte

The trouble is that this concern came a little late. A man of fine sense of honor, who had a real regard for the feelings of others, would before the deed have made sure of his moral right to use another's unprotected property.

At this time Harte's literary stature was rapidly growing. Those whom he dwarfed were ready to vent themselves against him, and *Outcroppings* gave them only too good an opportunity. While their enmity could not stop his growth, one cannot help thinking that some of the disrepute which marred his later life traced its origin to the time when he engaged in what should have been the innocent amusement of collecting a little volume of verses to catch the holiday trade.

CHAPTER XVIII

THE CALAVERAS SKULL

HARTE's second withdrawal from the *Californian* followed so closely upon the troubles over *Outcroppings* that one is likely to think him forced into retirement. More probably the reason was that he was too busy with other projects. Besides working regularly in the Mint, he was at this time under obligations to write for two Eastern newspapers, and was also planning the publication of a book.

As early as November 1, 1865, the *Californian* had announced that the 'condensed novels' were soon to appear in more permanent form. In February, 1866, just after his retirement, another mention of Bret commented: 'by and by, when he publishes that book with which he is big.' The project at that time was for the two friends, Twain and Harte, to combine forces. As one of the former's letters, January 20, 1866, explained:

Though I am generally placed at the head of my breed of scribblers in this part of the country, the place properly belongs to Bret Harte, I think, though he denies it, along with the rest. He wants me to club a lot of old sketches, together with a lot of his, and publish a book. I wouldn't do it, only he agrees to take all the trouble. But I want to know whether we are going to make anything out of it, first. However, he has written to a New York publisher, and if we are offered a bargain that will pay for a month's labor we will go to work and prepare the volume for the press.

Nothing came of these negotiations, and the joint volume never saw the light. As a first book of both men

Bret Harte

with both names on the title-page, what a prize it would have been for collectors!

While his luck with literary ventures rose and fell, Harte continued to draw most of his income from his position in the Mint, and to prosper in that work. His salary rose rapidly until it reached two hundred and seventy dollars a month. After a reorganization he became head of the General Department; as such he had twelve men under his direction and was responsible for the care of the building. In an institution which annually handled millions of dollars in gold, this was a post of responsibility and trust, and in it Harte left a good record.

The family life continued much as in earlier years. In 1865 a second son had been born, and named Francis King after the father and the beloved patron. Harte's income was now sufficient to let the family have a vacation away from the city in the summers, usually at San Rafael. In San Francisco, as *Neighborhoods I Have Moved From* shows, they moved annually or oftener. At the time of Harte's retirement from the *Californian* they lived in the wind-swept location at the western edge of the city described in *My Suburban Residence*. A large cemetery was close by, and funerals constantly passed. These at first afforded the household great excitement, but as the father noticed they soon grew blasé and refused to turn out for anything less than six carriages. The children, however, took to playing funeral, and delighted with the idea the father joined them with great zest. He usually took the part of the hearse, and, a feather-duster fastened upright on his back to represent the plumes, he marched on all fours at the head of the procession. It is no wonder that young 'Wodie'

(140)

was on such good terms with his father as to call him
'Bret.'

Webb coming to call one day in February, 1866, was
delighted with 'the two pretty little boys' and the scene
which he discovered:

It is amusing to see this young father playing with his
children. Calling on him the other day I found him in the
parlor, flat on his back, tossing one of his boys in the air with
his feet, precisely as Buislay *père* does Buislay *fils*, at the
Metropolitan.

It was very funny indeed. Not quite as dexterous as
Buislay is, he yet succeeded in turning the little fellow over
like a butter-ball, and making him throw all sorts of somer-
sets and hand-springs.

A summary stop was put to the amusement when Mrs.
Bret entered the room, and, from the rapidity with which the
curtain fell on the performance, I've an idea that she does
not wish to see her children made a circus of.

Life in this house seems to have been eventful. A
burglar visited it one night, but Harte, as a sensible
father of a family, remained discreetly in bed. Afterwards he bought a Newfoundland watch-dog and a revolver; the latter had a hair-trigger and both were
equally dangerous to approach. The dog proved more
useful than the revolver, for he supplied material for an
ironic essay *On the Sagacity of the Newfoundland*.

After four months, Harte returned to the *Californian*.
The situation had changed greatly. Webb was on his
way back to New York, having left San Francisco for
good; he had lost heavily on his journalistic venture,
and had long since relinquished financial control. The
Californian, so gallantly launched less than two years
before, was already a sinking ship. Between April 28
and August 18, Harte contributed eleven signed items,

and may also have acted as editor. Then J. P. Bogardus purchased a controlling interest, and the signature 'Bret' disappeared.

The next-to-last of Harte's contributions to the *Californian* was the poem *To the Pliocene Skull*, the background of which deserves commemoration as an indication both of Harte's ability to seize upon a timely theme, and of the time itself. Darwin's *Origin of Species* had appeared in 1859, and throughout the sixties even in isolated San Francisco interest was rife regarding evolution and the origin of man. Notices of the discovery of fossil human remains in California were common.

This interest came to a head — quite literally — with the announcement in 1866 that a miner had discovered a very ancient human skull. An account of the discovery which Harte himself wrote is breezy, yet accurate.

It appears that an honest miner, named James Matson, digging in a shaft in Calaveras County, came across this osseous fragment at the depth of two hundred and fifty feet. The relic passed into the hands of Scribner, merchant, who transferred it to Jones, doctor, who, in turn, handed it over to the state geological survey, where it exactly fitted a theory promulgated by the survey of the extreme antiquity of man on this coast. Professor Whitney has visited the shaft, and is confident that the position of the skull justifies him in ascribing its introduction to a period anterior to the lava deposits. This would make it antedate the mastodon, the pachyderms, and, indeed, most of the paleotheres.

Harte went on to consider how difficult life must have been among lava-flows, and great saurians for a defenseless man with a skull not unlike a Digger Indian's. He also described the confusion of the theologians:

Dr. Jones is reported to have given concrete expression to the opinions of the latter, by remarking in a peculiarly Cali-

The Calaveras Skull

fornian manner, as he took up the skull: 'This knocks h—ll out of Moses!'

He concluded:

Doubtless the society of pioneers will claim the skull as a member.

On July 16, 1866, Professor J. D. Whitney, distinguished savant and eponymous hero of the highest mountain in the United States, read a paper before the California Academy of Natural Sciences. He gravely exhibited the skull, told the circumstances, and stated the serious implications for the history of man.

Now the reports of the California Academy of Natural Sciences show that at that time it dabbled in everything from *Abies* to *Zua lubrica;* its popular reputation was that of the Academy of Lagoda, and it had already drawn the fire of John Phœnix, the first Western humorist. The whole matter of the skull, moreover, had every mark of the hoax. The Californian mining camp in dull times throve upon such carefully contrived humbuggery. We have only to remember the many hoaxes perpetrated by or upon Mark Twain. (One of the men involved with the skull was a Mr. Coons of Angel's, in all probability the same who shortly before had told Twain the story of the jumping frog.) Hoaxes often were highly elaborate like the proceedings of the 'stockholders' of the Pound Package Smoke Company of Jamestown, who for four months played with the fiction of importing smoke in pound packages by steamboat up Wood's Creek, this last a tumbling mountain brook. There was thus to the man in the street something profoundly funny in having this skull of doubtful parentage pompously discussed by learned gentlemen in frock-coats,

Bret Harte

and while they deliberated, a mischievous young journalist was loading his bomb. Taking the meter and mock-heroic tone of Holmes's *De Sauty*, he added in the address to the skull a parody of the popular *Skeleton in Armor*. Upon these he imposed skillfully the academicians' own terminology, and finally identified the skull itself as that of the famous Joe Bowers of Pike, hero of a popular song and a kind of Western John Doe —

> Which my name is Bowers, and my crust was busted
> Falling down a shaft in Calaveras County,
> But I'd take it kindly if you'd send the pieces
> Home to old Missouri!

This petard was exploded in the *Californian* a fortnight after Professor Whitney's report; the whole town roared, to the confusion of the Academy, and since that time no one with any common-sense has been able to take the Calaveras man seriously. The skull itself, a dilapidated and unhonored fragment, rests in the Peabody Museum at Harvard University, where the honest plaster-casts of Heidelberg and Piltdown doubtless snub it daily as a charlatan and impostor.

CHAPTER XIX

HIGHWAYS AND BYWAYS TO FAME

AFTER his final retirement from the *Californian* in the summer of 1866, Harte had for nearly two years no close connection with any magazine. He did a good deal of miscellaneous writing, however, and in various ways, some obvious and some devious, advanced his literary career.

Early in the year he had established himself as correspondent for two Eastern journals. His connection with Unitarianism through King had probably gained him this position with the Boston *Christian Register*, although there was something decidedly incongruous in his writing on the *Unitarian Conference in California* and the *Sanctity of Wednesday Evening*. With the *Springfield Republican* he was more congenially matched. Its editor, Samuel Bowles, had in 1865 visited San Francisco, and at that time had arranged for Harte's correspondence. The type-setters of Springfield were a little surprised to have letters from the Wild West written 'on thin, dainty, highly finished French note-paper in purple ink, in a delicately, scrupulously finished hand.' These letters were of more general interest than those sent to the *Register*, but by the end of the year Harte had ceased to contribute to either paper.

In '66 and '67 he had various connections with the San Franciscan newspapers, apparently acting as dramatic critic for the *Call*, and contributing special articles to the *Alta* and the *Chronicle*. Except for a few items in the *Bulletin*, however, the writing which he did for the local newspapers was apparently unsigned and can have been of little importance. The friendships established during his association with the journalistic world were of greater value.

In these years also he was widening his experience in many ways. Poverty and family ties no longer held him so close to San Francisco. He once spent a week camping in Yosemite Valley. In 1866 he visited the State Fair at Sacramento. In the next year he and Noah Brooks were there during the gubernatorial campaign, and observed an old-time politician who according to Brooks gave many suggestions for Colonel Starbottle. Harte apparently visited Virginia City at least once. He also went fishing, and this hobby may have taken him to out-of-the-way places. In the *Californian* during the summer of 1866, a series of articles described the happy-go-lucky angling party of Sacramentan and San Franciscan journalists who, after good sport on the upper forks of the American, crossed the summit and penetrated as far as isolated Hope Valley. It is possible that Harte was one of them. In any case several of his stories were to show a personal knowledge of the higher mountain country, and in a letter he once mentioned having often been ten thousand feet up in the Sierras. Many of his mining camps are suggestive of the utter decay of the later sixties — 'the disused ditches, the scarred flats, the discarded levels, ruined flumes, and roofless cabins.'

In 1867, Harte established his reputation the more firmly by publishing two collections of his own writings. For two years he had been considering a book of 'condensed novels.' Their reputation justified his attempt, for they had been reprinted frequently and had become known in the East. A critic of Artemus Ward's work in the *North American Review* of April, 1866, had mentioned Harte as 'a parodist of such genius that he seems a mirror into which novelists may look and be warned.' Carleton, although he had recently refused Mark Twain's *Jumping Frog* volume, finally undertook the publication of Harte's material. About the beginning of October, 1867, at last appeared *Condensed Novels and Other Papers*, by F. Bret Harte, with comic illustrations by Frank Bellew. The volume was inscribed to the memory of Thomas Starr King. As with *Outcroppings* the most unfortunate part of the book was the apologetic preface, which began:

The style and finish of the following sketches may make it sufficiently obvious to the reader, without further statement, that they are written with no higher ambition than that of filling the ephemeral pages of a weekly paper.

Hostile reviewers were not slow in commenting upon the resemblance to the earlier preface, and in pointing out that what purported to be humility was really egotism, since it suggested that the present pieces were merely tossed off and that the author, had he really tried, could have done much better.

The contents of the three hundred octavo pages included some of the *Bohemian Papers*, three Irvingesque myths of early California, and *A Night at Wingdam*, which was both the earliest piece admitted and the only one dealing realistically with the Western background. Neither version of *M'liss* was included. The volume was really an anthology of the author's prose work for his six years in San Francisco. The 'condensed novels,' however, as title and preface showed, were its core and *raison d'être. Fantine* and *La Femme,* the earliest of these fifteen travesties of popular contemporary novels, had appeared in the *Era,* the others in the *Californian,* where their introduction had announced that the magazine was now able to offer to its readers a three-volume novel in a single issue, 'or, so to speak, a seventy-five-cent book for ten cents.' Their success had been well deserved. Even today they are excellent reading, for Harte, with what seems fine critical penetration, chose to parody writers who are still known and read. Except for the omission of Thackeray and Hawthorne, he could scarcely have selected with better eye for the future. Dickens, Cooper, Marryat, Collins, Bulwer, Charlotte Brontë, Dumas, and Hugo are all there, and even T. S. Arthur, if forgotten as a novelist, is still remembered for *Ten Nights in a Bar-Room.*

Reviews were on the whole satisfactory, although Harte's old enemy, the *Territorial Enterprise,* took him to task for being imitative. The *Atlantic Monthly* granted a brief notice, and expressed mild admiration for the 'charming parodies, so well known in California.' Harte himself was not greatly pleased with the illustrations and general appearance of the volume — 'its circus clown's dress, and painted grins.' Almost the whole edition sold out immediately, but since the royalty was only ten cents a volume, the profit was somewhat less than two hundred dollars.

Only a few weeks after *Condensed Novels,* Harte's first book of original verse, *The Lost Galleon and Other Tales,* also appeared in the bookshops of San Francisco. It was, like *Outcroppings* of two years before, timed and designed for the holiday trade. The product of the local publishers Towne and Bacon, the small volume was immediately hailed as the finest piece of Californian book-making yet to appear. The binding was of brown cloth with a gilt emblem; paper and print were admirable; on the title-page the name of the title-poem and of the author stood out in mellow red. Like *Condensed Novels* the book was an anthology of work already published. There was no prose introduction, but with curious fatuity the author managed to give the suggestion of apology by some prefatory verses, and by the lines quoted as a motto:

> The earth hath bubbles as the water hath,
> And these are of them.

In contrast to *Outcroppings*, this volume of Harte's own verse caused no disturbance, and called forth only routine notices, generally laudatory. One reviewer — by this time the habit must have been established — objected to Harte's apologizings as 'an affectation of self-disparagement.' The *Daily Dramatic Chronicle*, under the heading *A Plagiary Poet*, indulged in some scurrility charging complete inanity except where relieved by thefts from Praed, Whittier, Holmes, Edward Pollock, and others. The local reviewers agreed that no such 'elegant' volume had ever before been printed in California.

During 1867, Harte also contributed irregularly to the San Francisco *News Letter* in both verse and prose. This little weekly was the bad boy of Western magazines; the students of the University of Michigan once petitioned the faculty to ban its ribald pages from the library. It offered Harte an excellent opportunity for the development of his satiric powers, and some of his prose contributions, although of no intrinsic value, are of great interest in the light of their author's later career. To understand their significance, however, one must realize their background and the attitude of mind in which Harte wrote them.

The original gold-rush of 1848 and the year or two following had had undoubtedly a tinge of the heroic. Strong and courageous men gambled their lives against gold. All ranks of society met in the struggle — the border desperado and the college graduate, the runaway sailor and the English gentleman. In a few years this had changed; rich finds became fewer and fewer; mining life grew humdrum; men of education and ability turned to other fields; miners came to be mere pick-and-shovel laborers, and were so regarded. As a miners' song of the middle fifties commented upon the 'Hangtown gals':

> They're dreadful shy of forty-niners,
> Turn their noses up at miners.

People who like Harte did not arrive in California until this time naturally assumed this attitude.

Miners, however, still constituted a large part of the State's population, and magazines like the *Era* were still, as late as the sixties, rendering at least lip-service in praise of the virtues of the 'honest miner.' The *Californian*, on the other hand, had tuned itself to the urban standard of San Francisco, and assumed that cultured people had no interest in reading about boors. Its youthful editors and contributors, who had not known the days of '49, looked upon the miner unsentimentally as a person who in intelligence and social position ranked with the ditch-digger of the city and the farmer's hired man. An editorial in the *Californian* of November 25, 1866, commenting upon the frequent use of the signature *Honest Miner* in communications to newspapers queried:

whether a gentleman who fried his beefsteaks and devoured saleratus bread was authority in matters of taste, whether a citizen who hanged horse-thieves and acquitted murderers was particularly sound as a politician, and whether the individual who contributed a fund of impious slang to the national vocabulary was peculiarly estimable as a moral teacher.

In the next issue Harte himself expressed a preference for the liquidity of Indian and Spanish place-names and commented upon the unromantic ugliness of American monstrosities such as Poker Flat, Red Dog, and One Horse Flat. In a letter to the *Christian Register* he noted cynically:

The less said about the motives of some of our pioneers the better; very many were more concerned in getting away from where they were, than in going to any particular place.

But these young critics of the *Californian* were too cock-sure. They failed to see that though the miner of the sixties might be only subject for ridicule, his forbear of '49, half a generation distant, with the haze of time magnifying his original not unheroic stature, was beginning to appear romantic. In 1865, for instance, a vigorous inland newspaper, the Sacramento *Union*, declared that the 'grand gold-hunting crusade' was a fine theme for an epic, a suggestion which Harte poohpoohed editorially.

Many of the critics of *Outcroppings* had objected to an anthology of verses on sunsets, birds, and flowers, when the real glory of the State was in its crude but heroic beginning. To these criticisms Harte had, as we have noted, struck back vigorously with two satiric re-

views of a pretended *Tailings*. From this imagined
anthology he had 'quoted' several selections illustrative
of what genuine Western poetry would have to be.
These were, of course, his own compositions, and in writing them he all unconsciously took a long step on the
road to fame. In one of them particularly, a parody of
Locksley Hall called *One Horse Flat*, appeared touches of
what we have since come to regard as his best humorous
style. It is worth quoting in part, for it reads like a pre-
study of the *Heathen Chinee*:

Bill took up the dice and shook 'em with a sweet seraphic smile,
Shook the dice and threw four sixes, and of course raked down the
     pile.

But he dealt the keards more deftly than was fit in one so young,
And my eyes on all his motions with a mute observance hung.

And I said, 'My festive William, speak and speak the truth to me:
How it is when I've two aces, that thou always dost have three?'

Then he turned, his whole cheek flushing — he was taken by sur-
     prise —
With a quiet imprecation in regard to his own eyes,

Saying: 'I have hid the bower, Pard'ner — I would do thee wrong,
And my boots the king and ten-spot have been hiding all along.'

Many an evening in our cabin did we sit with flaming dips,
And the spirits mixed together, that we tasted with our lips.

Many an evening with a neighbor did we turn the festive Jack,
Lightly dealt ourselves the bowers from the bottom of the pack.

The San Franciscan wits saw an opportunity for their
satiric powers in this arising of a sentimental interest in
the tobacco-chewing, unshorn gentry of the mining
camps. Satire is in the atmosphere of the *Jumping Frog*.
Prentice Mulford, who certainly knew the reality of
later mining life, contributed the *Life and Adventures of*

Highways and Byways to Fame

Barney McBriar, the Shootist, a keen satiric sketch of a frontier bravo. But chief among those who hurled stones was Harte. An opportunity came to him when in 1866 he read *The Life and Confessions of James Gilbert Jenkins, the Murderer of Eighteen Men,* who had been hanged at Napa two years previously. This lurid memorial presented the worst type of frontiersman — a dull-witted, lewd murderer in cold blood, not even saved by that spark of courage which lights up the portraits of most Western bad-men. Upon this confession Harte based his *Sylvester Jayhawk,* a vigorous if slightly unfair retort to those who were beginning to sentimentalize frontier ruffians as primordial giants of the heroic age. But the interest in a local literature was not to be killed. A year after Harte's final retirement, the *Californian* ran an editorial on Western writers. It granted that Harte was the most finished among them, but went on significantly:

We cannot now recall anything of his — we refer to his prose — that bears any intrinsic evidence, beyond some merely unessential local allusion, that it was written in San Francisco rather than in New York or Boston.

The article concluded with the prediction that a great reputation was yet to be made by a writer who should portray the life of the mining camps.

Harte would not have agreed. During 1867 his sketches in the *News Letter* continued in the satiric vein. They stressed the crudity and brutality, the callowness and the callousness of the miner and the frontiersman, but in them, strangely circumstanced, appeared names which were later in a different atmosphere to become famous. There were mentions of mining towns —

Slumgullion and Wingdam; and of people — Mr. Gash-wiler, Colonel Calhoun Bungstarter, and Judge Star-bottle of Mudsprings. The titles are a little confused, but there is no doubt about the names. Like Cervantes and Fielding, Harte began by creating a straw-figure for satire who later came to life as Colonel Starbottle, blue coat, pomposity and all, but who, like Don Quixote and Joseph Andrews, never quite escaped the trace of his origin.

Like Saul of Tarsus, to compare small things to great, Harte in '67 was yet breathing out threatenings and slaughter against the new gospel that any romance could come from the mining camps; a year later he was to be the chief apostle of the new faith. He has left us no confession of the light which he saw upon the road, but we can at least record the known events of the year which lay between the satire of, for instance, *St. Patrick's Day at Slumgullion Center*, and the sentimental romance of the *Luck of Roaring Camp*.

CHAPTER XX

THE OVERLAND MONTHLY

EARLY in 1868 the enterprising Anton Roman determined to establish a new magazine of a higher standard than any which had yet appeared on the Pacific Coast. The time seemed opportune, for the *Californian*, which once might have offered competition, was dying, and on February 1 finally expired. Because of the number of manuscripts presented to him as publisher, Roman believed that California could supply sufficient material for the enterprise. He considered also that the Far West, with San Francisco as its metropolis, needed and could support a good magazine which would as its primary function supply information on the development of the Pacific Coast and its vast unsettled back-country. He circularized the merchants, and soon had contracts for advertising which assured an income of nine hundred dollars monthly for a year. On his own part he guaranteed a circulation of three thousand copies monthly. He talked over matters of policy with friends, including Charles Warren Stoddard, who suggested Harte for editor.

No matter how suggested, Harte's name must have come up for consideration, for he was by this time often mentioned as the leading man of letters of the Coast, and had already had editorial experience. But Roman had doubts. He thought, not without reason, that under Harte's control the magazine would lean too much toward the purely literary, and shirk its duty of booming the West. He felt also that Harte, if free from editorial minutiæ, would be more valuable as a contributor.

Nevertheless, no one else in San Francisco could equal him, and Roman made advances.

Harte did not embrace the offer readily. He had already learned that the editor's chair was not the easiest of seats; he feared that a dearth of contributions would throw too great a burden of writing upon the editor; he doubted whether the new magazine, against the competition of Eastern rivals, could gain a sufficient number of readers to be finally successful. To convince him on this last point, Roman with a fine gesture pointed to the map of the two hemispheres hanging upon the wall to show how much of the world lay open as a field for intellectual exports from the Golden Gate; there was no doubt about the area, but one wonders what subscription list he expected from the broad blue expanse to westward or the almost equally uninhabited hinterland to the east.

Harte finally yielded, but with, for once, a streak of his grandfather's business capacity, he struck a good bargain. In addition to an adequate salary he stipulated complete control of contents, no signatures to any contributions, and an assistant editor. For the first six months, moreover, Roman himself agreed to be responsible for obtaining half of the articles. Harte also took the precaution of exacting promises of contributions from all his literary friends. Noah Brooks, of the *Alta*, agreed to act as assistant editor, and W. C. Bartlett, of the *Bulletin*, also offered help and support in this capacity.

These preliminaries were arranged by April, and the first issue of the magazine was set for July. In the interim for the completion of plans the Roman and Harte families practically set up housekeeping together. The

The Overland Monthly

Superintendent at the Mint must have been even more than usually complaisant, for the three months were largely spent in pleasant places far from the city. The combined families went first to San José; then, as the great wheatfields of the plain began to bake out, they moved to a retired spot in the Santa Cruz Mountains, and finally sought the ocean itself at Santa Cruz.

On July 1, 1868, the observing San Franciscan noticed a new magazine on the stands. At first glance, seeing only the quarto size and brown-buff cover, he might have supposed that the steamer had arrived earlier than usual with the month's consignment of the *Atlantic Monthly*, but he saw next that the title was the *Overland Monthly*, and examining more closely found that it was published locally and according to the motto — 'devoted to the development of the country.' Thus lured on to find out what inducements were offered to investment and what eulogies pronounced upon opportunities for wheat-farming and gold-mining, he was surprised to find the contents belying the statement of the title-page. There were, to be sure, articles upon various districts bordering the Pacific Ocean — Mexico, Hawaii, and Oregon — but whoever wrote them must have been interested in travel and description more than in possibilities for business. *Art Beginnings on the Pacific* — that was not the sort of thing to attract capital. In a poem called *San Francisco from the Sea* the writer (like the other contributions, this was unsigned) was scarcely even respectful in his references to the city:

> I know thy cunning and thy greed,
> Thy hard high lust and wilful deed,
>
> And all thy glory loves to tell
> Of specious gifts material.

although farther on he referred to

The glory of her coming days.

There were also other poems and articles, and a few
stories. The travel-sketch *By Rail through France*
might be by that clownish fellow, Mark Twain, who had
lectured on the Sandwich Islands, and recently written
a lot of letters to the *Alta* on the experiences of a ship-
load of Americans in Europe. At the end of the magazine were book reviews and an editorial section called
Etc.; that was like the *Atlantic* too. In fact, when you
considered it, the magazine was about as much like the
Atlantic inside as out — literary all through. What was
the meaning of *Overland*? The editorial page explained.
It seems that *Pacific Monthly* had been considered too
imitative. Other names like Hesperian and Occidental
had seemed too flatly sentimental, and anything with
Californian in it would not appeal to people outside the
State. So *Overland* had been chosen because it suggested
the new railroad on the old overland trail which would
be finished now in less than a year. Yes, that was a
pretty good idea for a name after all. As the editor
went on to say, the railroad might mean that San Francisco would absorb all the trade of the big mountain
country, sure to develop soon. Yes, *Overland* was a good
name, looked forward to the New Era. No more long
steamship passages clear down to Greytown. First
thing you know we'll be going through to New York in
ten days, maybe. Well, always a good thing to help out
local enterprises. So, pocketing his new purchase, the
San Franciscan went on his way, sensibly proud that his
city could produce a magazine so much resembling
Boston's best, but otherwise not greatly impressed.

The *Overland Monthly*

On the title-page he may have noticed that, again like the *Atlantic*, the new magazine carried an emblem — a bear upon a railway track, snarling at a presumably approaching train. This had a history. Mark Twain in fact declared it 'the prettiest fancy and the neatest that ever shot through Harte's brain.' The founders of the *Overland* had naturally selected for emblem a grizzly bear, the State's totem ever  since the raising of the Bear Flag. A grizzly was drawn, engraved, and printed, but he seemed insufficient. Let Mark Twain, at the time on a flying visit to San Francisco, continue his story:

> As a bear, he was a success — he was a good bear. — But then, it was objected, that he was an *objectless* bear — a bear that *meant* nothing in particular, signified nothing, — simply stood there snarling over his shoulder at nothing — and was painfully and manifestly a boorish and ill-natured intruder upon the fair page. All hands said that — none were satisfied. They hated badly to give him up, and yet they hated as much to have him there when there was no *point* to him. But presently Harte took a pencil and drew these two simple lines under his feet and behold he was a magnificent success! — the ancient symbol of California savagery snarling at the approaching type of high and progressive Civilization, the first Overland locomotive!
>
> I think that was nothing less than inspiration itself.

But one wonders whether Twain, Harte, or anyone else that day in San Francisco felt the full ironic significance of the emblem, or realized that the *Overland* in its very name suggested its own worst enemy. As long as California was isolated, it had a chance for its own cultural development; but once the railroad had made it a

Bret Harte

suburb of New York City, both the possibility and the
need of the *Overland's* survival disappeared. Instead of
making the inland country tributary to San Francisco,
the railroad made both tributary to New York. It
would be pleasant to think that Harte realized the situation, and drew those two lines under the bear in a spirit
of ironic fatalism. But even had he realized, he would
probably have been ready enough to exchange possible
individuality for the carloads of ready-made culture
and progress which the railroad seemed to bring. For
him the bear stood for the churlish crudity of the frontier from which he had revolted; the railroad for the
East and Europe which had long been his Eldorado, not
of the setting, but of the rising sun.

He must have been proud of the first issue of the
Overland. Even more than his books, it represented an
achievement. At the age of thirty-two he found himself
editor of a fine magazine to whose columns a group of
his devoted literary friends, the best talent of the West,
had supplied material. His own contributions were the
poem *San Francisco from the Sea*, most of the reviews,
and the editorial section *Etc.*

Such was the first number. Although it received good
press-notices, nothing in it is remembered today. For
the second number there was to be a different story, but
from it we need for the moment consider only a few
sentences from *Etc.*, in which Harte discussed the Californian gold-rush:

Three hundred years, and what a glamour shall hang
about it! How the painters shall limn and the poets sing
these picturesque vagabonds of 'forty-nine'; how romantic
shall become the red-shirts, how heroic the high boots of the
pioneers!

The Overland Monthly

Although he still wrote of 'vagabonds,' Harte had obviously gone a long way since the year before when he had been satirizing Slumgullion Center. His prophecy, moreover, must rank as one of the worst in history. The bit of writing which was more than anything else to make the red shirts romantic and the high boots heroic was contained in the same issue in which the editorial appeared, and the period which was to recognize the glamor, far from being three hundred years in the future, was distant by hardly that many hours.

CHAPTER XXI

GOLD FROM THE GRASS-ROOTS

DURING the early months of 1868, in the pleasant valley of Santa Clara, by the surf of Santa Cruz, and among the mountains while the sun baked out the aroma from the pines, the two friends Harte and Roman had had many a pleasant conversation through the cigar smoke. With the present rosy and the future hopeful, Harte had been in his best mood. Roman always remembered the charm of those weeks. At the same time with an eye toward the success of the new magazine he had kept urging upon Harte the possibilities for literary development which lay waiting in the yet untold story of the early mining days. His own memories of gold-digging and book-peddling had given him opportunity for conversation, and he had also supplied clippings and pictures to illustrate his point.

Is it possible that Roman in 1853 had offered his books for sale in the then flourishing camp called Yankee Jim's, high up on the narrow divide between the North and Middle Forks of the American? A worthless doctor in a drunken frenzy shot and killed his wife. The chivalrous miners, always quick to resent any wrong to a woman, immediately seized the doctor and hanged him. So hasty was their action that only after the doctor was permanently dead did they realize that they had left on their hands a fatherless and motherless year-old baby. A young fellow of sixteen, however, already acquainted with the child and the mysteries of his feeding and care, rose to the emergency and assumed the responsibilities of a nurse. The miners made arrangements to have the child removed to the care of a family in the valley, but by that time the 'nurse' had become so devoted that he left the camp in order to continue living near the child who had been so strangely thrust upon him.

The resemblances of this story to the *Luck of Roaring Camp* seem too great to be coincidental. The callousness of the miners, who offer bets 'Three to five that "Sal would get through with it,"' is paralleled by that of those who hanged a man without thought of circumstances. The devotion of Stumpy as nurse is equaled by the lad of Yankee Jim's. The greatest difference results from the fact that the story is dated in 1850 and the event in 1853, for at the earlier date a home in the valley would not have been available, and the miners, like those of Roaring Camp, might have had to keep the child with them. The essential situation is the same in both cases — a community of rough men suddenly entrusted with a helpless infant.

However Harte came by the idea, he was busy upon the story in the three months' vacation. At Santa Cruz he sketched the outline for Róman. Mrs. Harte and Mrs. Roman read the manuscript and were the first of the many who were to laugh and weep over the adventures of Thomas Luck.

The story got as far as proof, and then suddenly there was commotion. The proof-reader, a young lady, first shocked by association even through the printed page with one of Cherokee Sal's profession, next dumbfounded by references to obstetrics, finally threw down the sheets in indignation at Kentuck's embarrassed ejaculation over the baby — 'The d——d little cuss!' Deciding that such immorality in literature must not be, she hurried hotly to the printer. He, good man, recognized the gravity of the situation, and carried the proof-sheets (with the fire-tongs, perhaps?) to the publisher. Roman and Harte had gone to Santa Cruz for the week-end, and no assistant dared a decision. Brooks approved of the story, but others were doubtful. For a day or two it seemed that prudish qualms might blight Harte's career and wither in the bud the development of American local-color fiction. But on their return both Harte and Roman ordered the story to go in, and destiny was accomplished by the appearance of the *Luck of Roaring Camp* in the August *Overland*.

Among the miners there was a phrase which indicated the superlative for a claim. In such diggings there was no need to labor for days to strip the worthless surface-gravel; one had only to pull up the sod and shake 'gold from the grass-roots.' So it was with Harte's Californian stories.

The sudden appearance of the *Luck* was about as close to a miracle as one finds in literary history, for its author's previous writings had shown almost no indication of what was coming. The story's popularity, moreover, and the praise which it received for freshness and originality show better than anything else that it was not directly based upon any model, that it was something new for the world. In its mingling of sentiment and humor it owed much to Dickens. In form, however, it was largely new, for Maupassant and Stevenson were only young lads, and far from being based upon some book on the art of the short story, the *Luck* was to be one of the bits of material upon which such books have based themselves. Together with a wholly new subject-matter the story thus offered to the world in many respects a new form. In addition, the more miraculous, it represented for its author a suddenly and completely changed artistic attitude toward life.

The explanation of the *Luck's* unheralded appearance lies in fact somewhere very deep in Harte's mental history. His writings before 1868 had been, to put matters flatly, those of snobbery. He had never forgotten that he must impress his readers with a sense of his own gentility, a characteristic which one can ascribe to a childhood spent in a family never able to occupy the position to which its members felt entitled. To such a one the world is divided sharply between low persons and people worth knowing. [M'liss was merely a low person who by a miracle turned out in the end to be one worth knowing.] In 1867, Harte in the *News Letter* was satirizing miners as low persons who, because they were neither elegant nor genteel, were not even interesting. Many writers have begun in this way. Chaucer wrote of the highly proper Black Knight, that stuffed doublet, before he gave us the Wife of Bath, and learned that a lady might be all the more interesting when somewhat disreputable, and a knight when wearing a dirty shirt. Shakespeare wrote *Love's Labour's Lost*, that handbook of snobbery, before he was capable of Falstaff.

Some time shortly before August, 1868, Harte also must have had a new realization. Most likely after the manner of conversions it came suddenly, a great light upon the road. If he had been given to self-expression, he might have left us record of the day and hour when some word or incident gave sight to this blind-spot of his consciousness, when he realized that people for the artist are not sheep and goats, but all sorts of interesting and amazing hybrids. The *Luck* sprang white-hot from this realization. The famous sentence of paradoxes reads like a crude statement of the new gospel:

The greatest scamp had a Raphael face, with a profusion of blond hair; Oakhurst, a gambler, had the melancholy and intellectual abstraction of a Hamlet; the coolest and most courageous man was scarcely over five feet in height, with a soft voice and an embarrassed, timid manner.

But Harte had learned not only that outward may belie inward qualities, but also that the inward qualities cannot be finally judged by any ready-made moral or social standard. 'Stumpy, in other climes, had been the putative head of two families'; this bigamist, or worse, was undoubtedly a low person, but Harte, bold in his new faith, could make him the hero of the story.

Harte himself is the authority to the effect that California, not relishing such a picture of its past, refused to accept the *Luck* until the East had praised it:

The secular press, with one or two exceptions, received it coolly, and referred to its 'singularity'; the religious press frantically excommunicated it, and anathematised it as the offspring of evil.... Christians were cautioned against pollution by its contact; practical business men were gravely urged to condemn and frown upon this picture of Californian society that was not conducive to Eastern immigration.

As usual, Harte exaggerated to make a good story. Californian opinion showed no such unanimity of dissent. The San José *Mercury*, for instance, commented:

A capital little story from the pen of Bret Harte, entitled 'The Luck of Roaring Camp,' we shall transfer to our columns next week.

Even the *Daily Dramatic Chronicle*, which seldom lost a chance to attack Harte and all his work, bestowed high

Gold from the Grass-Roots

praise on the *Luck*. Although the story was not signed in the magazine, the press references show that locally its anonymity was never more than formal.

From the East, however, came the greatest acclaim of the story, and that which must have been most flattering to its author. After its doubtful reception in California, the August *Overland* went East by the long route *via* the Isthmus. Weeks passed while the author must have wondered anxiously what reception his boldly original story would meet with the larger public of the Atlantic Coast. Finally came the return steamer with — again to quote Harte:

newspapers and reviews welcoming the little foundling of Californian literature with an enthusiasm that half frightened its author.

The same mail included:

a letter addressed to the 'Editor of the Overland Monthly,' enclosing a letter from Fields, Osgood & Co., the publishers of the *Atlantic Monthly*, addressed to the — to them — unknown 'Author of "The Luck of Roaring Camp."' This the author opened, and found to be a request, upon the most flattering terms, for a story for the *Atlantic* similar to the 'Luck.'

That perfect lady, the proof-reader, had tried to stem the ocean with a broom. Nevertheless, she merits a word of praise, for according to her own lights she was a keen and honest literary critic. Had she been any less, she might have equivocated or shirked the duty, failing to sense the story's implications for future literature or arguing that under the circumstances even the recording angel might have pardoned Kentuck's oath. But with true crusader's spirit she realized that such things must

(167)

not be, that if the seemingly innocent 'd——d' was allowed to stand, the barriers were down. She lost. But if she still survives today, she probably points to contemporary literature to prove that she was right. Out of politely veiled references to an off-stage Cherokee Sal and her profession has come the unmistakable 'whore' spelled in five letters; from the reference to a woman's 'martyrdom' have sprung lurid obstetrics; from 'd——d' has grown pointed and vociferous six-syllabled swearing and bawdry. Literature is no more for ladies and gentlemen. And when the fashions of life change again and future generations put us on trial, they will decide that one of the first serpents to enter the paradise of Victorian-American gentility was a very timorous weepy little adder who promised never even to mention apples — and his name was *The Luck of Roaring Camp*.

CHAPTER XXII

THE EDITOR

As he laid away in his scrapbook the dozens of clippings which testified to the brilliant success of the *Luck* and the *Overland*, Harte could at last feel that he had won fame in that literary career to which he had dedicated himself ten years before. Into a luxurious office on Clay Street the fastidiously dressed editor fitted admirably. There a fine and loyal group of associates gathered about him — Stoddard, Brooks, Bartlett, Clarence King, Prentice Mulford, Josephine Clifford, Ina Coolbrith. They recognized him as both leader and friend; several have recorded the kindly assistance which he gave them with their own writing.

Among them all the editor with his old friends Ina Coolbrith and Charles Stoddard formed a sort of inner triangle. 'They were like brothers to me,' Miss Coolbrith said in later years, and to someone returning to California Harte once gave the message, 'Tell Ina Coolbrith I shall never forget.' The three used to meet in her quiet parlor, where, as Stoddard described it, the atmosphere was that of a long summer afternoon perfumed with lavender; through the windows to add an exotic note came the sound of water tumbling in a fountain outside. Limericks were in fashion and the three delighted to see what changes could be rung upon the fantastic names of California towns:

> There was a young girl of Yreka...
> There was a young man of Vallejo...

When the great day came for the opening of the overland railroad, Harte asked Miss Coolbrith to go to the celebration. She objected that she had work to do about her house, but he promised to help, if she would go. After they returned, he slipped an apron on, and with well-told stories kept everyone laughing while he peeled potatoes and shelled peas.

There is a noticeable absence from these scenes of that Mrs. Bret whom we last saw through the keen eyes of Inigo, squelching a little stiffly her husband's enthusiastic play with the children. She was older than her husband, well on in the hard thirties. She still kept up her singing. There was money enough in the household now for a servant or even two, and the family was flourishing. Her husband had advanced into far regions, but she, his friends said, no longer could share his aspirations. The firm mouth had grown firmer with years, and her husband, for all that he wrote of bad-men and gunfighters, was not master of his own house. He waited patiently (pathetically, his mother said) until wife and children were in bed before trying to write, but even then she complained that the light bothered her. Into the sanctum of the editor's own office she stalked by day throwing into a high dudgeon that fine young woman, Mrs. Clifford, the editor's assistant. Even thus in the presence of comparative strangers she laid down the law. She was going shopping and needed an escort; willy-nilly the famous editor left pen, shears, and congenial office companions, to carry packages. Whereupon Mrs. Clifford went into conference with Miss Dolson over the wrongs of their chief, whom they admired as man of genius, friend, and sympathetic counselor upon their own problems of authorship.

But not all of San Francisco gave to Harte that admiration which the Overlanders offered. No one can accomplish a meteoric rise in a small provincial city without making enemies. There were poets whose work had not appeared in *Outcroppings*, scribblers who nursed manuscripts returned from the *Californian* and the *Overland*, members of the Society of Pioneers and of the Academy smarting under the sting of satire, jealous writers who had known Frank Harte as a type-setter and did not see now why people in New York and London preferred his stories to theirs. For the moment his very success kept them quiet, for he was like a conqueror returned with the sack of many cities. But if he falters or fails, let him beware. He had supplied them only too many weapons. As one rises from type-setter to editor, the proportion of people worth knowing becomes smaller; as income grows, there is more chance to indulge in fine feathers. When the author of the *Luck of Roaring Camp* walked Montgomery Street, proud as a peacock of a huge overcoat with a great astrakhan collar, people noticed that he seemed to delight in being admired, but did not always have a greeting for those whose admiration he courted. His new gospel in fact applied only to art, not to life. 'Bret Harte,' Mark Twain decided, 'was one of the pleasantest men I have ever known; he was also one of the unpleasantest men I have ever known.' Anyone so temperamental as that is sure to have more enemies than friends, for people forget the pleasant moments and remember the snubs and the cutting retorts. His many and loyal friends defended him; his sensitive nature, they said, often made him repress kindly feelings, so that what had in an unimportant youth been recognized as mere shyness was counted snobbery in the famous man.

Bret Harte

Some, however, disliked Harte for more material reasons, for he had at times borrowed money in an easygoing way and forgotten to repay it. Stories even circulated of his refusing later to speak to people from whom he had borrowed, and of his accepting advance payment on a play which he never wrote.

After his success with the *Luck*, Harte had fortunately the good sense not to rush too rapidly with stories in the new vein. Since the time when he had written *Dolores* in three days, he had become meticulous. Once Stoddard found him pacing the floor trying to think of the proper two-syllabled word to fit into his prose. He could not always write. 'It's no use, Brooks,' he would say to his assistant editor, 'everything goes wrong; I cannot write a line. Let's have an early dinner at Martini's.' Then after dinner he might go back, and sit at his desk till late at night. He was usually reticent of work in progress, but once toward the end of 1868 he asked Brooks to help him calculate how long a half-sack of flour and six pounds of side-meat would sustain a given number of people.

Apparently the calculation proved too difficult, for in *The Outcasts of Poker Flat*, which appeared in the January *Overland*, the precise amount and nature of the food possessed by the snowed-in party was never stated. A result of this highly successful and thoroughly Californian story was a letter from Fields, Osgood and Company wishing to examine his stories of the West with a view toward their publication in a book. Harte was forced to reply that he had only two, but that he had others in mind and hoped to publish one in June. *Miggles* appearing in that month was hailed as another masterpiece.

The Editor

The success of these first stories was phenomenal. How often they were reprinted in America alone even before they appeared in a book, one cannot even guess. Laurence Hutton first discovered Harte by reading *Miggles* in a country newspaper; Taliesin Evans by finding the *Luck* in a cheap sporting sheet devoted, like the *Police Gazette*, to prize-fighters and chorus-girls, which he picked up in a barber-shop in the Ozarks. In England, Tom Hood was acclaiming Harte. Dickens himself got hold of the numbers of the *Overland* containing the *Luck* and the *Outcasts*, and although he recognized his own influence, the stories impressed him deeply. 'Rarely have I seen him more honestly moved,' declared Forster. Later he wrote to Harte an appreciative letter asking him to contribute to *All the Year Round*, and to visit at Gadshill. To Harte, since childhood a worshiper of Dickens, this letter must have been the final accolade. When it arrived, its writer was dead, and Harte had already composed his elegy *Dickens in Camp*.

The earlier part of 1869 was Harte's most prosperous period in San Francisco. To his regular salaries from the Mint and the *Overland* he could add for the family's expenses what he made by writing and Mrs. Harte by singing. Altogether the income was probably about five hundred dollars a month. The future, however, was threatening. A new President was in the White House, and Harte, as he had come in by the spoils system, could expect to go out by it. In addition, his arrangements with the *Overland* expired in June, and Roman had sold the magazine. Harte's actual resignation from the Mint on August 15, 1869, followed shortly on the arrival of the new Superintendent. Before this, however, he had re-established himself as editor.

Bret Harte

The new owner, John H. Carmany, had made his purchase for a business venture and was wise enough to know that Harte with his new reputation was the *Overland's* best asset. Harte realized his own value, and laid down very firmly his conditions, which included a salary of two hundred dollars a month paid weekly, in addition to regular compensation for non-editorial contributions. Only three days after this ultimatum, the *News Letter* made note that the difficulties resulting from the change of ownership of the *Overland* had been smoothed over; it offered congratulations to both Harte and California and declared that his retirement would have been equivalent to the magazine's 'early demise.' Harte probably obtained from Carmany all that he stipulated, but even so, the loss of his position in the Mint cut his income in two. At this time he must have begun to think seriously about leaving California so that he might more fully capitalize the reputation which he had established.

By September Fields, Osgood and Company were again negotiating. Harte offered to have a volume ready by October, but it did not actually appear until early in 1870. It comprised the first three stories, *Tennessee's Partner*, and the *Idyl of Red Gulch*, which, with ten early Californian sketches including *M'liss*, sufficed for a small volume. The reviews both in America and in England were highly eulogistic. A London edition with an introduction by Tom Hood followed shortly.

Meanwhile the *Overland* continued. It was not making much money for the owner, and its accounts may indeed have already begun to show red ink. Carmany later declared that he lost thirty thousand dollars to make Bret Harte famous. There was some friction between editor and owner, the result of the former's dilatory and easy-going methods of work. But on the whole he seems to have been a good editor. Although generally sympathetic with young writers, he could reject firmly, even icily, on occasion. A young lady, suspected of being the proof-reader who had objected to the *Luck*, once handed him a manuscript; glancing at the title he returned it with a polite bow and remarked: 'I will not trouble you to leave the manuscript; I am not publishing a Sunday-school paper.' He also rejected Joaquin Miller's *Peccavi*, and, very curtly, Walt Whitman's *Passage to India*.

In addition to his editorial duties Harte was the heaviest contributor to the *Overland*. In correspondence with the policy, he worked up two solid articles — one on the life of Grayson the ornithologist, and the other, supported by footnotes and a table, on Pacific steamship lines. Until August, 1870, he continued his editorial section *Etc.*, in which he often showed boldness and independence of judgment. He attacked, for instance, that powerful organization the Society of California Pioneers, and suggested that what the West now needed was a Society for the Suppression of Local Pride. With Brooks's assistance Harte also wrote the reviews. He frequently showed good critical ability, and as in his editorials was sturdily independent. In spite of their established reputations he 'scalped' both Lowell and Emerson, in the latter case laying his finger precisely upon the philosopher's weakest point, the failure to check sociology against experience. He objected regularly to highly wrought diction, sentimentality, and humor based upon mere misspelling.

Harte's first poetical contributions differed little from

the greater number of the verses in the *Lost Galleon* volume. He had lately, however, fallen under the spell of Browning, and early in 1869 he wrote a short Browningesque monologue in Western dialect, sentimentally revealing the death of Flynn of Virginia. Although Lowell had given poetic standing to one form of American local speech, there was still a smack of vulgarity about Pike dialect, and even after the success of his stories Harte was afraid of being vulgar. He offered his poem to the *News Letter*. Its editor at the time happened to be Ambrose Bierce, who usually had convictions and never lacked courage to support them. He told Harte flatly that the poem was too good to be lost in the ephemeral *News Letter*, and must appear in the *Overland*. Harte then published *In the Tunnel* in the March number. He was sufficiently encouraged by its reception to follow it with half a dozen companion pieces in the next year and a half. These poems suited the taste of the time, and were highly popular. Even with the necessary loss of their dialectical flavor, Freiligrath thought them good enough to translate almost immediately into German verse.

CHAPTER XXIII

THE HEATHEN CHINEE

THE world had by the summer of 1870 spoken decisively for the author of the sentimental romance of the Californian stories and poems. But there was also another and opposite Bret Harte — the satiric humorist of *Condensed Novels* and the *Pliocene Skull*. If the public had acclaimed these writings, their author might have remained a satirist, but he was probably glad not to be so fated. Some mental trait, comparable perhaps to his love of fine clothes and a good appearance, made him consider the writing of humor only a kind of buffoonery not suitable to his high aspirations. So in September, 1868, when he had written a poem which has since attained a place as a humorous masterpiece, he had not even admitted it to the *Overland*, but had abandoned it unsigned as a foundling to the charity of the *News Letter*. These lines, *Proceedings of the Academy of Natural Sciences at Smith's Crossing, Tuolumne County*, had been really the last gun of the campaign over the Calaveras skull, and to be most fully appreciated should be read along with his other satires against the Academy. Fortunately the *Society upon the Stanislaus*, as it was later called, was not wholly dependent on its setting; thousands who never heard of the San Franciscan Academy have luxuriated in:

> Nor should the individual who happens to be meant
> Reply by heaving rocks at him, to any great extent,

or the even more famous:

And he smiled a kind of sickly smile, and curled up on the floor,
And the subsequent proceedings interested him no more.

(177)

Bret Harte

The narrator in the poem thus fathered upon the *News Letter* gave his name as Truthful James. This veracious person was one of those mythical people like John Doe to whom Harte may have seen reference in Derby's *Phœnixiana* or may have manufactured by contraries from recollections of a hanger-on in the *Era* office who was called 'Lying Jim.'

Now, in spite of the public's decisive voice for romance, the old devil of satire would not die. Some time in 1870 this devil prompted Harte to put on paper some stanzas in which Truthful James described his experiences with a Chinese card-player. The rhythm of a famous chorus from Swinburne's *Atalanta* rang in Harte's head:

> Unto each man his fate;
> Unto each as he saith
> In whose fingers the weight
> Of the world is as breath;
> Yet I would that in clamor of battle mine hands had laid hold
> upon death.

Truthful James echoed it:

> Which I wish to remark —
> And my language is plain —
> That for ways that are dark
> And for tricks that are vain,
> The heathen Chinee is peculiar.
> Which the same I would rise to explain.

When Harte set out to write about the Chinese, he was usually serious. One of his minor satires in the *Californian* had glowed with indignation against the mistreatment of the oppressed race. At Union he had had enough experience with the white man's brutality. In his present poem, however, he was merely in a light moment parodying Swinburne, and developing the old

The Heathen Chinee

comic situation of the deceiver deceived. In the poem both yellow and white equally are rascals, and our sympathy goes to the former only because of the insincere moral attitude of Truthful James and Bill Nye's hypocritical battle-cry:

We are ruined by Chinese cheap labor.

This line, moreover, as the manuscript shows, went in as an afterthought replacing:

Or is civilization a failure?

The finished verses Harte dropped into a drawer, and apparently almost forgot. But material for one number was short, and the editor diffidently showed several yet unpublished poems to a friend in hopes that the latter might find something which he considered suitable. He did, but only after some persuasion was he able to make Harte send his verses to the printer. In September, 1870, *Plain Language from Truthful James* finally saw the light.

The success of this sixty-line poem is probably without parallel before or since. The *Luck* and its companion stories had reached about as far as a really literary production can, but the remarks of Truthful James swept beyond the comparatively narrow circle of polite readers, and like a popular song or a vaudeville joke became the property of the man in the street; picture and word of mouth carried it even to the illiterate. Almost immediately upon its publication cheap broadside editions were being hawked upon the streets of San Francisco and the other chief cities of the United States. Three or four song versions appeared in a few months. Its vogue leaped to all parts of the English-speaking world; the *Piccadilly Annual* of 1870 included it, and a

(179)

Melbourne edition appeared in 1871. Everybody knew it, and quoted it. It was said that President Grant had intended to take up the Chinese problem in his message to Congress, but refrained after the poem had made the whole matter the occasion of hilarity. An editor compared the Franco-Prussian War to the poem, with the Germans in the part of Ah Sin. The current argument of the day was whether the lines:

> In his sleeves, which were long,
> He had twenty-four packs —

should not really be read (the game being euchre) as 'twenty-four jacks.' The poem caused a literary epidemic; *Every Saturday* declared:

The familiarity of our poets with gamblers who cheat at cards and who have marvellous powers of versification without a corresponding correctness of orthography must be set down as one of the phenomena of current literature.

An article in the New York *Globe* of January 7, 1871, gave a good illustration and summary of the effect which the poem had produced:

Strolling down Broadway, last New Year's Day, we saw a crowd of men and boys, of high and low degree, swarming about a shop-window, pushing laughing and struggling, as if something new had appeared in the Metropolis of common interest.... Elbowing our way through the crowd, we discovered an illustrated copy of Bret Harte's poem, 'The Heathen Chinee' displayed to the gaze of the public, 'which I wish to remark,' for a sensation on Broadway 'was peculiar.'...

In all our knowledge of New York nothing like this has ever been seen on Broadway.... We have been obliged to produce it [the poem] twice in the Globe to answer the demands of the public, and we venture to say there is not a secular paper in the United States which has not copied it.

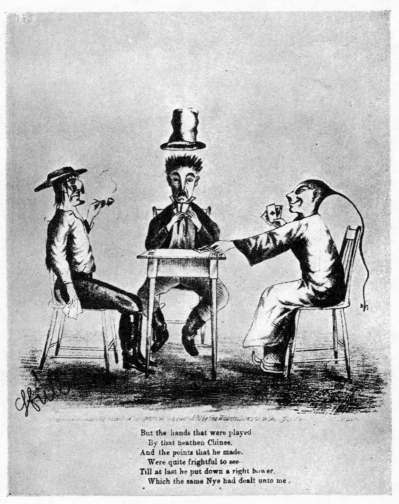

But the hands that were played
By that heathen Chinee.
And the points that he made.
Were quite frightful to see
Till at last he put down a right bower,
Which the same Nye had dealt unto me.

THE HEATHEN CHINEE

From an unauthorized edition of the poem published by the Western News
Company, Chicago, 1870

The Heathen Chinee

Meanwhile, the author of *Plain Language from Truthful James*, popularly known as *The Heathen Chinee*, sat in San Francisco experiencing a fellow feeling with that character in his beloved *Arabian Nights* who having carelessly rubbed a bottle set loose a world-shaking Djinn. The worst of it was that he seems never really to have liked the poem or to have seen why people made such a fuss about it, and to his dying day he was a little embarrassed when people referred to him as the author of the famous *Heathen Chinee* or talked about it in his presence. These seem to have been his real feelings, no mock modesty. He once remarked to some one whom he had just met: 'Perhaps you can have little respect for a poet who wrote such trash as the *Heathen Chinee*.' He is reported once to have called it 'the worst poem I ever wrote, possibly the worst poem anyone ever wrote.'

He disliked the poem partly, doubtless, because he knew that as its author the public would consider him merely a fun-maker. His real hope was for the summit of Parnassus, not for that lower shoulder to which the world, ungrateful, assigns the great jesters. But his dislike was also deeper-rooted. One of the basic feelings of his life was burned into him by the experiences in Union; in a dozen of his stories he was to hurl denunciations against ruffians who would set bull-dogs on inoffensive Chinese or murder a defenseless Indian. But in a moment of mere jesting he had played false to himself. Everywhere he heard himself quoted as authority (the popular mind was too dull to grasp the irony):

> That for ways that are dark
>   And for tricks that are vain,
> The heathen Chinee is peculiar.

Bret Harte

How many honest 'Anglo-Saxons,' justifying themselves
by these lines, have cheated Chinese? How much race-
hatred have they engendered? He had loosed the Djinn,
and could do nothing to control it. But no wonder that,
with the blood of an oppressed race in his own veins, his
dislike of that too clever poem attained the fixity of
hatred.

CHAPTER XXIV

GO EAST, YOUNG MAN!

In the eleven years since he had landed from the *Columbia*, Harte, like the hero of a juvenile, had risen from type-setter to editor, and going farther had attained heights to which even Horatio Alger never dared raise his heroes. In spite of all his success, his position in San Francisco was strangely insecure, for the *Overland* was financially precarious, and not a venture upon which a man with a family could count. In other ways the situation was not pleasant. He knew that he had enemies. He had never ceased, also, to think of himself as an Easterner, and he disliked many things in California — the bumptious *Society of Pioneers*, the loud professional boosters, the sea-fogs which irritated his sensitive throat. No wonder that he should long to turn over the leaf and begin anew among people who thought of him as a literary genius, and not as just Frank Harte, the type-setter, or the compiler of *Outcroppings* whom half the editors of the State had mauled.

Republics are ungrateful, but the State of California made a real effort to hold its most prominent citizen, known farther than Leland Stanford, or even perhaps than Jack Heenan, the Benicia Boy. On August 16, 1870, even before the appearance of *The Heathen Chinee*, the regents of the new University of California had offered him the appointment as Professor of Recent Literature and Curator of the Library and Museum, at the salary of three hundred dollars a month. The appointment, a fine expression of local pride, seems to have been distinctly planned as a bit of patronage to letters. But Harte was out for bigger game than a place in the infant university, itself to all appearances scarcely a more stable institution than the *Overland*. He declined the appointment, giving as his reasons that it would interfere with his writing and that he contemplated visiting the Atlantic States.

Carmany also made a desperate effort to hold Harte, for he realized that only by keeping the famous editor could the *Overland* be successful. According to his own statement, he offered Harte five thousand dollars a year, one hundred dollars for each poem or story, and a quarter interest in the magazine. He even agreed to finance a lecturing tour through the East. The terms were certainly generous, but after all, their fulfillment depended eventually upon the financial stability of the magazine, and Harte might well be skeptical.

At the same time tempting suggestions were coming from the East. Backers in Chicago offered support for a new magazine. The *Atlantic* held out open arms. Fields, Osgood and Company were bringing out an edition of his poems. Carleton had republished *Condensed Novels*. Enthusiasm for *The Heathen Chinee* swelled daily. By October he had definitely decided. By January 10, 1871, his plans were so settled that the papers announced his departure with his family for about February 1. Already he had sent his photograph, and on January 14, *Every Saturday* had the honor of introducing his portrait to Eastern admirers. The engraver had done full justice to the clear, piercing eyes, patrician nose, wavy black hair, and fine mustache and sidewhiskers. It was a young hero of romance that the East had a right to expect. (See frontispiece.)

Go East, Young Man!

As a farewell his literary friends in San Francisco arranged a dinner, and to it came that Bret Harte whom Mark Twain described as one of the pleasantest men he had ever known. Eleven sat down to table with their guest of honor; ten were old Californian friends and the other the famous editor of the *Springfield Republican*, Samuel Bowles. Dinner was in a private room of Louis Dingeon's famous restaurant, and as the courses came and went, and brilliant conversation played about the table, Noah Brooks noticed that the waiters occasionally changed as if in relays, a curious procedure:

Presently while the night seemed yet young, I saw Bowles furtively slip out his watch and look at the hour. The involuntary wave of surprise that swept over his face as he pocketed his timepiece without a word induced me to look at my watch also. It was twenty minutes to four o'clock in the morning. There was a general burst of astonishment when, an hour later, another inquisitive diner exclaimed, 'Boys, it is almost five o'clock to-morrow!'... The spell was broken.

It was the end; never again would he be one of the boys in San Francisco, glad to polish off a sketch for a few dollars. Even as he went out into the chill of that gray dawn, the task of maintaining a reputation rested on his shoulders.

On the morning of February 2, 1871, the Overland Express clattered away down the Peninsula toward San José. Woe to any crude Western grizzly who shall stand snarling in its way! In one of its new-fangled combination parlor-and-sleeping cars rode Bret Harte, his wife, and the boys. He had become too great for the city in which he had become great, the city which had both pampered and buffeted him and for which he bore no great love. But they had given him good send-offs,

(185)

the morning papers. The *Chronicle* had run a whole column reviewing his literary exploits; it commented:

None save a few jealous ones, whose lesser flames have cast shadows when the brighter light of Harte's genius was introduced, but will regret his departure.

The *Alta* had been equally friendly:

During a long residence in this state Mr. Harte has established not only a brilliant reputation as a literary man, but more enduring and hearty friendships than most men gain in his department of life.

The rails clicked beneath as the train gained speed. There was a long road ahead for it. It must rise to high levels and sink to low, labor up grades and scuttle down. But its most famous passenger was beginning an even longer and more varied journey.

PART IV
1871–1878

CHAPTER XXV

APOTHEOSIS

THE wheels clicked over the rails eastward, along the dreary Humboldt, through the high rampart of the Wasatch, across the plains. In the car sat Harte, his bridges burned behind, only hope ahead. He could have had no idea of what was about to happen. The situation was unprecedented in the history of the continent; indeed, it has not happened since, and is unlikely to repeat itself in the future. A writer in a distant isolated city had produced for a local journal first a series of stories which had charmed the nation's literary élite; he had followed with a poem which had attained as complete popularity as any piece of writing can well achieve. This author was now going East to receive the laurels already granted him. He was, moreover, personally almost unknown, and so piqued men's curiosity the more. Would he wear a beard over a red shirt, carry revolvers, and drink straight whiskey? Rumor had it that he was a professional gambler reformed. In any case he was the man of the hour in letters.

The wheels came to a stop in Chicago, and the Hartes prepared to alight. For this was the first city of hope. Before leaving San Francisco, Harte had received overtures from a group of men who wished to establish him as editor of the *Lakeside Monthly*. He had looked favorably upon the suggestion, and this definite expectation was one of the chief reasons which had encouraged him to leave the *Overland*.

A day or two after his arrival the supporters of the

Lakeside invited him to dine with them. Harte, who seemed pleased with the prospects, accepted, and all appeared to be happily arranged. At five o'clock he told one of his friends that he was going home to dress. The dinner-guests began to arrive. It was whispered that beneath the plate reserved for Harte rested a generous check which was to represent the immediate financial support of the magazine. With it Harte was to accept the editorship, and the greatest literary hero of the day was to be Chicago's capture. The hour of dining arrived, but no guest of honor. Time passed, and still he did not come. Finally, when all reasonable expectation was over, the famished diners took their places and ate. It was *Hamlet* without Hamlet. Nothing more was said of Harte's becoming editor of the *Lakeside Monthly*.

These are the unadorned outward trappings of an incident. When, however, one tries to discover what lay behind Harte's failure to arrive, one is confronted immediately with the impossibility of establishing truth when motives are concerned. Harte himself naturally slurred over the whole matter. His later explanation was that no guide was sent to escort him to dinner, and having waited for one until a late hour, he then considered it impossible to find the place alone in a strange city. So he sat down and dined *en famille*. Obviously this explanation is a little lame. He was past thirty, and surely did not need a nursemaid to conduct him about Chicago. It is incredible that for such a reason he should have so languidly let slip an opportunity of real importance and at the same time have let himself be put into the position of breaking his word. One Chicagoan, moreover, gave a flat contradiction to Harte's version by declaring that he himself offered to accompany the

chief guest to the dinner, an offer which Harte had declined as unnecessary, remarking that he knew the way.

A more subtle version is that offered by Mrs. Clifford,
Harte's assistant on the *Overland*, who, as we have seen,
had no love for Mrs. Harte. According to this story one
of Mrs. Harte's cousins was slighted in not receiving an
invitation to the dinner; that lady became so enraged
that she refused to allow her husband to attend. This
story is not incredible, but its basis is little more than
gossip. It is likely enough that Mrs. Harte had some
hand in the matter; if pique — a woman scorned — be
not a sufficient explanation, one may suggest that not
without reason she thought Harte's real opportunity to
lie on the Atlantic Coast, and made sure that he did not
remain in Chicago. The whole explanation, however,
may simply lie in Harte's almost psychopathic fear of a
public appearance which would demand a speech. The
same man who in San Francisco had lain sick on July 4,
1863, may in Chicago have suffered from funk at the
last moment. His later life was to offer another example.

So the wheels clicked onward. Eastward from Chicago and his fiasco, New York and Boston awaited him.
The four Hartes stopped a few days at Syracuse with
members of Mrs. Harte's family, and then came to New
York. They stayed five days with Harte's sister, Eliza
Knaufft, resting quietly while he interviewed some publishers and editors. He had no offers, however, which
seemed adequate while he still held his trump-card of
Boston and the *Atlantic Monthly*. For the whole family
had an invitation to visit for a week in Cambridge with
William Dean Howells, a young man of some reputation
as a writer and, of more significance, assistant editor of
the *Atlantic*. Again the wheels clicked eastward.

Bret Harte

In Cambridge, Howells awaited his guests with some trepidation. Harte's star had risen so suddenly and blazed so brightly that one had no precedents for comparison. There was the disturbing possibility of the red-shirted Californian, although the photograph and letters which Howells had already received made this seem rather unlikely. But the only thing certain about him was that he had snubbed a dinner-party of Chicagoans and, according to the story which Howells had heard, merely for punctilio, because forsooth they had neglected to send a carriage for him. Obviously a man who would do that must be treated gingerly. So Howells, deciding that there should at least be no question about a carriage, hired the handsomest hack to be found in Cambridge and himself drove it to the railway station. But on the moment of meeting, Howells lost all fear and constraint with the voice and handshake which, as he put it, 'were surely the most winning in the world.' The family piled into the handsome hack — one hopes they appreciated it — filling it completely, the men in front, Mrs. Harte and the two little boys of eight and six behind, and Howells drove them home.

As he drove, Howells sized up his guest, noting in addition to what he might already have seen in the photograph a medium stature, a 'jovial physiognomy,' an under-lip with a fascinating forward thrust, and as for clothes 'a child of extreme fashion.'

The week at Cambridge was for Howells a mingling of joy in Harte's company and of terror in the responsibility of getting him to places on time. He was, it seemed to his host, full of a boyish naïveté which kept continually bursting out. When Howells had, for instance, dilated upon the literary celebrities of the neighborhood, 'Why,' cried Harte, 'you couldn't stand on your front porch and fire off your revolver without bringing down a two-volumer.' He talked, Howells thought, mostly in irony, but never in the extreme of satire. He teased with kindness. You could never be sure just when he was earnest. Then, very inconsistently, Howells arrived at the amazing conclusion: 'Never was a man less of a poseur; he made simply and helplessly known what he was at any and every moment.'

But in piloting an irresponsible guest through Boston and Cambridge society, there lay the terror. He could not be got to luncheons and dinners on time. The carriage would be waiting at the door, Howells in despair, and then at last Harte would come dashing down the walk, his clothes still at odds and ends. In the carriage there would be much buttoning, pulling on of gloves, and adjusting of ties. About all this Harte himself was the least concerned. Hostesses might worry about overdone roasts, but they received from him no apologies. But hostesses were glad to have him on any terms. Such was the power of his name that one social climber had her invitations accepted for the first time because she had managed to capture the lion.

Luncheons, dinners, receptions, quiet talks with great men of letters — he was entertained every evening and often by day. Harte must have felt that he was at last in the full harvest season of life. Boston was still the literary capital. On his very first day he dined with the Saturday Club, and talked with Agassiz, Longfellow, Dana, Emerson, Lowell, and Holmes. Dinners were given for him at Longfellow's, at Agassiz's, at Fields's, at Lowell's. As man to man he talked with them —

these graybeards who had been literary gods when he a
child had spelled out their poems in school-readers,
whose supremacy was still unquestioned when he, himself a teacher in a little frontier school, had taught these
same poems to his Melissas and Clytemnestras.

Again, he lunched with Ralph Keeler, Howells,
Thomas Bailey Aldrich, and James T. Fields. Here,
too, was his old friend of San Franciscan days, Mark
Twain. Much water had flowed since they had scribbled
for the *Californian*. First Twain had made a reputation
with the *Jumping Frog* and *Innocents Abroad*; next
Harte had far surpassed him; then they had quarreled.
This quarrel may account for the *gaucherie* of Harte's
exclamation when some one spoke of the presence of
Twain, a Westerner, at a luncheon of literary Bostonians — 'Why, fellows,' cried Harte (and the false intimacy of the word rings badly) 'this is the dream of
Mark's life!' Even though Harte had been born in New
York instead of Missouri, an obvious retort in kind was
due. But Mark Twain was not in the habit of obvious
retorts, and the matter dropped.

This remark, however, is one of the few jarring notes
in the visit to Boston — that is, if one does not mind his
small-boyish way of thumbing his nose at New England's demi-gods and heroes. This flippancy, moreover,
was almost certainly an unconscious reaction from the
fear of seeming unduly overawed by the company in
which he was moving. He — the ink-stained devil of
Uniontown, the druggist's clerk, the type-setter for old
Colonel Lawrence's eight-page weekly — suddenly to
find himself in the same heaven where walked the writers whose benign faces looked out from the cards of the
game of authors and the surfaces of thousands of steel

engravings! To find, moreover, that, instead of expecting him to kiss the steps where they walked, they seemed glad of his friendship, and requested the pleasure of his company to dinner! No wonder he lost his sense of respect a little and burlesqued them to Howells privately. (Thank Heaven — if we may hazard a guess at his thoughts — no one knew about his having been a type-setter and so forth. They seemed to think instead that he had spent his time shooting Indians and highwaymen. No harm to let them. He could keep quiet about his past. No harm either to throw a few Western terms into his talk, to speak of shooting off a revolver from the porch. Of course in San Francisco he would never have made that sort of remark.) So he met them all, and they testified to his being 'at ease in every society.' He appeared that most intriguing of personalities, a distinguished and easy man of the world with a shadowy and sanguinary past. And so perfect and consistent a poseur was he that to his host he appeared no poseur at all.

He enjoyed his meetings with the great New-Englanders. He met Dr. Holmes, and the two gossiped as poet to poet about the difficulty we have in beginning a poem. And then after we get a start, something sweeps us off our feet and we swim! He met Julia Ward Howe, and at his request she sat down at the piano and sang the *Battle Hymn of the Republic* to her own accompaniment. He met Agassiz, who, gravely humorous, congratulated him for those scientific sympathies, rare among poets, which he had displayed in that now famous poem *The Society upon the Stanislaus*. Pressure of engagements forced him to decline an invitation to visit Whittier, who shared with him the memory of friendship

with Starr King. He met Lowell, however, and the by-
standers trembled at the gathering storm-clouds as they
heard the audacious Westerner voicing face to face with
its author an adverse opinion of *The Cathedral*. But the
clouds passed away as Harte suddenly began to pay
rare praise to some detail of the work. Nevertheless,
the clash was significant; the two never became friends.

Of all the Bostonians Longfellow alone awed the
Western *enfant terrible*. In a crisp night of the New
England winter the two walked home together from a
dinner at Lowell's. A fine contrast they were — the
younger man black-haired, dressed to the line of fop-
pery, with that walk which some called mincing; the
elder, patriarchal, hair silvery as the winter night, a voice
of deep baritone, his whole presence mellowed by age
and long-enjoyed honors into a gentle and modest
dignity. For once, Harte bowed down in reverence; he
offered no satire of Longfellow to Howells; on the contrary, the memory of the midnight walk through the
snowy streets of Cambridge remained one of his cherished recollections.

The week of the visit came to its end. Howells, on
pins and needles until he could get off his hands this
wildly irresponsible Westerner, began preparations for
leaving so early that he had the family safely ensconced
in their seats some minutes before the time of the train's
departure. He felt the lighter of his responsibilities. But
he had reckoned without his guest, for just at the final
moment Harte found that he lacked cigars and dashed
off the train to obtain some. He regained the car just in
time, and Howells, mindful of duty to the last, leapt on
again with him. Seeing the Harte family settled and
feeling the train in motion, Howells sprang to the door,

swung back to the platform, and suddenly turned deathly sick as he realized that in his haste he had just escaped being thrown against a stone archway by the rapidly accelerating train and having his brains dashed out. The Hartes were gone, but they had supplied gossip and anecdote for many a day. Nevertheless, Howells wrote to his father of the recent visitors, 'Till now Elinor and I have met no young people so congenial.'

Returned to New York, Harte soon found that his week in Boston had not been without material profit. He had conferred there with the editors and publishers of the *Atlantic Monthly*, and in a letter written on March 6, only two days after leaving Boston, he entered into a contract with its owners, Fields, Osgood and Company:

I accept your offer of ten thousand dollars for the exclusive publication of my poems and sketches (not to be less than twelve in number) in your periodicals for the space of one year commencing March 1, 1871.

This is said to have been to its date the largest sum of money offered by contract to an American author for a year's work. By 'your periodicals' the *Atlantic* was of course primarily inferred, but contributions to *Every Saturday* also apparently came within the terms. Osgood, moreover, was protected by the stipulation of twelve items. As to the quality of the work, he must have been prepared, like anyone else who deals in futures, to take some risk, but he could trust that Harte for his own sake would not wish to ruin his reputation by publishing mediocre work in a leading magazine.

The signing of the contract with Osgood was the final triumph of Harte's victorious storming of the East. Seldom had a man more suddenly found himself raised to a seat among the gods. Nothing shows better what a unique incident it was than the comments which it elicited from contemporaries. Howells has described it in terms usually reserved for royalty:

that progress Eastward from California which was telegraphed almost from hour to hour, as if it were the progress of a prince.

Every Saturday gave him an editorial even more flattering in its implications:

This young man... has had his progress from city to city heralded by the telegraph and the journals, as if he were a Chinese embassy, instead of the author of the 'Heathen Chinee'; or as if he were General von Moltke, rather than the writer of 'The Luck of Roaring Camp.' Almost as many towns as wrangled over the honor of having given birth to Homer have striven to tempt Mr. Harte to abide with them; dinners and drives have been lavished upon him, and California has been told in solemn editorials, how short-sighted she has been to let him go.

Even far away across the Atlantic reverberations of the great event sounded in the public ear. The London *Daily News* on March 21 gave Harte an editorial of more than a column under the lead, 'America has a new star.' It declared:

The East and the West contend for the reflected rays of his celebrity; cities dispute for the honor of his presence; Chicago beguiles him from San Francisco; New York snatches him from Chicago, and Boston plots deeply his abduction from New York. His slightest movement is chronicled in every paper, and where he stops for a few days, a kind of 'BRET HARTE Circular' appears in the daily press.

CHAPTER XXVI

AFTER THE FATTED CALF

WHEN the fatted calf had been killed, the elder brother rebuked, and the feasting ended, what then? The proper procedure was obviously for the prodigal to settle down and become a useful, hard-working son.

Harte's return had been somewhat like the prodigal's. He had never quite ceased to be an exiled son of the East temporarily forced to do swine-herding in California, and in the glorious festival of his return, the people of the East played the father's part. They saw him coming from afar off, they fell on his neck; they offered him the fatted calf, and indeed the golden calf as well. Even his obvious infelicities they accepted as the natural and excusable vagaries of one forced to live long in a far country. But after a few weeks the fine frenzy was over; the prodigal must now show himself worthy of his welcome.

The return from Boston in the first days of March roughly coincided with the end of the dazzling period of his reception. As an afterglow later in the month, however, one must mention Bowles's luncheon at the Brevoort House. Good solid Samuel Bowles had known Harte since 1865 when the latter was only a local scribbler; now relative positions were reversed, for Harte was the author of *The Heathen Chinee* and Bowles was still only a leading editor. The latter's comment on the luncheon shows Harte patronizing and Bowles, such was the glamor of Harte's greatness, accepting the patronage as natural.

Bret Harte

Bret Harte is brighter and nicer than I thought, and was very frank and kindly with me [!], and promises to come up with his wife and make us a visit. Indeed, he planted a hope in me that he might settle down in Springfield for the summer. He is very happy over his flattering prospects.

That a returned prodigal so royally welcomed should begin to think very well of himself was inevitable. Equally certain it was that he would soon come to look with disgust upon the far country and his former fellow swineherds. After his great reception in the East, Harte, who had never had much love for California, at once came to feel that it was a place in which he had, comparatively speaking, been fed on husks. He virtually abandoned all his Californian friends of whom at the time of leaving he had many. Mrs. Clifford, on her own statement, was the only one of them to whom he wrote in his first year of absence. On learning that Brooks was coming East to live, Harte showed his attitude by exclaiming: 'He and I will found the *Society of Escaped Californians.*' Roman on arriving in New York was snubbed so pointedly that he never forgave Harte. 'Too much of a change for so short a time,' he once said; and again: 'I think the adulation disturbed his head.'

But this disturbance of the head made him so carelessly self-confident that it lost him Eastern friends too; within a few months he had managed on two different occasions to present himself in a bad light to Boston. The first affair may not, indeed, have been Harte's fault. For the reunion of the Grand Army of the Republic in Boston on May 12, he contributed the poem-of-the-day — a stodgy monologue called *The Old Major Explains*; after his usual custom he sent the poem for someone else to read. But the audience, rightly or wrongly, had expected to see the great writer in person, and his failure to appear caused adverse comment.

The other affair, also involving a poem-of-the-day, was more serious. Harte had been asked to compose and read the Phi Beta Kappa poem at the Harvard Commencement — a real honor undoubtedly and to Bostonians probably the highest honor which an American poet could receive. But Harte was fatally careless about the whole matter, and proceeded throughout with bad taste. In the first place, with foolish temerity he decided to be humorous. Now a second *Heathen Chinee* would undoubtedly have been successful even at a Harvard Commencement, but rather than anything less uproarious he should have taken refuge in the usual pompous windiness of Phi Beta Kappa poems. And Harte, apparently confident that people would eulogize anything which he happened to give them, did not even go to the trouble to write a new poem. Instead, he took some old verses in the style of Tom Hood which he had written and published nine years before during his salad days with the *Era*. These he refurbished without improving greatly, and renamed *Aspiring Miss De Laine*. Then on Commencement Day he dressed himself somewhat more glaringly even than usual and took his seat on the platform. When he rose and began to read, all Boston's and Cambridge's assembled social and intellectual leaders grew, according to individual temperament, cold with vicarious embarrassment and hot with choler. His *green* gloves! His poem — flippant and silly without being really funny! His manner, too, was unfortunate. He placed both green-gloved hands on the table and spoke in so low a voice as to be heard only with difficulty. One reporter noted his manner as 'plainly indifferent, not to say contemptuous.' The same prosaic observer also commented upon the man and his clothes with what he must have considered a magnificent finality: 'his personal appearance comes near the unmarried girl's idea of what a poet should be.' Apropos of this last comment one should note that the only person recorded as having said a good word on this occasion was actually a young miss who was heard to remark how *wonderful* Mr. Bret Harte was — before she was properly squelched by an outraged parent. As to Harte's own reaction, testimony is contradictory. Howells thought that he took the disaster lightly, but Mrs. Aldrich that he realized the situation fully and was overcome with dismay.

Later in the year Harte, on visits to Massachusetts and New Hampshire, still further displayed how much, in spite of himself, his way of thought had become Western. While staying with the Fieldses, he was indeed greatly taken by the autumnal beauty of the countryside. But when they took him to call upon a certain lady, Harte, not impressed, noted her merely as 'a Mrs. Cabot (I think)'; the great names of New England apparently meant little to him. In October he went for a brief visit with Emerson at Concord. They walked by Walden Pond, Harte like all Westerners growing a little scornful of 'life in the woods' when he found the woods so close to civilization that one could be called in to dinner upon any occasion. But, although Longfellow had been impressive, Emerson certainly was not. His smoking amused Harte as a petty indulgence out of character for an Olympian. He chuckled inwardly (he who came from a country where men drank 'McCorkle's Whiskey — kills at forty rods') when Emerson proposed

that they have 'a wet night' and thereupon poured out
for his guest one glass of sherry. But the real clash occurred when they came to speak of Emerson's recent
essay on *Civilization*. It happened that Harte had lately
written a review of that work for the *Overland* in which
he had disagreed with its tenets, and at Concord, face to
face with its author, he stuck to his guns. Of this conversation Emerson noted in his journal of October 18:

> Bret Harte referred to my essay on Civilization, that the
> piano comes so quickly into the shanty, etc., and said, 'Do
> you know that, on the contrary, it is vice that brings them
> in? It is the gamblers who bring in the music to California.
> It is the prostitute who brings in the New York fashions of
> dress there, and so throughout.' I told him that I spoke also
> from Pilgrim experience, and knew on good grounds the
> resistless culture that religion effects.

A deadlock! The old and the new, the East and the
frontier, had clashed again. The confident old Tran-
scendentalist was talking a language strange to his
companion. And Harte was not likely to shift his beliefs.
He had sat in the hideous little frontier churches and
had his own opinion as to how much culture was likely
to come from those drab rows of bigoted worshipers. He
knew something of gamblers and prostitutes too, and he
might well wonder whether Emerson did. Transcendentalism and realism were grappling that day, just as,
less concretely, they were grappling at the same time
everywhere in American thought and literature. Transcendentalism, moreover, is well symbolized as an old
man of the East, realism as a young man of the West.

After his various encounters with New England, it
was apparent that, in spite of his contract with Osgood,
Harte was not to be one of those young Lochinvars like

Bret Harte

Howells, who had come out of the West only to make themselves as completely Bostonian as possible. When locating his family in the spring of 1871, he had naturally selected New York. He had known the city as a boy, and Mrs. Knaufft still offered him there a contact with his early years. New York was, moreover, rapidly becoming the focal point of American civilization; already it rivaled Boston as an intellectual and artistic center. The social life also was attractive, and Harte was constantly in demand — not only as a celebrity, but also for himself, for he made a charming dinner guest. During the first two years in the East, therefore, the Hartes made their headquarters with Mrs. Knaufft. Even so, New York can scarcely be called their home; the family struck no roots there, and Harte did not even get into the directory.

The more or less complete fusion of the two families cannot have been very satisfactory and Harte chafed under it. The trouble seems to have been that Mrs. Harte possessed little liking for, or ability at keeping up, a home. She seems really to have been less domestic than her husband; she liked the ease of hotel life and shunned the responsibilities of maintaining her own *ménage*. Harte's Bohemianism lay rather on the surface; he enjoyed the gayeties of society, but he had also a solid liking for his own hearth-fire. He was extremely fond of his children. At the end of his first year in the East, his daughter Jessamy was born, and, in a letter of that summer, the fond father noted: 'In the last two months the baby has occupied my attention as an author to the exclusion of all else.'

With ten thousand dollars to spend, Harte found living pleasant and easy. There was an elegance about even his new note-paper, with monogram of 'B. H.' and above it for crest a bear symbolic of the *Overland*. The family spent the first summer at Newport. It was expensive and the climate was not all that they had hoped. They met interesting and stylish people, however, and got along well with them. At one dinner, for instance, they came to know George Bancroft, the historian, and George H. Boker, the poet and dramatist. In the presence of new people Harte sometimes withdrew into himself and appeared only a highly modest and proper young man, but in a friendly atmosphere he soon blossomed out into an amazingly fine conversationalist, a raconteur full of anecdotes, a wit ready to pick out anything marked or peculiar in the people about him and humorously to satirize it.

During these months of the spring and summer, Harte was doing scarcely any work. People noticed his idleness as a bad sign, and began to talk of his being lazy. Walt Whitman, who must have shaped his opinions from hearsay or the newspapers, mentioned to a friend at this time that Harte had 'cultivated foppishness and superiority.' It was only natural, of course, that he should like to make the fatted calf last as long as possible. And besides the distractions of society and the mere pleasure of living with, at last, a sufficient income, there was the danger that he might write something unworthy of his present reputation. People everywhere were saying and writing wonderful things about his work. In London, for instance, *Chambers's Journal* came out on May 27 with an article on *A New Transatlantic Genius*. New editions of *Condensed Novels* appeared in both America and England, and although in 1867 the burlesques had generally received only brief notices and passing commendation, in 1871, now that their author was famous, critics saw in them the marks of genius and chorused in loud eulogy.

So for one reason or another the readers of the *Atlantic*, looking for the magical name of Harte, scanned in vain its columns in April, May, and June. He finally managed to get *The Poet of Sierra Flat* into the July number, but it arrived apparently at the last moment so that it was forced to stand inconspicuously at the end of the magazine. He wrote Californian stories for September and December, and these also, significantly, stood in last place. By the first of the year he had sent in three poems all based upon ideas which he had gathered at Newport; he was trying to branch out into new fields. The poems accordingly lacked his distinctive touch which was so closely bound up with his Western subject-matter.

> Ho, Starbuck and Pinckney and Tenterden!
> Run for your shallops, gather your men,
> Scatter your boats on the lower bay.

Those are vigorous ballad lines, but in hunting for them one would naturally take down from the shelves Whittier instead of Harte. To fulfill his contract he also contributed a new condensed novel and a poem to *Every Saturday*. But time was speeding, and Harte, like one whom the gods have stricken mad in order to destroy, sported and dallied. With March, 1872, the term of the contract came to an end. It was not renewed.

A good deal was gossiped and eventually got into print about the famous contract, and, although Harte was certainly culpable enough, the scandal-mongers dealt much too hardly with him, and as usual the more lurid version came with time to be accepted. Howells, for instance, writing after Harte's death, was criminally

careless of a fellow author's reputation when he declared
that he gave only one story and two or three poems in
the year! On the other hand, apologists have made the
mistake of trying to whitewash him too completely.
Actually Harte had supplied during the year seven contributions. He had therefore failed to fulfill the minimum of twelve. That his fault was dilatoriness, not
unreliability, however, is shown by the fact that he continued to hold himself responsible for material until both
the letter and the spirit of the contract should be ful-
filled. By September he had supplied the twelve. Osgood, however, apparently did not consider the contributions to *Every Saturday* as falling under the contract;
he continued to think himself entitled to more material,
and, at the time of his sale of the *Atlantic* late in 1873,
wrote his dissatisfaction to Harte apparently in decided terms. Harte's answer to this letter is preserved.
In it he listed the twelve contributions to the two magazines, declared, moreover, that Osgood had agreed to
accept *Mrs. Skaggs's Husbands* (published in book form)
as an equivalent to two articles for the *Atlantic*, and
finally stated that on receiving Osgood's letter he had
nearly completed another poem to be offered under the
terms of the contract. By Harte's system of calculation
this would have made fifteen contributions. There was
undoubtedly some misunderstanding about the arrangements, and without the complete correspondence no
final judgment can be made. As far as the evidence goes,
however, there is nothing to impugn Harte's good faith.
The quarrel, moreover, was not personally bitter, and
the two principals remained on good terms.

Harte's procrastination was the obvious reason for
his being dropped by the *Atlantic*. It must be peculiarly

irritating for an editor to have a Christmas story by a star contributor arrive only in time for the March issue, even though the story should prove to be so popular a one as *How Santa Claus Came to Simpson's Bar*. There was also a certain decline in the quality of the work. This was not marked, for the *Atlantic* stories were certainly superior to some of the *Overland* stories, such as *Mr. Thompson's Prodigal*. The real trouble was that the freshness of the *Luck* and the excitement about the *Heathen Chinee* had raised Harte's reputation to such a dizzily precarious height that anything which he did must seem an anticlimax. It was a great mistake, however, that he did not fulfill at least the letter of the contract — a mistake which no one will have much hesitancy in ascribing to the carelessness and bloated self-confidence engendered by all the flattery and adulation which he received during the first few months after leaving San Francisco. His failure with the *Atlantic* — for with all extenuations one cannot honestly call it anything else — was a real blow for Harte, the first which he had received since he had founded the *Overland* and begun his career of greatness.

CHAPTER XXVII

FIRST TRIAL — LECTURES

THE ending of his contract left Harte high and dry. Except for royalties he had no income, and his books, like most collections of short stories and poems, did not sell in great numbers. The next few years of his life, therefore, took form very clearly as a series of experiments, three in number, by which he attempted to gain financial security. Everything, his literary development included, was dominated by the economic factor.

Some months passed, however, before he seemed to recognize this necessity. His luck had been in for four years, and he could scarcely realize at once that it had left him as suddenly as it had come — he was still so highly praised almost everywhere, and moved in such good society. Besides, his was an easy-going disposition loath to face sooner than necessary the iron fact that he had suddenly become merely a workman without a job. During the year he had come to know plenty of rich men who had no objection, in fact were rather glad, to play Mæcenas to a famous writer temporarily in a difficulty, and credit with the tradesmen was fatally easy for one who always dressed so richly and was known everywhere as the great author. So he let drift until nearly the end of the year. He was not even writing much, for after March the title-piece of the volume, *Mrs. Skaggs's Husbands*, was the only new story to appear for more than a year.

During the last century there has always been, however, one obvious expedient for men of great reputation and little income. It is a means of which some — actors at heart — have made an honorable profession, but which to many has seemed nothing better than a downright prostitution. If the great man, the devil tempts, will only consent to make a display of himself on the lecture platform, he may be assured of much money; for whether or not he has anything to say, many will pay, just as they pay to gaze at caged animals, merely to see. Unfortunately, as his timid career as poet-of-the-day had shown, Harte was peculiarly averse to public appearance; he was one of that group for whom lecturing could never be anything but a prostitution. His debts, however, already began to be pressing, and the needs of his family left him no choice.

In the autumn he prepared a lecture, *The Argonauts of '49, California's Golden Age.* On December 3, he 'tried it on the dog' at Albany, his birthplace. Ten days later he went to Boston for his first real test.

Boston was still ready to receive him. There was a dinner for him before the lecture, but upon its gayeties fell a shadow, a very substantial shadow, unfortunately, nothing other than an officer of the law with a judgment for a tradesman's bill. There was hurried sending for Harte's publisher; there was promising of payment out of the proceeds of the lecture. But the shadow stuck close; it stood with the lecturer in the anteroom at Tremont Temple; it waited in the wings. Thus haunted, Harte walked on the platform with Howells and sat down facing the Boston audience — a critical assembly at best, but especially so for a Westerner who had already cheated it. As they sat together, Howells, with the thought of the bailiff in his mind, whispered across, 'Well, Harte, this is the old literary tradition; this is the

First Trial—Lectures

Fleet business over again.' Whereupon Harte smote his thigh 'joyously' and cried out, 'Yes, the Fleet!' 'Joyously' — perhaps it seemed so to Howells; one has one's doubts. But Richard Henry Dana, who had come back from California in the summer of Harte's birth, was on his feet making the introduction. One can only imagine Harte's agony during that speech. His situation was critical. He was about to make a public address — something which he feared and loathed. He was unaccustomed to speaking and bad at it. He faced one of the most demanding audiences in the world, and it was already half hostile. He knew that his own and his family's living depended on the next hour, that managers of lecture tours would watch the papers in the morning. The sinister shadow in the wings was evidence of the penalty for failure. The stakes were ruinously high and the odds heavily against him. Yet with a cold courage worthy of Jack Hamlin he rose, went to his place, and began.

First he sketched briefly the idyllic days of California before the *gringo* came, an account which drew largely, as all such must, from Dana's own book. Then he turned to a more familiar field and gave an impressionistic picture of early American California, interspersing his description with anecdotes and quips:

'I don't call that swearing. You should hear Bill Jones exhort the impenitent mule.'

'To think,' said Mr. Oakhurst, after a game of ten minutes from which he made five thousand dollars, 'to think as some folks believes that keards is a waste of time.'

As he spoke, the audience began to warm. It followed his descriptions; it rose quick and responsive to every joke, and bubbled over with laughter. And finally, when he concluded with some words about the Heathen Chinee, there was no doubt. He had triumphed. With that triumph the disconcerting shadow in the wings shrank to insignificance.

It was probably at this same visit to Boston that, just as the Aldriches were covering their fire, they heard the doorbell, and suddenly the 'buoyant, confident tone of Bret Harte' calling out at the foot of the stairs: 'Are you home, Aldrich? I have come to make a night of it.' He came up the stairs two at a time, chanting 'Polly, put the kettle on,' and asked for the spare room with the remark that the hotel was dreary and he wanted to be gay. They lent him room, pajamas and brushes, but he smoked Aldrich's cigars all night. The next morning he went to the hotel, his evening clothes ghastly in the daylight. Mrs. Aldrich, whose judgments on Harte seem much shrewder than Howells's, felt that all this gayety and insouciance may merely have covered a ruse to avoid the sheriff.

He went back to New York, where before his lecture of the 16th a letter from Fields gave him still further encouragement by declaring that people at Boston still 'boiled over with delight' as they recalled his speech. His New York lecture in Steinway Hall was another triumph. The *Times* gave a full column to report it, and stated that for an hour and a half he kept the entire audience in an increasing roar of laughter. The report gave a long excerpt from the lecture in which were scattered, like plums in cake, numerous neatly bracketed comments: [applause], [laughter], [great laughter], [continued laughter]. On January 7 a lecture at Washington was equally successful.

After his triumphs in the intellectual, commercial,

and political capitals, Harte was able to book many
engagements, and during three lecture seasons, which
covered the cooler months, he was frequently on tour.
No complete record of his engagements exists, but more
than fifty can be located so that one of his later advertisements is probably correct in its declaration that the
lecture had been delivered one hundred and fifty times.
His tours took him all over the Northern and Middle
States and as far west as Kansas and Nebraska; twice he
touched Canada and once penetrated far into the South.

Lecturing was profitable. His regular fee was one hundred and fifty dollars. Sometimes, of course, the managers were inefficient, and he did not get his full price; his
expenses, moreover, came out of his fees. Even so there
was plenty of money coming in. If he gave only one hundred lectures at one hundred and fifty dollars during
three years, this amounts to five thousand dollars a year,
and to this is to be added the income from writing. In a
letter of 1873 to his wife he expressed a wish that she
rent a house, and mentioned one hundred and twenty-
five dollars a month as a not unreasonable figure. In
the seventies this was assuming an almost luxurious
standard of living. The financial difficulty would seem
to have been solved.

But it was not. In the letters which he wrote to his
wife while on tour financial worry was the dominant
note. The ample income was spent as soon as, or before,
it came in. The family lived from hand to mouth, and
his lecture fees often had to be sent off post-haste as
soon as he received them. Frequently, indeed, post-
haste would not serve, and he telegraphed sums even in
amounts as small as fifty dollars. Still more disturbing
were the injunctions which sometimes accompanied

these remittances — pay Bliss, pay instalments to Rosen, Cooper, and Twill, pay an instalment to Arnold 'unless something else is more pressing.' Once at least the creditors became so pressing that they went to law; on July 6, 1874, Teats and Throckmorton, tailors, obtained in a New York court a judgment of $230.35 against Bret Harte for clothes made for him. Altogether it was often a harassed man who took the platform and stared out at his audience.

He generally managed to mask these troubles against the world. People who met him while he was touring noted him as boyishly exuberant, interested in everything. Doubtless, as even his letters show, he often thoroughly enjoyed himself. Sometimes he met people who pleased him, such as Professor Corson at Ithaca, and an anachronistic old Southern gentleman at Berkeley Springs. At Ottawa he spent a week-end with the Earl and Countess of Dufferin, and had his first taste of fine English hospitality.

The trip into the South in the autumn of 1874 was his most interesting and mentally profitable experience. His impressions filled two long letters to his wife — unusually affectionate letters, for she was awaiting the birth of another child. At Louisville it seemed to him that he entered a foreign country. He went on deep into the South, the home of those 'rebels' against whom less than ten years before he had been fulminating chauvinistic poems. Now he found himself strangely sympathetic with the Southern people and their problems. A monotone of sadness, he thought, dominated the whole land. At Macon, the cemetery of the Confederate dead — a thousand strong on the hillside — seemed to cover the whole town. He listened to these people of a past régime try to grapple the contemporary problem until he would have wept over their pathos had not his humorous devil tempted him to laugh over their quaintness:

I cannot keep the smile from my lips when I am with them — or the moisture from my eyes when I think of them, alone.

Politically (the South was still in the agony of Reconstruction) the situation seemed to him hopeless:

You wonder, dear Nan, to hear me talk so strongly of a political question — knowing how little interest I have in it usually. But I never before had such a fateful problem brought before my eyes — I never before stood by the bedside of a ruined and slowly dying people. If I were a statesman, I should devote my life to save them.

The Southern women appealed to him — not so pretty as those of New England, but finer ladies. His easygoing disposition loved the languorous tempo of Southern life. He was pleasantly amused, he who in the North was thought lazy, when a Georgian characterized him as quick, energetic, and decisive. His impressions of the South he utilized later in several stories.

Aside from the financial returns and the occasional interesting experiences, however, the lecturing had nothing to recommend it. The work was a spiritual poison to him. His intense dislike of public appearance never left him. He wrote once to his wife:

You can imagine the savage, half-sick, utterly disgusted man who glared at that audience over his desk that night, and d——d them inwardly in his heart.

Then, with that touch of humor in incongruity which saved him even from himself, he added:

And yet it was a good audience — thoroughly refined and appreciative, and very glad to see me.

The hour or two before each lecture was a time of depression amounting almost to horror. With this went naturally a sense of inability which also sometimes found humorous expression:

The people [of Hornellsville] seem to be preternaturally serious and depressed, as if they had come from my lecture instead of going to it.

Another anecdote, often told to illustrate Harte's wit, has also a more serious depth. Again in a small town with a depressing atmosphere he turned to one of his reception committee and asked:

'Is this a healthful climate?'
'Passably,' replied the committeeman.
'What's the mortality of this city?'
'About one a day.'
'About one, eh,' said Harte. 'Come this way a minute,' and he drew the committeeman into the recess of the bay-window, and then said to him solemnly, 'Is the man dead for today? I am going to lecture here tonight, and it would be a great relief to me to know that I could get through alive.'

Along with emotional went physical strain. In his letters while on tour were frequent mentions of colds, coughs, and fatigue. Trains left at all hours of the night; lecture halls were often cold and damp. On long trips he called upon his last reserves of strength:

I have missed no engagement yet. But I am drawing hard on my vitality to keep up. I was full of things to tell you, but I am so worn out, Nan, that I must lie down a few hours before the lecture to-night. I have only just arrived here, and to reach this place left Bloomington at half-past two last night.

Good night; Heaven keep you and the babies.

American railways at that time were highly unreliable and equally uncomfortable; the hotels in small towns were worse. His little sketch, *A Sleeping-Car Experience*, shows how badly the sensitive lecturer fared. Often he had to get into evening clothes in the cramped Pullman dressing-room, worrying whether the train would really get in before his audience had left; then would come a rapid, chilly dash by carriage from station to hall and the immediate entrance upon the platform, perhaps without any sufficient dinner. Once a Canadian audience waited an hour and a half while in a special train, an engine and one car, he careened toward them at seventy miles an hour. Again — and it was the only time when the golden flag of romance flew at the peak during these drab years — after the breakdown of an engine in Kansas, he quickly hired a saddle-horse and strapping lecture and blanket to his back dashed off like one of his own heroes fifteen miles across the bleak October prairie. Harte has been called irresponsible, but he certainly did his best to keep faith with his audiences.

Gradually, however, in spite of his initial successes, people began to realize and to spread the word that Bret Harte was not a good lecturer. He was in fact only a brilliant amateur who with the stimulus of a Boston or New York audience could be great, but who, when lecturing nightly, fell to mediocrity. The audience, as a reporter put it, was pleased, but not enraptured. In short, Harte lacked that spark of strange fire necessary for the great actor or public speaker. He labored, more-

over, under so many actual handicaps that the only remarkable thing is that he succeeded as well as he did.
His voice was weak. His nerves were troublesome so
that trifles — someone arriving late or leaving early —
upset him. In the depths of his brain he hated the work
and the people for whom he exhibited himself, and accordingly he could not escape seeming to his audiences
indifferent whether, as they probably put it, he gave
them the worth of their money. For a man who is damning his audience 'inwardly in his heart' can hardly help
displaying his thoughts outwardly.

Another not unimportant factor behind Harte's lack
of success was certainly his inability to look the part of
the returned Californian. If, as Joaquin Miller knew so
well how to do, he could have appeared mighty of limb,
bearded, booted, with gold nuggets serving for overcoat
buttons, people might really have been enraptured as
well as pleased. Harte himself believed it. 'I think, even
now,' he said twenty years later, 'that if I had been
more herculean in proportions, with a red shirt and top
boots, many of the audiences would have felt a deeper
thrill from my utterances.' Unfortunately no man can
change his stature, and for Harte to have shifted into
wild-Western regalia would have been equally impossible.

So with Harte's lecturing as with so many of his mines
— 'the lead played out!' On some of his later schedules
the names of small towns appeared in ominous number.
For a fresh start he tried preparing a new lecture,
American Humor, and with this he returned to the
larger centers for a few engagements in the season of
1874–75. It was not successful, and after the beginning
of 1875 no more lectures are recorded. His retirement

may have been precipitated by a difficulty over a contract with his agent, James Redpath, which put Harte in the embarrassing position of seeming to break his engagements. The deeper reasons for his abandoning the platform were his own hatred of the work, the undue physical strain, and a new literary venture.

CHAPTER XXVIII

SECOND TRIAL — NOVEL

DURING the period of the lectures Harte's family life had continued to be disturbed and unsatisfactory. Once he wrote back from a Western tour: 'Oh, Nan, I weary of boarding or living in a house with others. If we can find some quiet home of our own, this winter,... I think we will not regret it.' Between 1873 and 1876 they lived in Morristown, New Jersey, but as in New York they can scarcely be said to have established a home there. They resided during that brief period in four different houses, so that Harte might have added another instalment to *Neighborhoods I Have Moved From*. He disliked Morristown as he did small towns in general — 'bigoted, self-righteous, hypocritical,' he later described it. A second daughter, Éthel, was born early in 1875, so that with four children Harte's financial responsibilities were heavy. His mother and the old Colonel came to live with them in Morristown, and there in 1875 the former died. Harte continued to move in good society, maintained most of his old friends, and made some new ones. Most important among the latter were Charles A. Dana, of the New York *Sun*, and John Hay, whose *Pike County Ballads* had been suggested by Harte's dialect poems. He also came to know two prominent Englishmen — Lord Houghton and James Anthony Froude, both of whom proved to be real friends.

During these years Harte found, as others have done, that to be great is to be the golden mark for scandal. His marital life was apparently so regular that the scandal-mongers seldom attempted anything in this favorite field. Something was whispered to the effect that he drank too heavily. Harte certainly enjoyed good whiskey, and in the highly social life which he led he may occasionally, as most other men of the time and set did, have furnished some material for gossips. The best evidence, however, points to his having been a very moderate drinker. But his enemies had a real opportunity with his debts and his snobbery. Not unnaturally the worst attacks came from California. A vicious article in the San Francisco *Chronicle* called him a 'loose and not infrequent borrower of large sums and a cool ignorer of the gracious loaners,' and declared further that he had swindled contributors to the *Overland* out of their remuneration; in short, it characterized him as 'a rascal in the higher walks of life.'

In general the stories about his debts probably did Harte's reputation little harm, for they were merely taken as the amusing vagaries of a man of genius. In them Harte always appeared as a laughing, happy-go-lucky boy, entirely different from him of the letters telegraphing fifty dollars to stop the mouth of the most ravening creditor. John Hay, for instance, had his story: 'I was once complaining to Bret Harte of my lack of funds: "Your own fault," said the wise Argonaut. "Why did you fool away your money paying your debts?"' An often repeated story was that of the butcher's bill at Morristown. Harte was said to have paid this with stamps sent to him as return postage in numerous letters requesting autographs. Some female busy-body investigated the matter, and denied it 'on the authority of the butcher.' Harte, it is said, laughed over this story; doubtless he appreciated its real humor which lay in the fact that the lady did not make clear whether the butcher denied payment in stamps or denied payment altogether.

Of Harte's friends Brooks is the only one who has written soberly of his financial troubles. According to him Harte quickly contracted debts in New York. He always *expected* to pay these, but he simply lacked the strength of character as regards money, which we term in a word — thrift. Brooks, to show how destitute Harte was of what he terms 'money-sense,' told the story of a rich man, a patron of literature, from whom Harte borrowed small sums of money until the total reached several hundred dollars. One New Year's Day he received a letter from his wealthy friend enclosing all the I.O.U.'s cancelled, to let him have a fresh start for the year. Harte was immensely indignant at being made the object of charity: 'Damn his impudence!' he exclaimed to Brooks. And on being asked what he was going to do about it: 'Going! I have made a new note for the full amount of these and have sent it to him with an intimation that I never allow pecuniary matters to trespass on the sacred domain of friendship.' In this instance Brooks felt that Harte was fully serious; another anecdote, however, shows that the author of *The Heathen Chinee* could see the funny side even of his own liabilities. Having once gone out without his purse Harte borrowed car-fare of Brooks and later returned it, remarking: 'You hear men say that I never pay my debts, but [this with a chuckle] you can deny the slander.'

The years of the lectures were, largely because of the lectures, not very productive of writing. The lengthy *Episode of Fiddletown* was the only new story of 1873.

Second Trial — Novel

In the next year he was more productive with five stories in *Scribner's* and the *New York Times* besides a juvenile, *Baby Sylvester*, in *St. Nicholas*. The income from these writings was considerable. *Scribner's* is said to have paid one thousand dollars for the *Episode*, which was long enough to be run in three instalments; for one of his stories in the *Times* Harte demanded six hundred dollars and — a little to his surprise as his letter home shows — got it.

In quality these stories were on the whole better than those which he had written for the *Atlantic*. They generally showed a weakness at the end, but they were notable for apt touches in their openings, such as Colonel Starbottle's immortal reminiscence — 'blank me!' — of the too beautiful creole woman, which enlivens the beginning of the *Episode*. As regards weakness at the end, one must except *A Passage in the Life of Mr. John Oakhurst* which deserves to rank as one of Harte's best stories, and should certainly be read by all who think him incurably sentimental. The story has probably failed to receive its due recognition because of a curious lapse which has often disturbed readers. In the *Outcasts of Poker Flat* Harte had described the death of Oakhurst in 1850, but in the *Passage* the gambler reappeared in a stage of Californian society which must certainly be placed several years later than 1850. The incident was a good example of Harte's growing carelessness of minutiæ.

The cynically bitter atmosphere of the *Passage* is only one evidence that he was getting tired of always doing Californian stories with sentimental endings. A letter about *Baby Sylvester*, written to Mary Mapes Dodge, editor of *St. Nicholas*, showed his dissatisfaction; in de-

clining to alter the climax he wrote, 'I want a change
from the usual andante finale. I am sick of my heroes of
whatever genus — *homo* or *Ursa* [*sic*], dying in an attitude on my hands.¹ Harte was not at the end of his
literary growth; he needed a chance for quiet mental
development.

This chance, however, was yearly growing less, and
already some of his activities began to show how his
literary genius was being forced to slave more and more
at the collection of dollars. On July 17, 1873, for instance, he had 'covered' the intercollegiate boat-race for
the *Springfield Republican*, a journalistic assignment of a
kind which he had not done since the middle sixties.
More beneath his dignity was his contribution of two
poems — parodies of Tennyson and Longfellow — to
Nast's Illustrated Almanac for 1875; the other contributors to this cheap little volume were mere nonentities.

Although his reputation in America was perhaps falling off a trifle, it was at the same time spreading in foreign countries with a rapidity hardly equaled by that of
any other American writer. British critics eulogized
him. Hotten brought out a pirated edition of *The Complete Works of Bret Harte in Prose and Poetry* which sold
so heavily that almost every second-hand bookshop in
Great Britain now has a copy or two to show. Harte, of
course, much to his chagrin, could not collect a penny
from these sales. In Germany also he was proving
highly popular. Freiligrath's translations of his poetry
had appeared in *Gegenwart* early in 1872. Three volumes
of translated stories were published in the two following
years, and German magazines began to print translations of his work as it appeared. Two volumes of his
stories appeared in French in 1873. In 1875 he was paid

the unusual compliment of being translated into Hungarian. The introduction to this caused some amusement when a facetious American editor commented that in Hungary

Bret Harte has the reputation of being pár év óta nagy hirüve lett as Amerikai. This is exceedingly flattering; but, what will his readers think, when they find such a statement followed by the remarkable assertion that this popular author is known in Hungary as szerencsésen kikerüli?

After his comparatively prolific year in 1874, Harte's only publication in 1875 was the insignificant *Jersey Centenarian*. There was a sufficient reason, for he was busily engaged at last with a full-length novel. One need not seek far for the reasons which led him to try the longer form. In doing so he was only exemplifying what might almost be called a 'law' of literature — that the successful writer of short narratives will later attempt the novel. Hawthorne, Maupassant, and Kipling are, with Harte, outstanding examples. The motive force behind this 'law' is the tendency of mankind to judge quantitatively rather than qualitatively, and so to consider a mediocre epic or novel a 'greater' work of art than an excellent sonnet or short story. This feeling was stronger in the seventies than now, so that for Harte to assume full stature as a literary artist it was necessary, in the opinion of many people, that he become a novelist. Added to this was the hope of greater financial returns, for a successful novel could be expected far to outsell a collection of successful short stories.

His idea for the novel was manifest. As a writer he was associated preëminently with the Californian background. Good! In a three-decker he would tell a story which in its action would touch all phases of Californian

life. His earlier stories he had usually termed 'sketches';
they had been, to continue the figure, mere small line-
drawings or cartoons each displaying some two or three
characters placed in a tiny detail of the setting. But his
novel would be a colossal painting, a synthesis of innumerable sketches, the representation of a whole historical episode. Instead of a few characters he would
display the *tout ensemble* of California — miner, gambler,
stage-driver, vigilante, politician, priest, townsman,
man and woman, Spaniard and American. Instead of a
single scene the spacious canvas would have room for
high mountains, plains, and foothills, for towns, ranches,
and missions. To work!

The labor upon this vast cyclorama occupied a year.
He began writing in June, 1874. He found slow going —
a month for the first fifty pages. By the middle of summer he had completed the *Prologue*, a vivid narrative of
an emigrant train snow-bound in the high Sierras, suggested obviously by the tragic story of the Donner party.
He had already begun to find the problems of a novel
perplexing; characters could not be conveniently put out
of the way at the end of a few pages. As he wrote, somewhat naïvely: 'I have to dispose of my characters so as
to use them advantageously in the remaining "Books"
— it is the hardest work I have done.' Thereupon in the
same letter he added characteristically — 'meanwhile
how am I to live?' Some lecturing tours temporarily
solved the latter problem, but of course held up the
novel. In the spring he settled down to hard work at
Morristown, and ploughed along at better than a thousand words a day — very rapid progress for such a slow,
painstaking writer. Proof began to come in before the
manuscript was completed, for Harte had already made

arrangements with the American Publishing Company,
the firm in which Mark Twain was a leading member.
The title had been selected, merely the name of the hero,
Gabriel Conroy, which with the professional writer's eye
for business Harte had selected: 'the shorter the title,
the better the chance for its quotation and longevity.'
Osgood had been holding up for four months the issue of
a new collection of stories — *Tales of the Argonauts* — so
that his volume might be floated on the publicity attending the appearance of *Gabriel Conroy*. Then suddenly a
princely offer from *Scribner's Monthly* led to the postponement of publication for a year. For the right to issue the novel serially the magazine gave six thousand
dollars. Harte in a letter to Osgood bubbled over with
jubilation; he appended five postscripts, and threw in a
parody of Tennyson *gratis*!

The history of *Gabriel Conroy* is the best evidence possible that Harte's reputation did not — as many people
later came to think — go up like the rocket in 1868 and
down like the stick in 1871. The price which Harte received from *Scribner's* is said to have been the highest
ever paid for an American novel. In addition he received
a royalty of seven and a half per cent from the American
Publishing Company. To forestall any attempt at pi-
rating, an English edition was issued even before *Scribner's* had finished running the serial, and for this Harte
received an advance payment of five hundred pounds,
besides royalties. In 1876 also appeared a Canadian edition and a Swedish and at least two German translations. The novel proved immensely popular in Germany.
It has been stated that no fewer than fourteen German
versions appeared — an incredible number, but one
vouched for by good authority.

Bret Harte

On the whole, however, to the English-speaking world at least, *Gabriel Conroy* was a disappointment. There have been worse novels, but it was certainly not among novels what Harte's stories were among stories. It had the author's usual failings, such as a tendency toward melodrama. In its attempt to picture the whole life of the time, the story had grown unduly confused. It showed also, unfortunately, the marks of Harte's virtue as a writer of brief narratives — an episodic structure. People remembered it chiefly for striking scenes — the snowstorm, the meeting of Yuba Bill and Jack Hamlin, the death of Jack Hamlin. With an author's usual preference for a weakly brain-child, Harte cherished *Gabriel* as his favorite among his writings.

The results of this second attempt to gain financial independence strongly resembled the results of the first. Like the lectures the novel was for the moment highly remunerative, but offered no expectations for the future. After its comparative failure no publisher was likely to urge its author to a second attempt. Harte probably felt this the less keenly because almost before *Gabriel Conroy* was off his hands, he was, with a remarkable buoyancy and an energy which belies charges of laziness, already eagerly engaged with a new and entirely different venture.

CHAPTER XXIX

THIRD TRIAL — PLAYS

HARTE had long been interested in drama. The performance of *King John* was a treasured memory of childhood; during the San Franciscan years he had constantly attended plays, and for a time had acted as dramatic critic for the newspapers. Now in the late spring of 1875, when he had failed as lecturer and probably realized that he would not continue to be a novelist, he began to write a play. It was a natural enough undertaking, for a successful dramatist could count on a handsome income.

The appearance of several melodramas based on *M'liss* also probably aroused his interest. No less than three of these floated themselves on Harte's reputation about this time, so that with so many false Richmonds successful in the field he had reason to think that a genuine prince would be well received. At this opportune moment he met Stuart Robson, an actor looking for a play, who easily gave him the final push.

The manuscript of *Gabriel Conroy* must just have been off Harte's hands when he began a drama of California. In a letter to Osgood of May 26, 1875, he made facetious mention of an 'actor — whose fortune I am about to make — Stuart Robson.' He was working at Cohasset and Lenox in the summer and autumn. As usual, financial difficulties were assailing him, and his work suffered interruptions while he dashed off to Hartford and New York seeking advances on his novel. As the play progressed, Lawrence Barrett, another actor interested in Harte's work, read scenes aloud to a small group of actors and others who were staying at Cohasset. The readings were well received, and the play was declared highly promising.

On September 18 he ran up to see Fields, well satisfied with himself and bubbling over with humor which even a headache could not down. He won Mrs. Fields completely that day, and she noted him in her journal as a dramatic, lovable creature, with his blue silk handkerchief, red dressing-slippers, and quick feelings: 'I could hate the man who could help loving him — or the woman either.' He had reason to be light-hearted that day, for his play was finished.

For the plot Harte had taken one of the poorest of the *Overland* stories, *Mr. Thompson's Prodigal*. He elaborated the plot and reënforced it by introducing some of his favorite characters — John Oakhurst, Colonel Starbottle, and a Chinese laundryman. The setting, of course, was the old Californian fifties which Harte had already used so often that it was beginning to seem his private property. He dramatized, or rather melodramatized plot, characters, and setting according to the formula of his old favorite Dion Boucicault. Robson according to report bought the play for three thousand dollars, plus twenty dollars a night up to another three thousand dollars.

After an unencouraging trial in Chicago, *Two Men of Sandy Bar* opened in New York at the Union Square Theatre on August 28, 1876. Harte was present, and was elated with what seemed an enthusiastic audience. But the criticisms in the morning papers fairly wrecked the play. The *Times* began,

Third Trial—Plays

Last night probably for the first time in his career, Mr. Stuart Robson was an object of public pity.

The comment continued in even more damning strain:

The audience ˹assembled was brilliant, large, good-humored and indulgent, but the piece was too much for any good-nature, however strained, and it may be set down as the worst failure witnessed on the boards of our theatres for years.... The piece is utterly aimless, is without coherency of plot, definiteness of purpose, or action, and lacking in any sort of artistic symmetry in its model, or characterization in its *dramatis personæ*. Its sentiment is maudlin and mushy, its plot shallow, its pathos laughable, and its wit lachrymose. All in all it is a proof that the ability to write a comic song does not qualify one to write a play.

With such a reception *Sandy Bar*, as it was called for short, was not destined for success. The first-nighters may have enjoyed the performance momentarily, but perhaps they had cooler second thoughts. The play dragged through its scheduled five weeks, but it languished. Rumors got about that Robson was dissatisfied at the price he had had to pay, and that he and Harte were quarreling. 'I've been a good deal perplexed and irritated lately,' wrote Harte in a letter of this month.

The play went on to Washington at the beginning of October, and fared better there. 'We are doing an excellent business.... John T. Ford predicts even greater success in Baltimore,' Robson wrote back to Harte. And he added what seems a rather grudging admission: 'altogether I am well satisfied.' The play went on the road, and lingered for some time with little vitality. Probably one of its last appearances was at the California Theater, San Francisco, in September, 1878, the theater for the opening of which Harte had written a poetic address nine years before. It played four nights, and as usual the home-town critics took pleasure in lambasting the local dramatist. The *Alta* declared the play 'overweighted with a ballast of rubbish and inconsistencies.' These were harsh words, but on reading the play one feels them uncomfortably true; the only difficulty which one feels is in discovering how it was any worse than other melodramas of the time which were successful. In spite of its failure the play was published in both America and England, and was included in Harte's collected works. *Die Beiden Männer von Sandy Bar*, which appeared in 1877, showed the Germans' loyalty to their new favorite.

The failure of *Sandy Bar*, following so closely on that of the lectures and of *Gabriel Conroy*, might well have been enough to shake a better man, but Harte had still one shot left in his locker. The doors were scarcely closed upon the disastrous New York run before he was off with a fresh idea, and — one must admit — a dazzlingly good one. The acting of C. T. Parsloe as Hop Sing, the Chinese laundryman, had been the bright spot in *Sandy Bar*. Harte's idea was to write a play especially for Parsloe in a Chinese character, and for this play to take as collaborator, his old friend Mark Twain. If the two most popular humorists of the day could not produce something for which people would stand in line to pay their money — who could!

'Bret Harte,' wrote Twain on October 11, 'came up here the other day and asked me to help him write a play and divide the swag, and I agreed.' Twain, the letter explained, was to put in Scotty Briggs, and Harte the Chinaman from his previous play. The latter was to be *the* character and both were to work on him. Each was to do a plot and then the better was to be used or the two run together. They were to start work immediately. Twain declared that he had finished his plot — six days' work at eight or nine hours a day — 'nearly killed me.'

Harte was also hard at work. When the time soon came for closer collaboration, it was arranged by his coming to visit with the Clemenses in Hartford. The two did plenty of work, and the play progressed after a fashion, but otherwise things did not go well. To his hosts Harte seemed a discourteous guest — exacting, critical, and even sarcastic. We may perhaps find some excuses for him. Failure, debt, worry, and ill-health had goaded him until he was no longer the friend Sam Clemens had known in San Francisco. From our perspective we may see the pity of it, but his contemporaries saw in place of the former youthful jovial companion only a man of forty grown mean and irritable.

The history of his tale, *Thankful Blossom*, shows his deterioration sharply. In the first place, he had temporarily to break off the collaboration on the play to write this pot-boiler, and even so he had to ask Osgood for an advance on it before proof was finished. And if there ever was a pot-boiler, *Thankful Blossom* certainly deserves the title. It followed the fashion — a Revolutionary story for the centennial year. It was thrown together with the crassest materials — a plaster-saint Washington, local scenery of Morristown, reminiscences of Cooper's *Spy*, and stilted pseudo-eighteenth-century conversation which made the tough old Continental colonels talk like addle-brained Lord Chesterfields. The story according to Twain was thrown off in careless haste. He said, in fact, that Harte, with the aid of a bottle of whiskey, wrote it by sitting up all of one night, but this must have been only the finishing of the story, for no man, one would think, certainly not Harte, could write twenty-two thousand words at one sitting. The manuscript, too, shows changes in paper and in color of ink which indicate different times and places of composition. The slovenly manuscript itself, however, a contrast to Harte's usual neat pages, fully corroborates Twain's main contention of great haste. (The peculiar name of the heroine Harte said that he took from one of his own ancestresses, but the manuscript supplies the curious information that she was originally Nancy Peebles, and only became Thankful Blossom along with a shift from black to purple ink at page thirty-four.)

With the pot-boiler out of the way the collaborators finished the play in spite of personal friction. They bestowed on it the potent name of the original Heathen Chinee — *Ah Sin*. No copy of the text seems to exist, but synopses show it to have displayed the regular Californian touches. Some old characters — York, Masters, Uncle Billy Plunkett — joined themselves to Ah Sin in a setting upon the Stanislaus and manipulated themselves to produce a vigilante plot.

The *première* was set for May 7, 1877, at the National Theater in Washington. The two authors were both on hand helping with the rehearsals, but Twain fell sick and had to return to Hartford before the opening. For the first performance, Harte — conscious probably that he was firing his last cartridge — saw hopefully a large and fashionable audience assemble. Everything seemed to go well. Parsloe playing in the title-rôle was frequently called before the curtain by applause; Mrs. German as Mrs. Plunkett, a 'Malaprop' character, proved almost as popular. After the curtain, a characteristic note from Mark Twain was read to the audience and evoked great applause. When at the suggestion of this note the question as to the success of the play was put, the audience roared 'Aye!' unanimously. Harte wrote a congratulatory note to the actors and left the theater, thinking the play a success.

But again the critics were cool. 'The pleasure of the audience,' wrote one, 'was more in the novelty than in any genuine dramatic interest of the play; if changes are made as improvements suggest themselves, and the play undergoes a little pruning' — it might become — well, a better play. But one author lay ill and the other was a man who had already flogged his creative powers beyond their endurance and whose self-confidence was fast giving place to doubt and despair. On the third day after the opening, Parsloe, himself in despair, wrote to Twain bitterly blaming Harte — he was doing nothing to give the play the patching which it needed, especially at the end; he would do nothing but promise, and the actors had been forced to make changes themselves as best they could. 'I am not very well myself,' added the hard-driven actor, 'the excitement of a first night is bad enough, but to have the annoyance with Harte that I have is too much for a beginner.'

Harte in fact seems to have abandoned the play as a bad job. In the course of the summer, Twain labored over the text, pruning, paring, and rewriting much of the dialogue in preparation for the New York opening. Harte's desertion at this time must still further have estranged the two men.

The birth-crossed play opened the season at Daly's Fifth Avenue Theatre on July 31. Its advertisements had played hard on the great names of the authors, and it was announced as being 'produced under the immediate personal supervision of MARK TWAIN, who will have A WORD OR TWO TO SAY about it.' Harte himself was in Washington. The audience was large, and seemed to be amused. At the end of the third act came loud calls for the authors.

The critics who had blasted *Sandy Bar* were not unanimous on *Ah Sin*. The *Herald* and the *Tribune* said some good words, but the *Sun*, in spite of Dana's friendship for Harte, loosed a vicious salvo, although admitting that clever acting made the entertainment laughable and lively. The *Sun's* chief criticism was:

The plot of the play is weak, commonplace, and not at all original, the incidents are tangled and unconsequential, the language is often broadly humorous, and once or twice coarse, but never witty or epigrammatic, and the characters are mere sketches.

It termed the first three acts 'obscure, tedious, and somewhat inane,' and offered judgment in epitome, 'As a piece of dramatic work the play is beneath criticism.' The New York run lasted just through the month of August. On the road the play failed to maintain itself, and *Ah Sin* — the most interesting collaboration which the history of American literature records — faded into oblivion. It was never printed.

But the play, if it accomplished little else, at least wrecked a friendship, one which had in its best days been marked by honest admiration and warm loyalty on both sides. The readiness of Harte and Twain to collaborate shows their confidence in each other's ability even as late as 1876. The friendship had meant much to both men. The greater debt was Twain's; as he had written in a letter of 1871, Harte, during the *Californian* days,

trimmed and trained and schooled me patiently until he changed me from an awkward utterer of coarse grotesquenesses to a writer of paragraphs and chapters that have found a certain favor.

This debt Twain had striven to repay in different ways; he had helped Harte in various negotiations about *Gabriel Conroy*; he had lent him frequently large sums of money which remained unpaid. The trouble for Harte was that, while in 1877 Twain's debt to him was ancient and intangible, his debt to Twain was recent and only too tangible. This could hardly help putting him at a disadvantage, making him ill at ease and correspondingly irritable. There may never have been an out-and-out quarrel, but after the fiasco of *Ah Sin* the two dropped relations and there is no record that they ever even met again. Twain's later mentions of Harte were slighting, but Harte seems to have maintained a little of the old spirit, and in speech and writing he referred to his former friend with respect and gratitude.

CHAPTER XXX

DÉBÂCLE

THE end had come. For the last six years Harte had been like a general fighting a great battle. Defeated in the first encounter, he had refused to stand on the defensive; summoning all his forces, he had launched attack after attack. But the assaults had grown steadily weaker, and with the rout of the last he found himself, with reserves exhausted and morale shattered. It was defeat no longer; it was *débâcle*.

In 1877, everything was against him. In the *North American Review* for January, his work had been subjected to a searching adverse criticism for the first time in an important American magazine. Besides failing as lecturer, novelist, and playwright, he had ceased for three years to write short stories, and when he again attempted, it was evident that in his disturbed state of mind he had lost the art. In 1877 the best that he could produce was a series of miserable little stories and essays of which *Roger Catron's Friend*, *The Man whose Yoke was not Easy*, and *My Friend the Tramp* are typical. Naturally with such trifles, he could command no market, and Dana was probably moved half by friendship for Harte and pity of his situation when he published most of them in the *Sun* and paid one hundred dollars for each. There were nine of these bagatelles during the year, but even if he averaged something more than a hundred dollars apiece, Harte was not earning a decent living for a family of six, much less making head against his piled-up debts.

Débâcle

This very snarling of the wolf drove him at this time to dubious and undignified expedients. He published in *Harper's Magazine* the verses *On a Naughty Little Boy Sleeping*, which had already appeared in the *Californian*. It was also at this same time apparently that he sold his pen and name to those enterprising advertisers Enoch Morgan and Sons, and in a small pamphlet, a parody of Longfellow's *Excelsior* made known the merits of Sapolio. This product of Harte's destitution at the present day, ironically, brings a good price as one of the rarest items of Harteana, although bibliophiles are somewhat concerned at not being able to determine which among the slightly variant issues constitutes the first edition.

In the world of business one not infrequently meets an unfortunate man who once successful has in middle age had the misfortune of failing; thereafter his well-meant and even well-conceived efforts are rendered futile by a lack of physical and mental force. Although he was just past forty, Harte in 1877 appears such a man. We have already had to notice his pettiness at Hartford and his palsied incapacity at Washington.

A new hope kept him in Washington during the summer. With the fatuous optimism so characteristic of the broken man, he wrote to his wife: 'I think the tide is turning'; and again, with an added absurdity: 'Washington is the place for a literary man to make money.' He had become acquainted with John J. Piatt, editor and part owner of the *Capitol*, a magazine much like the old *Californian* in format and position, and as events proved equally unstable. In the first place Piatt offered Harte one thousand dollars for a story. This was rather more than the *Capitol* had any right to be paying, and there

Bret Harte

is in Harte's letters more than a hint of a mysterious man-behind-the-scenes which makes it look as if Harte were allowing himself to be used as a catspaw in some lobbying intrigue. The novelette itself, *The Story of a Mine*, lends strength to this supposition, for it dealt with the manipulation of land grants in Congress and was based, as Harte mentioned in a letter, on facts supplied to him.

He lingered in Washington to gather his material and write. He progressed slowly, afraid to put in careless work. He fell sick with 'gastric catarrh,' but not daring to give up, fought off the malady and lived 'on beef-tea and broth — eschewing all vegetables, liquors, or stimulants.' The tropical heat of a Washington summer sapped his strength. Yet he pulled himself together well enough to write a letter to a friend wittily composed in the style of 'My Lord Shaftesbury.'

All this time, he was almost literally penniless, and his wife sitting at some summer hotel was equally destitute. His letters to her were the broken cries of a man in torment; they touched depths of humiliation which make the very reader embarrassed. When possible he sent money, generally fifty dollars.

Dear Nan [he closed one letter], I have had no money since I have been here. I shall have none until the story is finished. I do not blame them. But it is hard. But it is not so terrible to me as reflection that you are left alone, penniless, at that strange hotel, with no money. If I could do anything by being *there*, more than I am doing here, I would come. *But I must come with money.*

God bless you, Nan; be patient a day or two longer.

Again:

My dear good, patient Nan, if you did not already know

Débâcle

how foolish I am about not writing bad news, you would guess, as I see by your kind letter you have, that I have had great trouble and perplexity here.

Yet the general tone of the letters makes one doubt very much his characterization of 'good, patient Nan.' He was too full of sympathy for her, too humble; one feels that her letters must have carried too much self-pity, too little sympathy and encouragement for him. It is a bad sign when a husband feels called upon to thank his wife for a 'kind' letter. And one grows hot with indignation when in the midst of his troubles he has to begin humbly and without complaint: 'I have written to you twice and telegraphed you twice within the past ten days, but have received no answer.'

So, in the worst days that he had ever known, he wrote *The Story of a Mine*. But the words were still-born from his pen. One follows without interest the action from the Coast Range of California, to San Francisco, across the continent, and to Washington. Yuba Bill appears for a moment, but he seems sick unto death. A group of descriptively named, lugubrious manikins — Mr. Joseph Wiles, Mr. Saponaceous Wood, Mr. Expectant Dobbs — play their set parts. But if to the general reader the story offers little, it is nevertheless biographically one of the most illuminating of Harte's writings. Despair lies over it like a dingy fog. There is a dull dreariness of atmosphere. Scarcely once does one glimpse the fresh sunlight of a really artistic touch. When the writer attempts satire, he merely whines. He makes reproachful reference to a Californian artist neglected by a Californian public. What are meant to be Juvenalian invectives against governmental corruption turn out to be merely clumsy vituperations of a tired hack-writer. On every page stand out italics — those raw stimulants which a failing writer desperately forces down the throat of a flagging reader. Only when the subject matches the mood do the words gain vitality, so that in a certain passage one can almost feel the breathless, humid city, sickening in the midsummer heat, with Congress and all who can afford it fled to hills or sea, and the asphalt of the deserted streets sticky underfoot.

As he worked, Piatt made him further offers — five thousand dollars a year if he would assume the joint editorship of the *Capitol*, or a smaller amount and a half-interest in the magazine. Harte was alternately hopeful at the fine words, and despondent when Piatt was scarcely able even to meet his engagements of advance money as instalments on the story came in. The necessity of writing for the *Sun* caused delays, and people again said ugly things about his breaking engagements. 'It lost me, I fear, many friends,' he wrote cheerlessly.

Then came catastrophe. The *Capitol* itself was involved in debt; far from paying five thousand dollars to an editor, its proprietors could not even pay for the manuscript already delivered to them. 'But I shall tonight finish the story,' Harte wrote from the depths on September 21. 'Please God, I may yet get a couple of hundred dollars out of it from Osgood, and, mayhap, something from England. It isn't a bad story — some of it has been written in the sorest trouble I have ever had.' A little while later, creditors attached the assets of the *Capitol*.

Harte was a broken man, far gone toward a complete physical and nervous collapse. He was downright ill a

Débâcle

second time in September. His very writing showed his mental distraction; such a crude tautology as that to his wife 'penniless... with no money,' he would surely not have permitted when master of himself. His manuscripts of the time show it. The ordinary sheets which he sent to the printer were written in a fine, neat hand, and in spite of last-minute corrections were admirable copy. *A Sleeping-Car Experience*, however, is badly written on odds and ends. *My Friend the Tramp* is scrawled on three or four kinds of paper, largely scrappy, some of it scarcely better than brown wrapping-paper. Across the top is written in pencil 'Proof to be sent to B. H. 45 Fifth Av. by 4 P.M.' Toward the end of *Morning on the Avenue* a mind scarcely functioning clearly has scratched out a word, rewritten it and rescratched it four times. Even so, for the sentence to read as it now does, it must have been changed again in proof.

In some way he managed to get through the winter, but he himself was sick and the family almost destitute. Memory of that time remained a nightmare for him. 'That *awful, terrible last* winter!' he once wrote, and in another letter, 'I could not, and *would not under any circumstances*, again go through what I did in New York the last two years and particularly the last winter I passed there.'

A man, however, who has in his day eaten dinner at so many good tables as Harte had, is not likely to be let starve in the gutter. He still kept some friends in high circles. With their encouragement, in spite of his dislike at soiling himself in what he called 'political mire,' he at last found himself, like poor Mr. Expectant Dobbs, of whom he had been recently so scornful, sitting in Washington hotels and in secretarial anterooms while his

friends saw 'what could be got for him.' John Hay was
in the State Department and the Assistant Secretary
was Frederick W. Seward, whose father had been a
college mate of Harte's father and stepfather. So 'Mr.
Expectant Harte,' who had come down to Washington
with only twenty dollars in his pocket, was in good
hopes. In the meantime, he wrote some verses as pot-
boilers, a four-hundred-line Byron-and-water satire
called *Cadet Grey*, in bastard stanzas not quite either
ottava rima or Spenserians. Before long the Secretary
of State was won over; next, President Hayes granted
him an interview and gave the cheering information that
he had been included in a list of proposed names for
consuls. Hopes were even held out of a diplomatic appointment in some small European country, and he
might actually have had First Secretary of Legation at
St. Petersburg if he had not feared that the cost of social
life would eat up the salary. Finally matters became
definite. He called on the Assistant Secretary again, and
Seward remarked:

Mr. Harte wouldn't you like to take the map and look at
some of the places talked of for you.... Here is "Crefeld,"
near Düsseldorf, in Germany, on the Rhine, not much to do
and it's worth about two thousand dollars now and may be
raised to three or four thousand. What do you think of it?'

The man addressed would have thought very well even
of an appointment near Hades, on the Styx.

Of course [he confided to his wife], I was wise enough not
to commit myself — although you can imagine that, with all
my disappointments, this seemed like a glimpse of Paradise.

At the last moment a rival faction sought to influence
the Secretary, alleging that Harte on account of debts

Débâcle

and extravagances would not be safe in a governmental post involving a financial trust. Fortunately, Harte remembered his services in the Mint, and so was able to counter with a highly commendatory letter from the Comptroller of the Currency, who had once visited the San Francisco Mint as inspector. Harte, sick again with a cold and a cough, was assured of the place. On May 11, 1878, he addressed his first letter to the Department of State enclosing bond and accepting the appointment as Commercial Agent of the United States at Crefeld, Germany.

PART V
1878–1902

CHAPTER XXXI

TIMON AM RHEIN

IT was the afternoon of June 28, 1878, the hottest day of the season. The passengers wilted and sickened in a heat of 92° as they cleared the docks at Hoboken. The engines throbbed and the ship moved down past the Battery; Harte was still going eastward into the unknown. This time he was alone. There was simply not enough money to take the family along, especially since consular appointments were notoriously insecure. As it was, he had had to borrow from Dana to keep things going at home until he could begin drawing an income from his office.

His fellow passengers on board saw a still elegantly dressed and handsome gentleman. He was almost forty-two, and his full head of hair, worn long enough almost to cover his ears, had already turned a golden gray. Even so it made only the better contrast with his dark mustaches and side-whiskers. During the voyage he passed as a good sailor, because he never took to his berth, but actually heavy and miserable, he envied those who could be really seasick and then well. There was no physical vigor left in him. Indeed, there was no mental vigor, either. He had failed, and then, being offered the choice between certain destitution and uncertain exile, had perforce chosen the lesser evil. His self-confidence and his self-respect — both so necessary for happiness — were shattered. As the *Suevia* rolled in the Atlantic swells, his spirit as much as his digestive organs caused his misery.

After ten uncomfortable days at sea, he landed at

(249)

Plymouth. On the run up to London, he had the American's usual rapture over his first glimpse of southern England, but in London he lapsed into misery. Perhaps he felt the contrast to his glorious reception in Boston seven years earlier. He stayed five days, hoping that someone would look him up and take notice of him as a celebrity, not daring to make the advances himself. But his coming had not been heralded, and, besides, it was summer and everyone out of town. He wrote to his only English friends, Houghton and Froude, but had no answers. He went to see a few publishers, who seemed cool, although Trübner showed him some courtesy. London appeared 'a sluggish nightmare,' and he felt unutterably lonely and beaten. England like America must know him for a failure. He went on to Paris for three days, where two of his wife's nieces gave him a little companionship; but Paris seemed only 'a confused sort of hysterical experience.' Then, after a tedious, sleepless night on the train, which brought back all his weariness and despondency, he came to Crefeld. That evening he wrote to his wife:

It's been uphill work ever since I left New York, but I shall try to see it through, please God! I don't allow myself to think over it at all, or I should go crazy.

The next day, on July 18, 1878, he who had been a world conqueror took possession of his Elba, the tiny consular office in Crefeld.

A trim, small city with shaded, clean streets, delectable *Haus-platten* and neat shops where red-cheeked *Mädchen* smile and say: '*Bitte schön!*' — this is Crefeld today, for all the cloud-heavy skies of the Rhenish lowlands as pleasant a little German city as one can wish to find. It was probably much the same fifty years ago. But it was not so to the bilious exile who came there to eat bitter bread in loneliness and humiliation. His first letters were the spewings of a Timon. The city was uninteresting and monotonously ugly. Its inhabitants were fat-witted satyrs become pimply about the nose and streaky in the face from daily overeating, and swilling of Rhine wine — 'guzzle, guzzle, guzzle.' For all that, the German cooking was damnable. His room in the hotel was the most uncomfortable 'hole' that he had ever lived in. A *fest* was distasteful and childish. The former Vice-Consul was — the description has a misanthropic thoroughness — 'a very narrow, mean, ill-bred, and not over-bright, puritanical German.'

With such opinions one cannot wonder that he got away from Germany as soon as he could, especially since among his first letters he had found friendly notes from Houghton and Froude, the latter being a warm invitation for a visit. By the political customs of the day, one man received the pay and another did the work. Accordingly Harte, who, unable to speak anything but English, was helpless in his office, quickly arranged with a young German, who spoke also English and French, to do all the routine work as Vice-Consul for a remuneration of five hundred dollars annually. Having accomplished this in less than a fortnight, Harte was comparatively free, and immediately set off on what was to him more important business.

For one thing becomes immediately clear from his actions — pressure of circumstances may have forced him to become a minor governmental official, but he had no intention of remaining one indefinitely. He was still too ambitious to rest in Elba. Although temporarily unstrung (he felt that he should not even try to write for six months), he knew himself a writer of world-wide reputation, and he meant to regain the position and the perquisites which went with his attainments. In America he had ruined himself; on the Continent he was linguistically helpless; England remained.

At the end of July he left Crefeld. He stopped a few days at Paris and probably at this time negotiated with *Figaro*. The editor offered him any price which he might set, if he would write about Parisian life. 'But,' said Harte, 'I know nothing of Parisian life.' Like trout to fly, the Gaul rose to the epigram, replying with the inevitable shrug: 'So much the better!'

Harte went on to England, where his visit of a month was as pleasant and successful as his previous one had been the opposite. He stayed with Froude in Devonshire, and was charmed by the country, the quiet hospitality, and the deference shown him. Returned to London, he found editors receptive, and thus encouraged set in immediately upon a story for *Belgravia*. Then, through the good offices of Joaquin Miller, who always admired Harte, although the latter scarcely reciprocated, he received an invitation to visit with the Webbs of Newstead Abbey. Here, besides the Byronic associations, the open hospitality delighted him. He met many socially fine people, even a live duchess — the Duchess of St. Albans — who took a great fancy to him and urged him to pay a visit to her country-seat. He went back to Germany in September better pleased with himself and the world than he had been in many months; he had been kicked and cuffed so much in the last few years that a little kindness and praise was balm to him.

Timon am Rhein

The situation at Crefeld, however, was almost as distasteful as ever. He really settled down now to his consular work. In more than four months he was absent apparently only upon two brief trips — once for a few days to pay his visit to the St. Albanses and again to earn a needed hundred dollars by a lecture at Wiesbaden. His situation as a consular officer of the lowest grade was highly uninspiring. Strictly speaking, he was not a consul at all, but only a Commercial Agent of the United States; in title-adoring Germany this sometimes put him into uncomfortable positions. As a Commercial Agent, moreover, he had no regular income, but was paid, so to speak, on a commission basis out of the fees which he collected. Fortunately, the manufacturers of Crefeld did a steady export trade in silks and velvets so that he was able to collect regularly his maximum allowance of twenty-five hundred dollars in addition to what was allowed him for office expenses. The examination and certification of invoices upon the exported goods was the chief official activity. Vice-Consul Schneider attended to most of this routine, but Harte had to be responsible for the monies collected, make reports, and attend to minor miscellaneous duties. His letters to the Consul-General at Berlin in his early months showed him often entangled in the toils of bureaucratic red-tape.

Of his life during these months one has difficulty in gaining a just impression. In letters to his wife he represented himself as uniformly dispirited to the point of despondency, suffering from rheumatism and dyspepsia, unable to eat, worried by financial straitness, oppressed by the grim and dark winter. In later years he often spoke of his terrible loneliness in Crefeld, the hateful

(253)

evenings when he walked aimlessly along the blank, empty streets longing to see a familiar face.

This memory may have been of the first weeks, however, and as for the letters, we must remember that an exile is likely to feel sorriest for himself and most homesick when he is writing home. Actually, numerous incidental references in letters show that he was enjoying a reasonable amount of social pleasure. He accepted invitations from various German friends, and sometimes visited for several days. He was on intimate terms with the family of his Vice-Consul, to whom he sent gifts on Christmas and on birthdays. He made little excursions into the surrounding country and across the Dutch frontier. He attended concerts and operas at Düsseldorf and Cologne, although with a spleen which seems a little provincial he reviled German operas as produced by Germans. Upon most of these occasions he was with companions of high standing — such as the general commanding at Düsseldorf — with whom he was on friendly terms. One of his letters written in December, 1878, also shows that he had developed ties of intimacy:

My dear Mr. Jentges,

Both I and my cousin would like so much to be able to enjoy your hospitality, and see a German Christmas under such pleasant auspices, but we have already promised ourselves to Mdme Fay in Düsseldorf, and I do not see how we could, without discourtesy forgo our engagement.

Won't you convey Miss Cooper's regrets and my own to Mrs. Jentges, and assure her that we are deeply grieved at our inability to accept her thoughtful invitation.

(There is no mention of Miss Cooper in the letter to his wife, and I have been unable to locate the name among Harte's cousins.)

Timon am Rhein

In spite of his feeling that he needed a six months' rest, he had stories constantly on hand during the latter part of the year. He found it a great relief to know that he had an income from his office and so was not forced to write under pressure. Nevertheless, the stories of this period, such as *An Heiress of Red Dog*, showed no marked improvement. The Germans were gradually becoming conscious that their admired author was in their midst, and various publishers negotiated with him. Little came of this, except that on the death of Bayard Taylor, he wrote for the *Berliner Tageblatt* a brief article which is probably unique in being an essay by one American writer upon another which was published in German, but never in English.

During these months, however, Harte's real thoughts were upon the future. In England lay his hopes. During his brief visit in November he had made tentative arrangements for some lectures, and, although he could still characterize lecturing only as 'agony and misery,' he was ready to go through with it to earn some money and at the same time to be in England long enough to cement his friendships.

CHAPTER XXXII

THE GENTLEMEN OF ENGLAND

In the last days of January, Harte left Crefeld to deliver his lectures. He found his English friends making long faces, not without reason. The manager had blundered by scheduling the first lecture at the Crystal Palace in Sydenham, and in the announcements of that bourgeois temple of amusement Harte had the chagrin of finding himself sandwiched between a pantomime and a presti-digitator on equal terms with both. In Victorian England, so sensitive to propriety and good introductions, this was an ominous beginning. Except for his contract, Harte in despair would have withdrawn entirely.

Seven on the evening of January 28 saw the large bleak hall moderately well filled, both in the reserved seats at half-a-crown and farther back at a shilling. At a quarter-past Mr. Bret Harte — 'the celebrated American poet and humorist, author of "The Luck of Roaring Camp," "The Heathen Chinee," "Sensation Novels," etc.' — quietly entered from a side door, walked to the reading-desk and commenced to talk, without, to the horror of the half-crown ticket-holders, any formal speech of introduction. He read his lecture, *The Argonauts of '49*, in a conversational tone, pleasant to those who could hear, but inaudible a few yards from the platform. Now this was no docile American audience; the shilling seats were full of true-born Englishmen reared to the traditions of heckling and learned in the ways of Hyde Park. Before ten minutes had passed, there were noises from the rear benches and cries of

HARTE CARTOONED IN 'VANITY FAIR'

'I think it's poor and does not contain any one of my characteristics, but still it might be worse. . . . It's considered a very *swell thing* here to be caricatured in "V. F.," and I suppose it will help my lectures.'

The Gentlemen of England

'Speak up!' Then a gentleman was upon his feet — a stony-faced, determined-looking person with gray beard and side-whiskers. Making himself the spokesman of the discontented shilling tickets, he addressed the lecturer at some length. The audience, like the Etruscans at the bridge, at once divided into those before and those behind; the shillings cried their champion on and the half-crowns called on him to sit down and let the lecture proceed. The lecturer was reduced to silence and embarrassment. At his wits' end, the best he could do was to invite the chief malcontent to take one of the dozen vacant chairs on the platform. Spoken probably in all seriousness and in extreme mental torment, this remark saved the situation. For the half-crowns and the shillings had both come to hear American humor, and they suddenly decided that this must be it. Loud laughter and cheers rang through the hall; Harte had won his audience and the gray-beard had to subside. A quarter of an hour later, indeed, he was again on his feet proclaiming the good English doctrine that 'he had a right to hear.' He failed to gain a following this time; the lecturer managed to continue successfully, and finally to conclude amid warm applause.

All things considered, the papers were very kind in reporting the lecture. It even inspired in the *News* a column of editorial on American humor in which Harte was compared favorably to Mark Twain and Artemus Ward. Nevertheless, there was no denying that only by the merest grace of luck had he escaped complete failure. Harte was somewhat unstrung by the experience, and after such a dubious beginning decided on the advice of his friends to postpone the tour. Accordingly, he lectured only in the four other places where definite dates had been set. The financial results of the lectures disappointed him. The visit was, however, a social success, for invitations were showered on him so lavishly that he had to decline many.

In the middle of February, he returned to Crefeld, but he was again in England for the end of March and half of April to fulfill his postponed lecturing engagements. This time the agent had made better arrangements, and properly dignified persons were at hand to introduce the speaker. Harte, of course, had his ups and downs. At Birmingham he seems to have been thoroughly successful, although in ignorance of what was expected he walked off under cover of his applause, leaving the gentleman who was to make a complimentary speech without anyone to whom he could address it. At Brighton the lecture almost fell flat between the shillings who could not hear and the half-crowns who felt called on to be fashionably bored. Brighton, nevertheless, with its usual blatancy presented him with an illuminated scroll, apparently a credential of honor for his having lectured in its world-famous aquarium — 'a very elegantly and eloquently prepared piece of parchment, like a patent of nobility,' at which Harte was in secret immensely amused.

The real importance of these visits to England lay not in the financially disappointing and the always irritating lectures so much as in the opportunity of making friends. The proceeds from the lectures and the sale of an occasional story meant little, but the reëstablishment of his own self-esteem meant everything. And after he had once broken the ice, he found himself in England almost in the same position which he had held in the Eastern States in 1871. He was making friends rapidly. To Froude and Houghton he had first added the Webbs and the St. Albanses. His lecturing visits strengthened these friendships and added among others the Pembertons of Birmingham, and the Van de Veldes, the families who were most to shape his later life.

Everywhere he was delighted to find people accepting him warmly and entertaining him in friendliest fashion. If he had remembered of his Froissart anything more than that misundersood statement about the sadness of the pleasure-bent Englishman, he might well have quoted the good old canon's conclusion when he came visiting King Richard's court: 'The gentlemen of England are courteous, tractable, and glad of acquaintance.' He might have added, 'and the ladies of England also,' for it was the hostess more often than the host whom Harte mentioned in his letters home.

After his return to his post in April, he just escaped wrecking completely the good impressions which he had made. In its circumstances the incident strangely repeated the Chicago fiasco of February, 1871. In England, Sir Frederick Leighton as President of the Royal Academy had asked him to respond to the toast to 'Literature' at the annual dinner. It was a high honor, especially for an American. Harte, of course, disliked the idea of speaking, but was unable to bring himself to a flat refusal. But when in Crefeld he received the official invitation, which should have been a mere formality, he had completely lost courage and, what was worse, was so stricken with mental paralysis at the very thought of after-dinner speaking that he could make no answer at all, either yes or no. The time was short, and in England Leighton was tearing his hair and calling upon mutual friends to spur Harte to action. Finally he telegraphed, and Harte, forced to a decision, sent a return telegram, so short as to be hardly courteous, declining the invitation with the lame excuse of pressure of consular duty. Then Froude wrote to Harte; Harte wrote to Leighton; and Leighton, mollified, telegraphed regrets to Harte. It was now too late in decency to ask anyone else to speak; so Froude let himself be taken as Harte's scapegoat and replied to 'Literature,' a toast for which some of his critics probably said he was better suited than for one on 'History.'

Harte thus just missed making the same error which he had made under similar circumstances eight years before, but that he did is significant. He had learned his lesson. He knew now that no one was so great as to be able to ignore the decencies of social behavior. In 1871 he had let his head be turned; in 1879 there was no question of this; in fact his opinion of himself remained constantly too low. When he had come to Chicago and Boston he was confident and ready to become overconfident; when he came to London he was timorous. Adulation in '71 was his ruin; in '79 his salvation.

So at about the time of the Academy dinner, Harte attended a state banquet at Düsseldorf, where he met the Prince of Hohenzollern and was bored by sentimental speeches in German which he could not half understand. He went on approving invoices at Crefeld, and one hopes that he appreciated the irony of his telegram to Leighton about important business. The unworthy use to which the world has put its literary men is an old and lengthy song, with Burns as a whiskey-gauger being the favorite verse. Another can be made of the experiences of Harte at Crefeld, especially of a curt letter from the Appraiser of the Port of New York requesting the Commercial Agent to ascertain and forward 'as full and exact information as possible, respecting the cost of manufacturing, and the market price of hatbands.' At the end of his first year, he found that he had had to keep the office open after hours on three days and that business had increased by one third. On these grounds, he requested an additional allowance for clerical aid, and was granted an extra two hundred and fifty dollars *per annum*. He derived some satisfaction from this increased business, although one cannot see how even the best Commercial Agent could have done anything personally to increase the American demand for German velvets.

Nevertheless, his reports dating from the beginning of his second year showed that he was no longer a tyro at consular business and also that his spirits were on the rise. There is a touch of joy in well-turned sentences which recalls the lively columnist of San Francisco. Once a departmental circular called for a report on weather conditions; this was one of Harte's sore points, and in replying, he commented:

The table is compiled from the observations of a competent local meteorologist. In mitigation of the fact that it has rained in the district in the ratio of every other day in the year, it may be stated that the general gloom has been diversified and monotony relieved by twenty-nine thunderstorms and one earthquake.

Again, a demand for information as to possible Mormon proselyting in the district gave play to his pen:

A prolific household with *one* wife seems to exclude any polygamous instinct in the manly breast, while the woman, who works equally with the husband, evinces no desire to share any division of the affection or the profits. The like may be predicted of the manufacturers, with the added suggestion that a duty of 60 per cent, *ad valorem*, by engaging the fullest powers of the intellect in its evasion, leaves little room for the play of the lower passions.

Socially Harte continued to make little advance. He still thought Crefeld and the Crefelders provincial, especially when some of them took offense at the picture of their own city presented in his romantic little tale *A Legend of Sammtstadt* — that is, of Velvettown. He took to living at Düsseldorf — by train less than an hour distant from his office — where he had more friends and more opportunities for amusement. He continued to work at the language, and learned how to talk with 'a reserve verb in his pocket' to finish off the sentence.

On account of his health, he took a month's vacation in Switzerland during the summer. His comments on this trip were as misanthropic as his first impressions of Germany, and showed him indeed a little provincial in his dislike of things foreign. He noted with implied disapproval that the Germans said Mainz instead of Mayence, as other people did. The river steamer was inferior to an American one and the Rhine to the Hudson. The cathedral at Strassburg was very ugly; the hills at Zurich not better than those behind Oakland. To do him justice, he praised the beauties of the Alsatian plain and the colors of the Swiss mountains. But when it came to the Swiss themselves he rose to a minor masterpiece of invective which deserves collection into an anthology of hymns of hate:

A race of 'Yankees' [to the New Yorker only New-Englanders were Yankees] — more intolerant and bigoted than the poorest downtrodden peasants I ever met — are these 'hardy mountaineers,' with their sham sentiments, their sham liberty, their sham chamois (an ugly cross between a goat and a jackass), their sham *jödel* — that awful falsetto as musical as a cat's serenade; and nothing real about them but their hideous *goitres*.

At intervals during the year, as lecturing engagements, consular duties, and health allowed, he did some writing, but his efforts were experimental and opportunistic. He had already tried once, in *A Legend of Sammtstadt*, to make use of a German background, but in this he had merely applied Irving's technique to Germany as he had in the early sixties applied it to Spanish California. Early in 1879 he began for the *Berliner Tageblatt* a series of articles giving his 'frank, outspoken "impressions" of Germany, but the reception of the first essay proved that the German public did not care for frank, outspoken impressions, and so the series went no further. In *Peter Schroeder* he made the first of his many and generally unsuccessful attempts at picturing a Californian in Europe. Finally, with *The Twins of Table Mountain* and *Jeff Briggs's Love Story*, he returned to purely Californian settings. Evidently he was merely drifting. He himself seemed to sense the futility of what he was doing, as he wrote to his wife: 'I grind out the old tunes on the old organ and gather up the coppers.'

His personal problems continued as usual. With the income from his office plus what he could pick up from lecturing and writing, he managed to make ends meet. Every month he sent one hundred and fifty dollars to his wife. He was firm in his resolve to keep himself free from the financial entanglements which had wrecked his peace of mind in America; '*I will not make a single debt*' was the statement underlined in one of his early letters. In reality he did even better than this, for in the first year he managed to pay off his debt to Dana.

At first arriving in Crefeld, he had considered the possibility of having the family join him, but had found that to live properly in Germany was not so cheap as he had hoped. The matter was let drift, and with every month the change of administration and his possible displacement became more imminent. In addition, his own discontent with Germany grew chronic, and with continuing ill-health made him feel that he could not endure to remain long in the sodden lowlands. Sore throat, colds, toothache, rheumatism, neuralgia, dyspepsia — one begins to feel that sickness was the determining factor in all Harte's later life. If *The Twins of Table Mountain* is not much of a story, one should remember that Harte wrote it when half dead with neuralgia. While writing *Jeff Briggs's Love Story* he was so afflicted that he often could accomplish only a page in a day. By the end of 1879, he had become convinced — and German doctors confirmed his belief — that he could never be well in Crefeld. In October, along with a request for two months' leave on account of his health, he also ventured to request a change of station.

He spent the first part of his leave in England, although there is certainly something incongruous in an invalid's going to spend January in London. The fact is that, although Harte's illnesses were genuine enough, he was beginning to look upon England as home and was willing to run physical risks for the social pleasures of which he was sure. In addition to his other friends, he was coming to know many of the literary folk — George Eliot (who delighted him), Du Maurier, Hardy (who, he thought, resembled anything but an author), Gilbert,

The Gentlemen of England

Sullivan (who invited him to a dinner with the Prince of Wales which Harte had to decline), Henry James (whose English manners grafted on Bostonian breeding Harte doubly disliked). He was elected one of the first members, and became the second president of the Rabelais Club, which included some three or four score literary men.

In the meanwhile, Harte's friends in the State Department were working to have him transferred and at the same time promoted. In the last days of March, Harte, laid up with a sore throat in Germany, read in the London *Times* that President Hayes had appointed him to Glasgow. Except that climatic conditions were little if any more favorable, the change was in every way an improvement, and Harte, the end of his Rhenish exile in view, ticked off his blessings complacently. He would have full consular rank, in the second city of Great Britain, a regular salary of three thousand dollars, with fees which should total another thousand. He would be within comparatively easy reach of London, and even closer to his friends' country-seats in the Midlands.

When he left Germany on April 18 to spend in England the remaining five weeks of his leave, it was as if he were already shaking from his shoes the hated dust — although Harte would probably have declared that Crefeld had so much rain as to make this apostolic gesture an impossibility. He went to England for lectures at Oxford, Cambridge, and Norwich, and, at last, to respond to the toast to 'Literature' at the Royal Academy dinner. For Leighton, with a forbearance which was almost more than Christian, had again offered him the honor.

(265)

Bret Harte

On Saturday evening, May 1, 1880, there gathered at Burlington House a group to which even the *Times* was obliged to refer as a distinguished company. Sir Frederick presided, flanked by His Royal Highness the Prince of Wales, and His Royal Highness the Duke of Cambridge. At the tables sat other members of the Royal Family, Her Majesty's Ministers, many of the ex-ministers, foreign ambassadors, both archbishops, a maharajah, peers and M.P.'s innumerable, the Lord Chief Justice, the Lord Mayor, the greater number of the Royal Academicians, and (as the *Times* concluded) 'other gentlemen of position and influence.' Some listed under this last category, curtly by initials, are better known today than the members of the Royal Family, as, for example, T. Huxley, A. Sullivan, J. A. Froude, A. Trollope, and R. Browning.

Time came for speeches. The Prince of Wales graciously responded to the toast to the Royal Family; the Duke of Cambridge for the Army; Admiral Inglefield for the Navy. Mr. Gladstone, just returned to office, spoke at some length in a Gladstonian fashion in response to 'Her Majesty's Ministers'; Sir James Paget spoke for Science; Sir Frederick rose to propose the toast to Literature:

In coupling a name with literature, I propose to take a rather unusual course; for I shall call upon a writer who owes us no allegiance save that of friendship to the country in which he is now a guest [cheers] — an English writer, nevertheless, for English is the tongue in which he delights the innumerable host of his readers; English is the tongue in which he has clothed a humor racy and delicate at once, and has married it to a most subtle pathos — a pathos so deep, so tender and so penetrating that we rise from his pages half believing that wrong is an untoward accident in the world, and goodness the one abiding, inextinguishable thing. [Cheers.] This company will be glad, I am confident, of the opportunity thus offered to it of welcoming in its midst the great American humorist, Bret Harte. [Loud cheers.]

Under cover of the loud cheers rose to his feet in this brilliant porphyrogene company the former printer's devil of Uniontown, wishing undoubtedly that he were, that moment, in Uniontown or even farther away. As the cheers subsided, he began: 'I presume I am selected to answer to this toast as a native of a country which reads more English books and pays less for them than any other nation [a laugh].' He went on with a few harmless remarks about American humorists and humor with a reference to the respective climates of England and America. He was interrupted once by a cheer and several times by laughter. He concluded by thanking the president, and the ordeal was over. Speeches by the Lord Mayor and the Archbishop of Canterbury concluded the proceedings. After dinner the Prince of Wales asked that Mr. Bret Harte be presented.

This was the man who in America had cooled his heels in departmental anterooms seeking a two-penny appointment, had been called a played-out writer, had been dragged through the newspapers as snob, swindler, and drunkard. In England he listened to his eulogies recited at a public dinner before a 'distinguished company'; he was a fellow speaker with the Prime Minister; he chatted with the heir-apparent. Yet there are people who try to find something subtle or salacious in Harte's remaining in England.

CHAPTER XXXIII

THE CONSUL OF ST. KENTIGERN

AFTER the dinner Harte ran off to Scotland to have a look at his new post, and found it prepossessing only by contrast: 'As to Glasgow. It's a big city — about as big as New York — very smoky, very damp, they say. But it's a relief to Crefeld.'

A few days later, he returned to Germany, and after another month turned over the office to his successor on June 18. He left with no regrets. Although the Germans continued to read his books with avidity, they too apparently felt little sorrow at losing him in person. His only valedictory seems to have been a poem in nine unrhymed stanzas, *An Bret Harte, Zum Abschied*, in the *Kölnische Zeitung*, which in turgid and almost unintelligible language entreated him to nourish himself from Germany's spirit rather than from England's mountains of gold.

Nevertheless, to England he went as rapidly as possible. His official papers for Glasgow had not arrived, and he found himself pleasantly footloose for a month. Happy in his promotion, delighted with the invitations which poured in upon him, still glowing with memories of the Academy dinner, he was at his best during this time. He was again that pleasantest of companions, most brilliant of raconteurs, wittiest of conversationalists, that old Bret Harte in fact who had been well known in San Franciscan days, but who of late had been too little in evidence. One observer remembered him

(268)

The Consul of St. Kentigern

during this month as a great favorite in the highest
Bohemian circles, picturesque in appearance and personality, wearing his hair long and affecting velvet
coats and soft hats, larding his conversation with vivid
phrases and swear-words which struck weirdly upon
English ears, telling extravagantly humorous stories,
liking to gather about him a group of kindred spirits.

Among these last was William Black, who came to
know Harte about this time and was delighted with
him. Sir George Wombwell took the two and some
other friends on a driving tour to visit the abbeys of the
East Riding. In the evenings Harte and Black vied
with each other in anecdote and repartee. They went to
Brighton together, where, as Black commented, 'If we
didn't amuse him, he certainly amused us.' Then
Harte went to visit Black at Oban, where they looked at
Highland scenery and played poker. Black summed up
his new friend in a letter: 'He is the most extraordi-
nary globule of mercury — comet — aerolite gone drunk
— flash of lightning doing catherine wheels — I ever
had any experience of.'

On July 24, Harte was able to take over his consulate,
but a letter of four days later was — an ominous portent
— dated from Paris. He had fled there to get 'one ray of
blessed sunshine' after three weeks of continuous rain in
Great Britain. With a discontent at the actual, which
was becoming a more and more pronounced trait with
him, he was already wishing himself located at some
place other than Glasgow. Not until late summer, however, did Harte begin really to make the acquaintance
of that great gloomy city of the Clyde, which in his
stories he called St. Kentigern. He soon found that he
owed his promotion almost entirely to John Hay, and

before long he received a warming letter from the loyal
Assistant Secretary.

> I do not know what Heaven meant [wrote Hay] by creat-
> ing so few men like [Clarence] King and you. The scarcity of
> you is an injury, not only to us, but to yourselves. There are
> not enough of you to go round, and the world pulls and hauls
> at you until you are completely spoiled.

Harte kept this letter by him to read when he was low-
spirited.

The appointment to a more lucrative office immediately brought to the fore the problem of his wife and
family. The uncertainty attending the election, only
four months distant, still raised difficulties. Nevertheless, Harte's letter left the decision open to his wife, and
since this lady's character was a decisive one, we can
only believe it was she who concluded not to come.
That he was not merely gesturing about having the
family rejoin him is shown also by a letter of this autumn
to an English friend in which he mentioned: 'I have been
hoping that some of my relations would come to Glasgow this year, and justify my setting up a home.'

When Harte finally settled down to the consular
work, he found that he had inherited a jewel from his
predecessors in the person of the Vice-Consul, William
Gibson. Consuls came and went by presidential whim,
but Gibson remained. He had been Vice-Consul since
1874, and was to remain through Harte's term and
afterward. An efficient, clear-headed, Scots lawyer of
high standing in his profession, able to meet his shrewd
countrymen on their own ground, he was eminently
better fitted than Harte for the routine of consular
work. As a Vice-Consul he was, indeed, one may say, so

good that he was bad. If Harte had not had an efficient aide, he would of necessity have had to remain in Glasgow, but Gibson made it easy for him to run off to London, or Bestwood, or Newstead upon any and every occasion.

While in Germany, Harte had on the whole remained at his post conscientiously. His absences without official leave do not seem to have amounted to more than about ten per cent of the total time, and from what one knows of American political life in the seventies this was probably an excellent record. There is no way of determining just how much he was absent from Glasgow, but it was certainly enough to make him a standing joke in the consular service. He was called 'Consul of the United States at Glasgow, resident in London.' Preserved at Glasgow is a collection of letters and telegrams from Harte to Gibson numbering five hundred and sixty-two. Some of these were probably sent while the Consul was on official leave, but their very number makes certain that he must have been away from Glasgow an extraordinarily large proportion of his time. This voluminous correspondence, damning as it is from one point of view, is equally saving from another. For making allowances for periods when Harte was in Glasgow and on official leave, one sees that at other times he must have been in daily communication with his office. The letters show, moreover, that he was not merely letting Gibson do the work, but was directing, deciding, and in short being responsible. The correspondence also shows him by no means deficient in business sense and administrative ability — no rubber-stamp for his subordinate, either, for he did not hesitate to make suggestions or amendments when he considered these necessary. The historian of the Glasgow Consulate vouches for the efficiency of Harte's administration: 'Although it is said that Consul Bret Harte, while in charge of this consulate, was often absent from his post, the business of the consulate was kept up to date and the records carefully entered and compiled.' He adds a special commendation: 'Consul Bret Harte was very prolific in his reports to the Department of State and wrote extensively on all matters of interest.' These reports were, of course, the work of the office force, but the correspondence shows that Harte knew what was going on and sometimes put in a hand. He probably had little or nothing to do with their actual language, so that the historian seems unnecessarily complimentary in the statement, 'His dispatches make most interesting reading both on account of their varied subjects as well as their literary merit.'

As to the varied subjects, the historian was certainly right. At Crefeld, Harte had sent in reports apparently when the department requested and not oftener. At Glasgow, it seems to have been his settled policy to take the initiative and report voluminously upon any matter which in his opinion might be of interest to the Government — on two British warships building in the Clyde; on some engines being constructed for an Italian vessel; on the exportation of cement fire-bricks from Scotland; on the system of buying individual apartments in a building; on an invention for collecting the gases evolved from furnaces; on the improvement of the Clyde; on the sugar industry at Greenock; on the market price of white Highland wool at Glasgow; on the Scottish deer forests. These are only some of his subjects. The reports were frequently long; one on labor conditions filled eighteen and a half closely written large pages. For this unusual activity, he several times received special letters of thanks from the State Department.

The consular work at Glasgow was in every way both more important and more difficult than at Crefeld. Harte had under him the Vice-Consul and four clerks, and in addition an agency at Greenock. Three of the clerks were paid by the Consul himself. The routine work, as at Crefeld, was principally with invoices which averaged forty-eight hundred a year and represented an annual export trade of nearly ten million dollars, mostly in pig-iron, textile products, and chemicals.

In a busy seaport special problems constantly arose with which Harte in a quiet inland city had never had experience. He was hardly settled in office before the American barque *Bessie Wittich* dropped anchor in the Clyde with a record on her voyage of 'unseaworthiness, brutality, and inefficiency.' The Consul received from the crew a letter of appeal — pathetic and misspelled, lavish in its use of 'sir.' 'The captain,' noted the Consul in his report, 'was intoxicated, violent and overbearing in the Consulate.' Harte's experiences with the *Bessie Wittich* gave him the opening for his story *Young Robin Gray*.

This was only one of many difficult situations in which he seems to have conducted himself well. He negotiated tactfully and successfully with the Duke of Argyll (or was it Argyle? he inquired of Gibson) concerning the erection of a memorial over the bodies of nineteen American seamen shipwrecked years before and buried in His Grace's property of holy Iona. A certain George W. Gile, claiming to be an American citizen blown out to sea while fishing, came into port on the British vessel which had picked him up. Since he was not a seaman, no funds were available for his repatriation; the Consul recorded simply in his report: 'I supplied his wants out of my own private means and procured a passage for him to America.'

During his first two years Harte had to contend with these difficulties of a new and troublesome post under most distressing personal conditions. On September 13, when he was scarcely yet established at Glasgow, he went shooting on a Scottish friend's estate. An overloaded gun recoiled violently, and the hammer, striking him in the face, cut his upper lip severely. A few minutes later, as he lay under the surgeon's hands and needles, his host's small son pushed timidly into the confusion, and managed to announce audibly: 'Tell Mr. Bret Harte it's all right; *he killed the hare!*' This elegy which, with Stevenson's 'He clung to his paddle,' a man might be glad to have as an epitaph, amused Harte greatly even under the circumstances. Three days later, his lip properly stitched and his face a mountain of bandages, he quoted the boy's remark in two letters, and with characteristic carelessness of detail, although the letters are dated the same day, he gave the quotation in the second as: 'Oh, I say, tell him he killed the hare after all.'

At the time of writing these letters Harte was not worrying about his hurt except for the possibility of a scar. Loss of blood and shock, however, proved serious for his already weak constitution, so that the superficial wound brought on a period of debility and almost continuous illness which lasted until well into 1882. The foggy climate of Glasgow aggravated his troubles and made his recovery doubly difficult. 'My transfer from Crefeld here, on account of my health,' he wrote, 'resolves itself into a ghastly farce.' His desire to enjoy a modicum of physical comfort must be urged as an extenuating circumstance of his absences from his post at this time. He was able on account of illness to get some official leave, but in addition he also spent much time in England either in the homes of his friends or at such resorts as Bournemouth and Harrogate. The severity and the continuity of his illnesses is shown by the fact that this period was a literary blank. Between the middle of 1880 and the beginning of 1882 he produced no story. The only year of his residence abroad in which some volume of new work failed to appear was 1881.

CHAPTER XXXIV

RECOVERY

In the summer of 1877, five years past, Harte had first fallen ill. His illness had been both physical and, whatever word one may choose, nervous, mental, or spiritual. The latter was the first to be cured, and after the summer of 1880 there was in his letters no evidence of abnormal depression. The physical troubles were more tenacious, and only by the summer of 1882 did he begin to show a more or less permanent improvement. His recovery in both cases may be considered the result of his English contacts. The flattering reception culminating in the Academy dinner nursed and coddled his pride in himself. Later, while Consul at Glasgow, he found in the comfortable homes of his English friends the refuge and shelter which enabled him at last to regain some degree of bodily vigor.

Nevertheless, Harte had in England not nearly so large a circle of friends as has often been represented. To visiting Americans and to the socially humble literary and dramatic folk who knew him, he appeared indeed by comparison the darling of the whole British aristocracy, one whose life must be a continued rout of social adventures. J. L. Toole, the actor, told of once meeting him in company with three gentlemen whom Harte introduced as the Duke of St. Albans, Count Bismarck, and Sir George Trevelyan. The comedian, convinced that his leg was being pulled, made some flippant remark only to be chagrined later upon discovering that the three were all genuine.

(276)

Recovery

Although Harte was thus on intimate terms with some members of the aristocracy and had an acquaintance with many others, he was on the whole in the middle eighties beginning rather to restrict than to expand his circle. Having obtained an entrance into high society, he had the common enough experience of discovering that he did not greatly care for it. Once he coolly declined a week-end invitation from a countess for no more reason than that he wished to attend to some literary business. He had reached a stage of life in which he found that a few intimate friends sufficed him. 'The Webbs of Newstead Abbey, the Duchess of St. Albans, Froude' — these along with the Van de Veldes were the only friends which he thought it worth mentioning when in a letter to his wife late in 1882 he gave a sort of summary of his way of life.

This same letter, while only mentioning his other friends, gave a long paragraph to the Van de Veldes. It was a significant testimony of the way in which this association was rapidly coming to be the predominant one in his life. He had met Monsieur and Madame Van de Velde on one of his early visits to England. Arthur Van de Velde was Chancellor of the Belgian Legation in London. In this case as in some others, however (the Frémonts and the St. Albanses, for instance), the closer friendship was between Harte and the wife. Born of the old French nobility, Belgian by marriage, Madame Van de Velde had been at some time a resident of most of the Continental capitals. Her two anonymous volumes of reminiscences are full of the gossip of half the courts of Europe — what the Empress said to the Emperor apropos of the Countess de Castiglione, the daily habits of Queen Isabella, the huff of the Countess Montijo. As a girl she had in 1857 visited the United States, where she had met Prescott, Longfellow, and Agassiz, and been delighted with the country and its people. Harte once characterized her, along with her husband, as 'intensely *un-English.*' Being un-English, she was also un-Victorian; she wrote a volume on French fiction in which she defended Gallic frankness on sex.

Like thousands of others in Europe, Madame Van de Velde had read and admired Harte's stories. She had also her predetermined liking for Americans. At the beginning of their acquaintance in 1878, she had doubtless been to him merely one more of those *grandes dames* with literary yearnings who at one time or another had 'taken him up' as a social lion. The friendship developed rather slowly, but by the end of 1880 the two were in correspondence. By this time also he had probably made the acquaintance of that spacious home in St. John's Wood, in the fashionable northwest of London, which housed the Van de Veldes with their *nine* children and a corps of servants almost equally numerous. The real cementing of the friendship seems to have come in the autumn of 1881, when Harte had been at the worst of his illness. At that crisis the Van de Veldes took him to their summer residence at Bournemouth, kept him a month, and finally, since he was still weak, escorted him back to Glasgow. It is no wonder that Bournemouth was the only English watering-place for which Harte cherished a liking.

Shortly after this, the Van de Veldes set aside in their town house a room which was to be Harte's. When he was in London, he occupied it; when he was elsewhere, it remained vacant. With a pretty sentimentality something of his own property always remained in the room so that he might feel some share in ownership and, as nearly as possible, imagine himself in his own home. The house at Bournemouth was equally open to him in the summer. Harte appears to have been not a little mystified at all this kindness; with what seems to be perfect frankness he wrote to his wife: 'They have adopted me into their family — Heaven knows how or why — as simply as if I had known them for years.'

Obviously he was no longer merely a captured literary lion, but was being cherished affectionately for his own sake. A mother of nine children, Madame Van de Velde was ready to care for another. This tenth was a man, but he needed the care of a child which his wife (whether his or her fault, no matter) was not giving him. But Madame Van de Velde saw in Harte more than a pathetic and at the same time fascinating human being to be nursed into physical health. She knew him also for an author whose writings had once stirred the world, but who was now fallen upon strangely evil days. It became her aspiration to restore to the world the great Bret Harte of earlier years. To this end her home offered him domestic comfort, freedom from worry over the daily routine of living, and a refuge when actually ill. In this favorable environment, she herself often acted as his amanuensis, thus easing the physical strain of authorship. She translated some of his stories into French. Of greatest importance, she stood always ready with suggestions and kindly criticism, so that he needed no longer, as he had in Germany, compare himself to an organ-grinder playing before closed shutters without knowing whether or not his listeners wished him to move on. As one of his closest friends wrote, Harte's 'happily renewed industry as an author was largely due to the kindly interest of his good friend, Madame Van de Velde.' He himself, writing in 1883, thanked her for labor over his manuscripts and for suggestions, and sent the gift of a portfolio to his 'amanuensis, translator, critic, and above all — friend.'

With this aid the stream of Harte's stories, which had dried up entirely in 1881, began again with *Found at Blazing Star*, the manuscript of which is significantly dated '15 Upper Hamilton Terrace, London, January 1882.' The stream was only a trickle at first, and the water was generally muddy. *Flip*, with a weak imitation of M'liss in the title-character, was the only other story of 1882 and the next two years offered only six titles.

In truth, however, much of Harte's energy was at this time being expended upon dramatizations of his earlier stories. In spite of his failures, thoughts of a lucrative play were coming to obsess him as thoughts of gold-mines and oil-wells haunt other men. At this particular time his imagination was fired by his having seen *Jeff Briggs's Love Story* presented as 'a pretty little parlour piece for private theatricals.' The dialogue had been word for word from his own text, and he grasped at the idea that if amateurs could so readily and successfully dramatize his stories, he himself might as well do the dramatization in a professional way. Early in 1882 he was working hard upon a stage-version of *Thankful Blossom*. It was a bad selection, for the story was neither one of his best nor one of his best-known; in addition, its Revolutionary setting made an English production very unlikely. He had hardly finished this before he was at work adapting *The Luck of Roaring Camp*. In this case the title had good advertising value, but the production of the new play under the old title would have been little less than a swindle on the public. The actual story formed only the prologue of the play with the additional changes that the Luck was to be a girl (was Stumpy to say, 'I proclaim you Thomasine Luck'?) and was of course to escape drowning and be the leading figure. Except for the prologue the scene was in Europe whither the Luck himself (excuse me, herself) and various members of Roaring Camp were to be transported. After the completion of this travesty, Harte collaborated with Edmond About in dramatizing from the French the latter's novel *Germaine*.

Harte negotiated with various producers about these plays, but none of them saw footlights. They cannot have been entirely without merit, for Frohman made an offer for the *Luck*, and terms were finally agreed on. It was to have been produced at the Madison Square Theater in the autumn of 1884, but Frohman finally decided that it needed radical revision. Harte was so discouraged that he thought he would rather write a new play. As a substitute he collaborated with Madame Van de Velde on a version of his recent story *A Blue Grass Penelope*. This was no more successful, and the only money which Harte seems to have derived from all his work was a small forfeiture from Frohman apparently for failure to produce the *Luck* according to contract.

Needless to say, Harte had expended on the plays a great deal of time and energy, neither of which he could well spare. Never, he declared, except when he was in the Mint and editing the *Overland* at the same time, had he worked so hard, for in spite of all the joking the consulate was not a sinecure. His lack of physical vigor, also, was still a drag. Gout troubled him. 'Think of it!' he wrote to his wife, 'I who am an anchorite, and for the last two years almost a teetotaller — a subject for gout!'

With work on stories and plays, with consular duties and visits to London, the seasons rolled on. Every month two hundred and fifty dollars went to America. Multiplied by twelve, this represented three thousand dollars, his complete regular salary as Consul. Out of the money which he derived from consular fees and from his writings he supported himself, sent extra money to his wife for Christmas and for summer trips, relieved the needs of particularly destitute American citizens, and occasionally sent a little to his sister Eliza, who had fallen into financial difficulties. Harte himself was probably able to live on comparatively little. Except for his love of clothes and good cigars he did not have expensive tastes; as a single man he did not need to repay social debts in full; the generous hospitality of his various friends must have taken care of a considerable proportion of his daily living expenses. For one of the few times in his life he seems to have been free from serious financial cares. Once he wrote to his wife — unnecessarily, one would think from the record — 'do not mind a little extra expense.'

The marital situation was anomalous. There had never been any real break; Harte's letters regularly contained expressions of affection for both wife and children. Yet the difficulty of a few hundred dollars for traveling expenses was enough to keep them apart indefinitely. The boys were approaching their majorities and beginning their own careers; the girls had grown out of recognition in their father's absence. After a Republican President had been safely elected and Harte had solidified himself with the new administration by writing a preface for Mason's biography of Garfield, the time would have seemed ripe for the establishment of at least Mrs. Harte and the girls at Glasgow. But the assassination of Garfield again made the political situation uncertain. As regular as the swing of the sun northward were the plans of a visit one way or the other, but something — pressure of work, temporary financial straitness, the political situation — always caused postponement. Out of all this discussion there materialized only a short visit of his son, Frank, to his father in 1884. And naturally, although they got along well enough, the reunion of a middle-aged father and a youth scarcely out of adolescence was not the feast of joy which a sentimentalist would like to imagine. To his friends in England the relation to his family must have seemed highly incongruous. He talked to them of his wife and children, sent money and presents, encouraged correspondence between his children and theirs — but he kept the ocean between. The situation, however, seems to have been slowly defining itself; there was apparently no great quarrel to separate husband and wife and no great love to bring them together. The barriers of space and expense which divided them were not impenetrable; any strong desire of either party could have burst them in an instant. But they had been apart for years now; on both sides of the ocean had developed new threads of association which it seemed scarcely worth while to break. So the Consul swung between Glasgow and London, and ended his letters, 'Love to all' and 'Kiss the children for papa,' signed with his pet name 'Limick' or the now almost forgotten 'Frank.'

Of what Harte himself was becoming in these years

we have an interesting self-portrait in the Consul of St. Kentigern who appears in several stories. He was a quiet, middle-aged man of the world, observing rather than acting, amused and sympathetic with the vagaries of human nature, never shocked or intolerant, a pourer of oil upon troubled waters, a perfect week-end guest. He was a trifle proud of his knowledge of feminine nature, and not afraid of a passing flirtation, but was not to be entrapped into more serious dalliance. He admired the British gentlefolk and their ways, but he guarded his Americanism jealously and almost belligerently. This is doubtless an idealized portrait — Harte on full-dress parade — but from what we know from other sources it does not seem much removed from the actual.

With the Glaswegians themselves — 'the righteous St. Kentigerners of the tribe of Tubal Cain, great artificers in steel and iron, and a mighty race of engineers before the Lord' — the Consul remained on cool relations. He lived in dreary lodgings or equally dreary hotels and took meals at what seemed to him an even drearier club. If any fellow clubmen did drop in, they could talk only of steamships, iron, and wool. His Vice-Consul, Gibson, was probably the only man in the city for whom he had any affection. With Scottish character the Consul could never be wholly sympathetic. The story told of his first coming to Glasgow, although doubtless apocryphal, is illuminating. Having arrived late at his lodging, he dashed out to get dinner, and left his landlady to unpack his bags. On returning he found her in the doorway, arms akimbo, stern-faced: 'I've unpacked yer kists,' she stated, 'and whaur's yer Bible?' To one caller he burst out, showing very bad manners himself, into a diatribe against the bad manners of the

Recovery

Scotch, apparently without any thought of reflection upon his guest. 'Why,' he cried, 'it is marvelous. Here in this lodging of mine even the table-girl cannot hand me a plate except in the spirit of aggression!' He went on to declare that the Scotch even got drunk like no other people: 'There is no gayety, no brilliancy, no sense of enjoyment visible, but a stern, stupid aspect of business in it all as if they were intoxicated from a sense of duty.' The caller thus rudely assailed later came to know the Consul better, and like many others has recorded that once Harte was warmed by friendly company no one was ever more charming and more entertaining. Only once does Harte seem to have entered into the life of the city. For some unknown reason — perhaps some humorist was thinking of the *Society on the Stanislaus* — he was asked to deliver a lecture in a scientific series. Harte, however, having like Elmer Gantry only one masterpiece available, blithely set out upon *The Argonauts of '49*. The audience expecting science refused all chances to laugh and waited for the science. Finally, one bolder than his fellows burst into a hearty roar and carried the rest with him. Thenceforth the lecture was successful, if not scientific. What the St. Kentigerners thought of their Consul has, unfortunately, not been well recorded. He left behind him little except the vague reputation of a man-about-town.

In the later years of his consulate its cares seem to have rested but lightly upon him. His assistants were well-trained and efficient in routine; he himself was a veteran in the service. Destitute *soi-disant* Americans of all kinds, an alleged murderer among them, might turn up to claim the Consul's good offices, but the Consul was able to satirize them all in a rollicking poem:

And I think I know all fancy styles of active mendicancy, from the
    helpless Irish soldier who mixed in our country's war,
And who lay in Libby Prison in a cause that wasn't his'n and I sent
    back to the country — that he never saw before!

I know the wretched seaman who was tortured by a demon captain
    till he fled in terror with his wages in arear;
And I've given him sufficient to ship as an efficient and active male-
    factor with a gentle privateer....

I have tickets bought for mothers and their babes — that were an-
    others — and their husbands — who not only could be
    claimed as theirs alone.
Till I've come to the conclusion that for ethical confusion and im-
    moral contribution I have little left unknown.

But the careless lines did not indicate that he had grown
callous. He replied to a letter from Gibson:

I suppose we must pay the passage home of that poor
woman and child, and draw upon the Beneficent Goodness,
payable on our own *post obits* for a return. See if the Secretary of the Foreign Relief Society (to which I belong) will not
take a share in this secure investment. . . . If the Society wont
do anything — pay her passage, give her a pound or two for
expenses, and charge to my a/c.

The continuation of this letter shows the perfection of
the accord between Harte and his Vice-Consul; it could
not have passed except between friends too certain of
each other to fear misunderstanding:

But why, my dear Gibson — why is it that no sooner is my
back turned upon Glasgow than I find you surrounded by
distressed women and babies appealing to you for succor?
Why is it, as I pass out of one door, they appear to you at the
other with dishevelled locks and mute pledges of affection in
their hands? Why do they 'bring their wounded hearts and
tell their anguish' to you, and fly when *I* approach? Why
are you — so stern and uncompromising to masculine in-
digence — melting towards feminine mendacity — either

with or without child — or obviously gestating? Perhaps in the interests of propriety I had better return promptly to the Consulate. There — tho' I may succumb to impoverished tramps, who have never seen America or the salt water — tho' I may give largess to bachelors for the support of imaginary wives; though I may restore unhappy orphans to their fathers, and succor starving men with whisky for passage money to the next port — I will at least uphold the unimpeachable moral integrity of the flag, and keep it from becoming the swaddling clothes of illegitimate posterity, and the advanced banner of vague paternity.

But in truth the Consul did not inflict upon himself, more than he could help, the settled gloom of that office and its sordid callers. Wilder and wilder tales were told of his absences. The papers printed a story that in the fourth year of his consulate he put his head out of the train-window on its arrival at Glasgow, and asked: 'What station is this?' Naturally some of these rumors got back to the State Department, and he once received a letter, an inquiry and at the same time a warning, in the matter of his absences. (Quite characteristically Harte was in London when this dispatch arrived in Glasgow.) His reply in its evasion of the main point at issue reminds one of some of Sir John Falstaff's defenses. Harte himself seems to have had an easy conscience in the matter. When he chose to hire three clerks at his own expense and then administer the consulate efficiently by letter and telegram, he apparently considered that he had done his duty. In Glasgow there were no complaints of any inefficiency. 'In fact,' Harte wrote to his wife, 'I'm *rather* a good Consul.' And in fact he and Gibson constituted probably one of the best consuls which the service could boast. The officials of the State Department also must have thought that Glasgow was well administered, for in spite of the fact that his notorious absences continued after the departmental letter of inquiry, he remained in office throughout Arthur's term.

March 4, 1885, saw the inauguration of Cleveland. Within six weeks the now Democratic Department of State sent curt notes to Harte and a number of other consuls calling attention to certain mistakes in some of their reports. Harte excused himself as best he could. The matter itself was trivial enough, but the Democrats were in power for the first time in a generation, and the henchmen were clamoring for spoils; everywhere consular heads were being laid to the block. Harte waited his turn while some Democratic friends in America did what they could. On July 18 he saw the expected bad news in the London *Times*, where five years before he had first read of his promotion. The newspapers declared that he was being removed for inattention to duty, but, as with his position in the Mint sixteen years earlier, there is little reason to believe that he lost his consulate for any real cause except for the change of administration. On August 20, 1885, Harte turned the Glasgow office over to his successor and, a white-haired man of forty-nine, faced the world again with no resource but his pen.

CHAPTER XXXV

GRUB STREET DE LUXE

WHILE awaiting his successor Harte had visited with the St. Albanses in Ireland — a depressed, dull, and preoccupied guest. Of the many problems which faced him the most immediate was the question of his return to the United States. A few years earlier he had intended, if he had lost his consulate, to return; but by 1885 the situation had changed. He had become — so evil was the memory of '77 and '78 — almost superstitious about even visiting America:

I cannot call it a dread [he declared]; the word is too large to express my meaning; it is not a *presentiment*, exactly. Perhaps it is because I have been *singularly lucky while I have been here in Europe.*

When he finally faced the decision, only two arguments favored America, the more suitable climate, and a sentimental patriotism which, in spite of everything, kept him always a foreigner in England. These were as nothing in the face of the overwhelming economic fact that on account of copyright difficulties he could not live in America and effectively control his English market, which alone would afford him a living; for in America he was still in eclipse and could receive only a pittance for his writings. In addition, he had now many more friends and pleasant associations in England than anywhere in the United States. So he decided to remain — temporarily at least — until he finished some stories already undertaken for English magazines. Since the arrange-

(289)

ment was 'temporary,' the family situation was to remain as it had been for the last seven years.

The year 1885 was marked also by several other important occurrences in Harte's life. It had seen, even while he still was Consul, a renewed literary vigor. At about this same time, he had established relations with A. P. Watt, his literary agent, and A. S. Boyd, his illustrator; the latter was to be an efficient aide, the former an essential partner in his later literary life. In 1885 he made also one other important decision; he went to live as a permanent resident in his room at the Van de Veldes'.

After so many important occurrences Harte's life, which had been so varied, suddenly became static. For the next eight years — one may state it in mathematical terms — it was composed of four factors, and since the components remained constant, so did the life as a whole. The factors were his financial liabilities, his residence with the Van de Veldes, his association with Watt, and his literary activities. One need only discuss these components to present Harte's life between 1885 and 1893; within these dates the seasons and the years are not significant.

To classify Harte's family under his financial obligations may be a little too cynical, but it is certainly the obvious arrangement. He carried on, indeed, a correspondence with his wife and with each of his children, but he had frequent occasion to complain that his letters were not answered. The boys had left home; Griswold was attempting to follow his father's path in journalism; Frank was on the stage under Boucicault and Barrett. The girls were becoming young women. The family's visit to England or his visit to America was consid-

ered yearly, and still something always prevented it.
There was still correspondence about a permanent reunion in America or England, or even, in the hope of
cheaper living, in Germany. (Wolf! Wolf!) The gap
was widening positively too. When Harte had lost the
consulate, he had had no word of sympathy from his
wife for so long that he was embarrassed when people
asked him what his friends in America thought of his
displacement. Although her letters are not preserved,
Mrs. Harte also probably had her grievances. But the
one solid and enduring tie between Harte and his family
in these years was the financial one. Although with his
office he had lost more than three thousand dollars annually, he resolutely set out to make up that amount by
literary work. He pledged himself to continue sending
his wife two hundred and fifty dollars monthly, and
monthly it went. 'I enclose the usual draft,' was monotonously the beginning or the ending of his letters. This
amount plus what he needed for himself constituted his
financial liabilities.

The second factor in his life was his residence with the
Van de Veldes. In the cooler seasons, he lived in the
London home; in the summers, the family rented a
country-house and he went with them. They gave him
the physical comforts of a home. Daily, Madame Van
de Velde constantly ready to aid, he did his stint of
writing. He was still not a strong man and was often ill,
but on the whole his health was better than it had been
for years. Nevertheless, it had a queer look, this living
in another man's family. In the days of the old Queen,
one did not do so. With 1885 seems to have come a sudden dislocation in some of his closest friendships. There
was no more mention in his letters of visits to the Duke

and Duchess at Bestwood or to his 'English cousins' at Newstead Abbey. Perhaps to this time dates Harte's liking for the motto of the Earls Mareschal of Aberdeen, which he had learned in Scotland; in his later years he was very fond of quoting it aloud with quiet scorn: 'They say. What say they? Let them say!'

The third factor in Harte's life was the efficiency of A. P. Watt. Mr. Watt laid claim to having founded the profession of literary agent, and the firm, continued by his sons, is still a leading one in the field. He and Harte had established relations in 1885 or perhaps shortly before. His first triumph was with *Maruja* which he placed in *The Illustrated London News* and in *Harper's Weekly*. This was the first time since 1878 that any of Harte's stories had been published in America except in the New York *Sun*, which in spite of Dana's friendship paid him only paltry sums. In England also his establishment of relations with the liberally paying *News* marked a new era. In a formal letter of commendation Harte showed his pleasure in the result and his appreciation of Watt's services.

The association soon became invaluable to Harte. In spite of his good record in the consulate, he had never been successful in his own business affairs. Like most authors, he loathed dickering coldly and meanly over the sale of his work. Watt immediately relieved him of this trouble and worry. Harte had no more direct contact with editors and publishers; even the proofs were transmitted through the agent. Watt also increased the proceeds, for in his hands a story was a piece of goods to be sold to the highest bidder, so that without emotional disturbance he could peddle it among possible buyers until he had got the best price. To aid his work he even developed the 'bluff' that his client had other income and was in no immediate need of selling his stories. In Harte's opinion this was of great importance, since it kept editors from thinking that they could squeeze him. In addition to selling finished work, Watt soon came to feeling out the market ahead and obtaining contracts. In his later life Harte seldom began a story without knowing where it was to be published, exactly how much he would receive for it, what length it must be, and what must be its general nature in order to satisfy the buyer and evoke another contract.

One immediate result of his agent's activity was that Harte ceased to write almost exclusively for the New York *Sun* and *Longman's*. Watt placed stories in many different magazines, among others, in England *The Illustrated London News*, *Graphic*, *Macmillan's*, *Strand*, *Black and White*, *Idler*, *English Illustrated Magazine*; in America, *Harper's Weekly*, *Scribner's*, *Lippincott's*, and *The Saturday Evening Post*. In addition, Watt saw to the collection and publication of Harte's work as books — one, sometimes two a year in England, America, and Germany. The volumes were usually thin; a single story like *Maruja* or *Cressy* sufficed to fill one. Often they were cheaply bound in luridly colored board covers picturing some wild-Western event from the story — early California ludicrously interpreted by a British illustrator. They were little better than 'shilling-shockers,' but they brought in money, and that was the essential matter. He was able to make up the three thousand dollars lost with the consulate.

In view of all this, Watt is considered better as a partner than as an agent. Harte and Watt, Ltd., formed an organization like that of a manufacturing firm. Harte represented production; Watt, sales. As an efficient sales-manager the latter saw to it that the factory had contracts placed ahead and did not have to risk forced selling in an open and perhaps glutted market.

Harte represented production; his brain was the factory. This was the fourth and final component in his life. The factory turned out standardized Californian stories of a little varied but always popular pattern. One need not sneer at this or decide that the factory was incapable of producing anything new. One does not blame the manager of a cloth-factory, if on the word of his sales-manager he turns out herring-bones to meet the public demand; on the contrary, one would think him insane if he set to manufacturing exquisite but unsalable checks. You who are ready to cast the first stone at a broken, white-haired man, consider whether you would, for any ideal such as Art for Art's Sake, take the chance of letting yourself, your wife, and two young daughters go destitute.

His manuscripts of this period were no longer the disordered scribblings and scraps of the later seventies; they were, instead, what the products of a well-ordered factory should be. In them Harte displayed only one bit of artistic caprice; he often wrote first across sheets of about four by eight inches; later someone pasted the sheets together by twos to make them approximately the usual size. They were often a good deal scratched, for he was still a slow writer. What most displayed them the standardized products of a factory were the careful notes attached, as, in *A Knight-Errant of the Foot-Hills*, '8,881 words/Feb. 1889,' or the even fuller description in Harte's own script:

Grub Street De Luxe

MS of
'Young Robin Gray'
written for
'Good Words'
About 7000 words
Begun 20 October /93
Finished Novem 17 /93

One almost looks for the little card which some efficient manufacturers insert: 'In case of defect in this article mention in complaint N°03093.'

In quality, the stories were better than they had been in the bad times of '77 and '78. They were more like those of the early seventies — good in parts. The opening of *Snow-Bound at Eagle's*, for instance, was wonderfully vivid; it might be called the classic of the Western stage hold-up. This opening, it may have been, which caused Hay to write to Harte in 1886 — more in friendship than in judgment one fears — that he had only just arrived at the real maturity of his powers. *An Apostle of the Tules*, gave Hay some further justification for his feeling. Two mentions of this story in his letters show Harte's own pride in it. It was certainly all in all the best story which he had done in ten years and the only one of the eighties which would give a critical friend confidence that he had not lost the art. Of the general run of his stories one need say little. Although they were Californian, few dealt with events of the mining country. Harte's mind seemed to be running to other times — Spanish, or Civil-War days, and other scenes, the snow-bound High Sierras, the marshes of Humboldt Bay, the bare valleys of Contra Costa, the cafés of San Francisco.

His slavery to contracts naturally had some bad

effects upon his work. Often editors wanted stories much longer than the *Luck*, or the *Outcasts*, and he whose best narratives had been so concise was forced to spread his incidents out too thin. Again, other American writers popularized certain *motifs*, and Harte was not above doing them over in 'Californiese.' Thus the feud in *Cressy* really belongs in Miss Murfree's tales of the Southern mountaineers, and the mulatto wife in *Through the Santa Clara Wheat* in some story of Cable's Louisiana.

Still, people liked his stories. Year by year he went along. He was not buying bonds, but he was not making debts. He was a Grub-Street hack. It was Grub Street *de luxe*, perhaps; it generously allowed him evening clothes, a club or two, and some amenities of life. But well as Watt might conceal the fact, Harte had no illusions; he knew himself the slave of his pen. He had become a factory to produce stories, to meet the factory's financial obligations, to buy supplies of food and clothing, so that the factory might produce more stories to buy more food, and so to grind on in the circle until the factory eventually wore out. Income and expenditure balanced so that no surplus was ever built up, and the factory could never stop. He worked steadily, summer and winter, in sickness, often, as in health.

This, then, was the end, the end of that high dream of a life devoted to literature to which he had in all youthful freshness dedicated himself on New Year's Eve, 1857. 'When literature' — the epigram is Sheridan's — 'is the sole business of life, it becomes a drudgery.' One must not think that Harte acquiesced willingly. He still had dreams. He had nearly given up poetry now, of course; 'the gentle muse,' he wrote, 'is too expensive

Grub Street De Luxe

and exacting a flame for my old age,... *prose* is a better housekeeper and more profitable.' Yet one day, as he seemed to be watching the smoke of his cigar float over his after-luncheon cup of coffee, he said suddenly: 'I should like to have time to write a long poem.'

A long poem he knew was merely a dream, but he still cherished hope for a play. Whenever the factory had got a little ahead on contracts, he established what commercial language would call a 'development division'; that is, he tried to develop drama as a new 'line' of products in addition to his standard and universally known stories. All the time which he took from regular work reduced the income visibly, but he took the chance; it was his only hope. Between 1885 and 1892, he prepared a new scenario of the *Luck*; he wrote a two-act farce for Toole; he did preliminary work on an adaptation of *Gabriel Conroy*; he collaborated with Hatton on a version of *M'liss*. He made nothing from any of them.

All this while he kept himself and the family going with stories which he frankly called 'bread-and-butter' work. His letters showed what he thought of the situation. He wrote to his wife urging her to write often; 'You,' he added, 'cannot possibly hate pen and ink as I do who live in it and by it perpetually!' He was approaching despair again, not the acute despair of '77, but a sort of chronic middle-aged despair; he wrote: 'Sick or not, in spirits or out of spirits, I must work, and I do not see any rest ahead.'

Yet he had his little triumphs — petty compared with those of the *Luck* or the *Heathen Chinee*. In 1887 he let himself loose with three exclamation points when announcing to his wife: 'a little story I have engaged to

(297)

do for the great Parisian journal — "Lettres et Arts"!
— the finest and most expensive pictorial magazine in the
world! Each copy costs about seven hundred dollars!'
Madame Van de Velde did the translation, and *L'Épave
de Bois-Rouge* appeared before *A Drift from Redwood
Camp*.

Personally, in character and appearance he was changing little. In 1890, John Pettie, of the Royal Academy,
requested him to sit for a portrait. It was a long undertaking, principally because Harte was forever interrupt-
ing the sitting by telling stories, but the final result
showed the real man as no photographer ever caught
him. The almost haughty posture (Let them say!), the
wavy hair half covering the ear, the carefully groomed
drooping mustaches, the patrician profile with its keen
eye and sensitive nostrils! And then the emphasis on
the clothes, the richly furred overcoat, the shining white
cuff, and the glove fitting without a wrinkle! But if the
Academician caught the man head up, facing the world,
not less true and significant was the little pencil-sketch
which his friend Boyd drew informally one November
day in a hotel at Leamington. In it one sees only a
drooping, prematurely old man of fifty-seven, the
overworked factory-slave, wearily pushing the instrument of his servitude, a pen.

Eight years passed, hardly to be distinguished one
from the other. He was still Grub Street's man; *The
Home-Coming of Jim Wilkes*, appearing in 1892 in an
advertisement for Sunlight Soap, showed that. The
four factors remained constant — he produced; Watt
sold; the Van de Veldes sheltered him; his wife received
her money. There were only two threats to the indefinite prolongation of this equilibrium.

BRET HARTE IN 1890
By John R. Pettie, R.A.

Grub Street De Luxe

One was his own ill-health. Although he was stronger than he had been in the years of his consulate, rheumatism, colds, and sore throat troubled him often. He feared the time when he could no longer fulfill the contracts which Watt brought him. Then, too, old age came on. Pettie's brush showed that even his mustaches were getting a little gray.

The other disturbing factor was the improvidence of his wife. He sent her more money than was necessary for her absolute needs. Frequently he urged her to lay a little aside; he wrote her of his fears that he might fall sick and leave both of them penniless. His exhortations accomplished nothing. The most charitable explanation of her actions is that she believed the newspaper stories rather than his letters and imagined him living opulently in London while he dealt out to her a monthly pittance, which was scarcely better than hush-money. Otherwise an incident of 1887 is scarcely credible. Harte received from his wife, apparently by cable, an unexplained demand for money. The call was embarrassingly sudden and the amount large, but fearful of some emergency he procured and cabled the amount. Thereafter for nearly a month he remained in anxiety about his wife and children; he at last received a letter acknowledging receipt of the money and the explanation that it was needed for the expenses of a trip to the Adirondacks.

CHAPTER XXXVI

GHOSTS IN LANCASTER GATE

'MEN like me has their day, and revolvers has theirs; the world turns round and the Bar fills up and this yer river changes its course — and it's all in the day's work.' Philosophical passages are so rare in Harte's stories that in the words of that simple-souled frontiersman, 'the bell-ringer of Angel's,' one may properly feel a reflection of the writer's own mood. He was not actually old — only fifty-seven — but sickness had made many of his years count double; the world of his youth was a generation of men and thousands of miles away; death had just struck close to him, and threatened the eight-years-enduring balance of his life. The bar was filling up and the river changing its course.

In 1892 the great epidemic of influenza had swept over the world. Harte, the weakling, had passed unscathed, while his friend and host, Arthur Van de Velde, whose strength and vigor he had often envied, had fallen sick and died.

While the family affairs were being settled, Harte lingered on in the hospitable house on Upper Hamilton Terrace. Madame Van de Velde was called to Berlin by the death of her stepfather, and left Harte as temporary guardian for the children. In July, 1893, more than a year later, he was still living in the now half-dismantled house, and wrote to his wife in the old strain, 'it looks now as if I might be able to make some preparations toward our near meeting.' Shortly afterwards, however, Madame Van de Velde and the children estab-

lished themselves at 109 Lancaster Gate, and Harte
went to occupy a room in the new home. 'They say.
What say they? Let them say!'

In his room just off Bayswater Road, with its clatter-
ing cabs and busses, the ageing white-haired man probably cared little enough what they said. Men like him
had had their day; revolvers had had theirs; it was all in
the day's work. He had gone through too much to care
greatly about many things. He was fast becoming a
ghost. The life with which through his constant writings he was most closely bound, had long ceased to exist.
The Stanislaus, which he remembered so turbid with
slumgullion, was clear now; the ditches were weed-
choked; the flumes wrecked; the sluice-boxes long rot-
ten. California was growing wheat and fruit, and setting
bait for tourists. 'Wingdam' was dust and forgetful-
ness, a crying-place for coyotes; Los Angeles was growing
great in the land.

He was plainly out of touch. Even in London, though
not old, he was the relic of a past age. It was as if he
were one who had dined with Dr. Johnson or remembered Queen Elizabeth. New kings reigned in the
literary world — Hardy, Meredith, Wilde — they
meant little to him. A new drama was being born, but
Dion Boucicault, of the *Colleen Bawn* and the *Octoroon*,
remained his model. The star of Kipling rose in the east
— what of that? His own star had blazed just as
brightly in the west when this same Kipling was a tod-
dler. Once, indeed, he met Kipling, but at the same
dinner he sat next to Lord Roberts; he confessed himself
more interested in the man of action than in the one
who like himself merely spoiled clean paper with ink.

He began to haunt more and more the Royal Thames

Bret Harte

Yacht Club, of which he was a member. He cared nothing for boats, but there he was safe from all literary talk. He sat contentedly smoking while his fellow members — there are no greater hobbyists than yachtsmen — talked endlessly across and to their passive listener on gaffs, keels, and rigging, and sailed old voyages over again. He did not even make literary capital out of the club; no sailors appeared in his stories, for although Robin Gray owns a boat, he is scarcely a yachtsman.

New ideas in other fields also failed to interest this ghost of a past epoch. A niece and her friend turned up to visit him once in 1895; they were full of strange talk which made him feel more out of touch than ever, although his description of them is not without a gleam of the keen old irony.

They are both [he wrote blandly to a friend] enthusiasts of a new kind of religious 'fad' which, they tell me, is sweeping America, called 'Christian Science.' They wonder I have never heard of it! Have you? They have books upon it, they expound it to *me*. Our conversation is not flippant nor wildly entertaining. My niece is serious, and her friend teaches *Latin* and cognate things in a seminary in Baltimore.

Besides a ghost, he was also becoming a legendary character, although the two, both being immaterial, may perhaps be considered the same thing. Twice in the earlier nineties he broke his old habit and granted interviews. There was method in it (Watt's hand shows); for he was contributing to the magazines for which he was interviewed. Both reports played up the contrast between the man as he was and as he had been — or as people thought him to have been. The latter seemed to the interviewers the more real. Moreover, if the report in *McClure's Magazine* is a correct version of the conversation, Harte was beginning to make something of a legend out of his own early days. People in England, even his intimate friends, told and believed all sorts of things about him. He had been a Colonel in the Army of the Potomac; he had fought Indians; that scar on his lip — he had got it when attempting to show a friend how in Western style one pulled a trigger with the toe. It is amusing to be able in some cases to trace the source of these legends. One of Harte's friends declared that the latter told a certain story as one of his own experiences. A woman was standing, rope about neck, ready to be swung into the air by a Californian vigilance committee. With a fine feminine gesture, she suddenly raised her hand to her neck and, like Sir Thomas More saving his beard from the headsman's axe, withdrew a braid of hair caught within the noose; then nonchalantly presented herself for execution. Whether Harte ever told this as a personal experience, one cannot be sure, but where he did tell it was in his sketch *With the Entrées*, and there it was presented neither as a personal experience nor even as a true incident, but merely as one of a series of 'whoppers' about Western life.

The influence of the legend upon Harte's own mind was shown most clearly in one of his letters. He had been born in 1836 and two extant documents of the sixties show that he then accepted that date. When, however, the newspapers began to publish biographical sketches, the date 1839, perhaps in the first place the result of a mere reversed numeral, established itself. In 1895, when Harte wrote to his friend Colonel Collins, he had rejected the true date and accepted the legendary one by calling himself 'an old mustache of fifty-six.'

Bret Harte

If his own youth was becoming hazy, his California was now scarcely more than a ghostly country from some past existence. He made Charles V responsible for land-grants in California; he introduced Joaquin Murrieta in a story of Civil-War times, although that notable bandit's head had been pickled in brandy and publicly exhibited in San Francisco eight years before Bull Run. Such anachronisms, however, have to be forgiven most authors. His inaccuracy in place-names may also be explained, for Californian names had always been to Harte mere convenient counters, and he had made little or no attempt to have his description of the place tally with reality. So he wrote of the dense Carquinez woods, although the hills along Carquinez Strait were grass-covered, and made Bolinas the name of a vast plain, although actual Bolinas lay closely pressed between the surf and rugged mountains. Of more significance, he began in his old age actually to forget the natural characteristics, the local color of the State. He wrote, for instance, of the ocean side of San Francisco peninsula being baked for six months of the year by a pitiless sun. He made his worst slip, however, when, doubtless with memories of English wheatfields in his mind, he wrote of Californian poppies as 'crimson.' This break elicited some *Plain Language to Bret Harte* in the *Overland Monthly* — a brief poem, which is, incidentally, one of the cleverest parodies of Harte's most famous poem:

> Which I wish to impart,
>   And I hopes not in vain,
> That I think that Bret Harte
>   Should come back again
> To the land that is called California,
>   And the reasons I now will explain...

Ghosts in Lancaster Gate

> But what kills me plumb dead
>   Is to see where he's writ
> That our poppies is red —
>   Which they ain't red a bit,
> But the flamingest orange and yellow —
>   Oh Bret, how could you forgit!

In harmony with Harte's feeling for California as a ghost-land was his curious tendency to refer to it in the past tense; he wrote once in a letter, 'California was a land of flowers,' as if the land had sunk beneath the sea, or the poppies, azaleas, and lupins withered with the mining towns.

Yet, in spite of all the haziness, he seems occasionally to have had one of those clear visions of his earlier experience which are traditionally associated with the approach of death. In 1893 he wrote *An Ingénue of the Sierras* and *A Protégée of Jack Hamlin's* which displayed the best local color and were the best stories of nearly twenty years. If we add to these *Colonel Starbottle's Client* of the preceding year — a story good in its beginning — we have assembled the components of which all his best later work was formed. The three stories were built respectively about Yuba Bill, Jack Hamlin, and Colonel Culpepper Starbottle. They were ghosts of the past, all of them — the shrewd politicians of the Gilded Age had killed the old 'war-horse of the Democracy'; sober business men had killed the gambler; the railroads, if they had not killed, had forced the stage-driver to the back-roads and stripped him of his glory. One likes to think of the three ghosts gathering about a bottle of Scotch in the room in Lancaster Gate. The Colonel, blue-coated, ruddy, and pompous, 'ready, suh, to hold myself, personally responsible, suh'; Bill, gigantic and hard-fisted, his irony devastating as a

Sierran avalanche; Jack, slight, quiet, most dangerous of the three, talking with suave cynicism, coughing at intervals. What would they talk of? What better subject than Joe Briggs of Tuolumne, Jeff's father, who had owned Chiquita, had that bad run of luck at White Pine and blown out his brains down in 'Frisco, that ghost character who like Cap'n Flint in *Treasure Island* is mentioned as a celebrity but never appears? And as the three ghosts from afar so strangely gathered in fashionable Lancaster Gate discuss Joe Briggs, doubly a ghost, there moves among them (scarcely more real than they), filling their glasses and offering his mild cigars, the one who had created them to their ghostly but vivid existence — a slim, dapper, white-haired, slightly drooping old gentleman.

As he aged and grew ghost-like in Lancaster Gate, the seasons moved on uneventfully. The death of Arthur Van de Velde proved only to have threatened, not actually to have overthrown, the equilibrium of his life; the four factors, slightly reproportioned, still controlled it.

After the readjustment seems indeed to have come a more definite break with his wife. There are no published letters dated between July, 1893, and January, 1895; even after this time there are generally only brief notes enclosing the monthly remittance, never the long gossipy letters of earlier days. After 1893, moreover, there was no more planning of visits or of a reëstablishment of the family life. The cause of this, likely enough, was the new situation at Madame Van de Velde's. If even the old arrangement seemed strange, perhaps equivocal, the new one must have seemed to the man of the world — unequivocal. Mrs. Harte could probably have gained a decree in any divorce court.

Ghosts in Lancaster Gate

There are, however, subtleties of human relationship which the world's coarse thumb cannot sense or the clumsy scales of justice weigh. Madame Van de Velde was the mother of nine children, and, just as her youngest was ceasing to be a baby, Harte had appeared. She had taken him in as she might an outcast child; she had nursed him in body and in mind; for seven years her husband and she had given him a home. She had made develop a new Bret Harte reconstituted as man and artist, whom she may well have felt to be her own creation. Whether she ever felt differently for him is, I think, a question which will never be answered. It has after all only a curious interest. In any case, she could not have done more for him than she did. It is not too much to say that whatever is of value in Harte's later work the world owes to Madame Van de Velde.

In comparison with this relationship, the others of his later life meant little. After his son Frank came to live in England in 1893, he had a home at which he could visit and relax himself by running mechanical toys for his small grandchildren. He visited Froude occasionally, and the Marquess of Crewe, son of his old friend Lord Houghton, now dead these several years. He established also a new and pleasant friendship with the Earl of Compton; he visited several times at Compton Wynyates, where the venerable residence inspired him to the not very inspirited *Ghosts of Stukeley Castle*. A. S. Boyd, his illustrator, and Mrs. Boyd were among his friends and with the latter particularly he was in frequent correspondence. He kept up his lifelong interest in the theater, and had a few theatrical friends, such as Sir Charles Wyndham. In town he saw much of Colonel Arthur Collins, who was his frequent companion at the theater. He was no recluse, but in comparison with ten years before, his social activities were few. He was no longer the gay companion, ready even to make a night of it by going the rounds of the music-halls. His fellow club members — except for the yachtsmen — saw him little; they missed him at the Beefsteak, the Rabelais, and the Kinsmen.

He was too busy to waste his meager strength upon social excursions. He sat at his desk for long mornings transferring ideas from his brain to paper, by means of a handwriting which grew yearly a little finer and less legible. In spite of constant practice he remained a slow worker; a thousand words a day was about his limit; often he wrote less. Having finished one story, he began to consider the next. For several days, he might not write at all, but would merely turn over his ideas, pacing the room or sitting blankly before blank sheets of paper. He would talk over the idea with Madame Van de Velde or some other friend: 'Do you like that? Do you think it is good?' Satisfied that an idea would be fruitful, he recommenced writing. Beginnings troubled him, so that often he painstakingly rewrote with slight changes the first lines on several pieces of paper. Once started, he went more surely, but always slowly. Sometimes — it is probably characteristic of the story-teller as opposed to the moralist — he would say: 'I don't know what the winding-up will be, but I do know what my characters are, and they will work out their own conclusion.' He never let a day pass without adding something to the manuscript. Having finished one story, he began to consider the next.

Aside from the reëntrance in strangely renewed power of Jack, Bill, and the Colonel, there is little which need be said about the fruits of this writing in the earlier nineties. There was perhaps a slightly upward trend. The quantity also increased a little; two volumes, six or eight titles, constituted his yearly average. Some stories, such as *Clarence*, were long enough to pass as novels.

His work generally went with him on visits, and he seldom took a real vacation. In August, 1895, however, after twelve continuous years in the British Isles he left for six weeks on the Continent, partly with Colonel Collins and other friends, partly alone. They went to Cologne, thence up the Rhine and to Switzerland. He enjoyed the Rhine, and Switzerland too this time. To be sure, he remembered Daudet's epigram about Switzerland being all a gigantic hotel company. When a green sickle moon rose over the Alps at just the right moment, he felt that the company was really overdoing a bit, and suggested to his companion that they call the hotel proprietor and ask him to have the crescent taken down.

The most interesting feature of this brief trip lies, however, not in any importance of its own, but in the demonstration of his character given by the letters written from Switzerland. Since his previous visit, he had mellowed considerably; he was genial where in the bad time of 1879 he had been misanthropic. Years in London had leached the provincialism out of him. But the characteristic which stood out most strongly was his romanticism — his desire to escape from the present and adjacent, to regain the distant in time and space. Germany and Germans he had certainly disliked enough when forced to live there among them, but no sooner was he there again than he began to blat, 'just like old times' and 'old days,' like any alumnus back to reunion. In the beauties of the Alps he became maudlin about 'the dear old Sierras' which he had appreciated little enough when near them.

This romanticism was nothing new in Harte (even in California he had longed for the 'East and Europe'), but it was a trait which seemed to grow intenser with age until it became dominant in both his character and his work during his last few years. At this time when asked to contribute to a series of articles by literary men called *My Favorite Novelist and his Best Book*, Harte selected nothing by Dickens, but Dumas's *Count of Monte Cristo*. The selection, and even more the essay itself, showed how slight — again a ghost-like trait, perhaps — he was coming to feel the connection between literature and reality. In his best work the connection had been fairly strong, although the reality had been an unusually strange life; he had attempted to calculate with care, one should remember, the amount of provisions for the *Outcasts*. In his later work, except perhaps when Jack, Bill, or the Colonel appeared, he was content to employ accident and marvel — flood, fire, and earthquake. This was not carelessness, for his friends were always highly impressed by the endless pains which he took with his work; it was simply that melodramatic incident did not clash with the artistic theories which he held at the end of his life. The close of the essay on his favorite book gave a fair statement of his own position.

But 'Monte-Cristo' is *romance*, and, as I am told, of a very antiquated type. I am informed by writers (not *readers*) that this is all wrong.... But if they [the readers] have been lifted temporarily out of their commonplace surroundings and limited horizon by some specious tale of heroism, endeavor, wrongs redressed, and faith rewarded, and are inclined to look a little more hopefully on Jones's chances of promotion, or to Mrs. Jones's aunt's prospective legacy — why blame them or their novelist?

This romanticism explains something else about Harte. Once, for instance, in congratulating Froude on a brilliant historical essay, he wrote:

How I envy you! Have you nothing to spare for a poor literary man like myself, who has made all he could out of the hulk of a poor old Philippine galleon on Pacific seas?

The natural answer would have been: 'Do not envy — emulate! if you cannot return to America to hunt material, the British Museum has already scores of volumes from which you may harvest the records of human experiences in early California. Search, and find material for your stories.' Such advice would probably have been lost on Harte; hunting in old books he would have thought a waste of time. Enough for him if he could evolve from his brain 'some specious tale' no matter how incredible, which would allow Mr. Jones to escape momentarily from himself into some land of illusion.

CHAPTER XXXVII

THE MARINE ANIMAL

'A MARINE animal,' wrote the schoolboy, 'is completely surrounded by its environment.' Unfortunately, this applies also to all human beings, although with some it is more noticeable than with others. Harte in his later life was one of those most like the marine animal, for economic necessity, determined by his decisions of many years past, threw him upon Grub Street, and thenceforth circumstances dominated him. But even among creatures of the sea there are some, the flying-fish notably, which seek constantly to escape from their environment or at least to exchange one environment for another. Such a one was Harte; the wings upon which, flying-fish-like, he sought to escape were his dramas; and once almost at the end he thought for a little while that he had succeeded.

One of his stories of 1895 was *The Judgment of Bolinas Plain*, a regular Californian fiction designed to turn an honest penny and to give Mr. Jones his half-hour of illusion. Among others who read it in the *Pall Mall Magazine* was Mr. T. Edgar Pemberton, of Birmingham. He had known Harte for fifteen years, and had once given him the embarrassing present of a St. Bernard puppy. They had since drifted apart. Pemberton, however, was struck by the dramatic possibilities of the *Judgment*, and, being himself something of a playwright, he immediately wrote Harte for permission to use the story. The latter was from experience pessimistic, but with the gambler's infatuation he could not resist another throw of the dice, and suggested a collaboration. With his usual energy in new literary ventures, he got to work immediately, but pressure of contracts interfered and progress was slow. They were a strange pair of collaborators; Harte scarcely better than an invalid for twenty years, and Pemberton for ten under sentence of death from Bright's disease. Upon the slight framework of the story, they built a full-length play. They expanded a single paragraph into Act I. They introduced a ministerial character to chaperon Sue and so save her reputation. Act II contained most of the actual story. Act III brought in a trial scene by a vigilance committee. In a melodramatic climax Sue stood with clasped hands and heaven-cast eyes and the vigilantes placed bets as the acrobatic villain-hero leapt through an upstairs window to save himself (off-stage) by catching the branches of a tree. This incident, together with much misuse of soliloquy and many artificial entrances, showed Boucicault still dominating Harte's ideas of drama.

They first expected to produce *Sue* in England, but Pemberton managed instead to place it with Frohman. The first night was set for September 15, 1896, at Hoyt's in New York. As the date approached, Harte was too anxious to contain himself; it was nearly twenty years since he had had a play produced, and now neither he nor his collaborator could be present to supervise the rehearsals. On the morning of September 16, however, Pemberton had Frohman's cablegram: 'Well received. Fine acting. Press praises.'

Harte had at last written a successful play; at least one may honestly, if not enthusiastically, call it a suc-

Bret Harte

cess. The captivating Miss Annie Russell in the title-rôle was perhaps as great a factor in the play's favorable reception as was its own merit, but all dramatists are indebted to good acting. After playing New York the company went on tour, and kept going for two seasons. The collaborators actually made some money, but Harte failed to realize his dream of a restful old age supported by the profits of a successful play.

In 1898, Frohman brought the company to London, and opened on June 10 at the Garrick. The play ran until July 27; the critics gave high praise, but the financial returns were poor. Harte concluded despondently that the full houses must have been largely 'paper.' He had the melancholy comfort of being told that the play was an artistic success, something about as satisfying doubtless as a moral victory. *Sue* appeared again in America, and as late as 1900 was still a 'live' play on Frohman's list. It was, besides *Sandy Bar*, the only one of Harte's plays to be published; in comparison with that earlier work it shows much improvement, but it is far from being a great drama.

The natural result of success with *Sue* was an intense stimulation of Harte's dramatic efforts. Before the end of 1897, he and Pemberton, partly at Frohman's suggestion, had dramatized three others of Harte's stories. None of these was ever produced. A curious evidence of how play-writing obsessed Harte's mind in these years is his occasional casting of whole pages of his stories in dramatic form.

So, in spite of his gallant effort, Harte, like the flying-fish, tumbled back into his old environment. He continued writing his neat notes — the factory-record — upon his manuscripts:

The Marine Animal

Three Vagabonds of Trinidad
For Punch supplement   4000 words
Begun Feb. 1, 1900   London
Finished Feb. 14, 1900   Camberley.

Having finished one story, he began the next. He was more confident in himself, and often broke away from Californian subjects. There were English, Scottish, and German stories; he even made use of his brief experiences in France and Switzerland. One fallacy about him is that he could never absorb anything except California; on the contrary, he seems to have been unusually susceptible to the influence of every place with which he ever came into contact. Naturally, however, editors preferred from him his standard Californian wares. Another fallacy is that he always remained 'a promising young writer.' He was really, however, so fully professionalized by the end of his life that he could take any *motif* at an editor's needs and do it 'Californian'; he wrote Californian Christmas stories, Californian juveniles, Californian sentiment, humor, adventure, mystery—what you will. He was so fully professionalized that he had little or no trouble in finding subjects; he could take any third-rate idea and dress it up well enough to please editor and public. He was so fully professionalized that he considered the whole business of literature about as boring a way to earn one's bread-and-butter as type-setting or filling out invoices. He had, finally, that last touch of the professional — the pride in doing good, careful, honest work under all conditions. And occasionally still, when he came by the right idea, his best could be surprisingly good.

As he labored at plays and stories his health began

to fail again. Ailments preyed upon him in Job-like multiplicity—colds, neuralgia, rheumatism, toothache, sciatica, ulcerated throat, gout, lumbago, tonsillitis, dyspepsia. But he kept on writing.

With illness his life became more circumscribed than ever. In 1895 he had left 109 Lancaster Gate and moved into his own rooms at No. 74, a short distance off. The move made little difference in his life; he frequently visited for long periods with Madame Van de Velde at her country-house near Headley in Hampshire and later at Camberley in Surrey. He was a constant correspondent with his friends. Christmas was his great joy, and he never failed to send gifts. He took up a pathetic little hobby of photography, and exchanged letters with similarly interested friends over adventures in developing and toning. People often noticed his fondness for the weaker creatures of the earth such as puppies, kittens, and children. He was one of those whom approaching old age makes mellow, not cynical. But he did not turn to religion; in fact after the children had grown up, even the conventional 'God bless you and keep you all' disappeared from his letters.

The last years of the century saw some decisive events in his family. Jessamy married in 1898, and the father could give only a mournful *dimitte*:

I can only congratulate her upon finding a husband who can take the place of her father and his precarious fortunes. It is hard to face this fact, which for the last six months I have been trying to avoid.

Early in the same year his wife had come to England, but she lived with Frank and his family. Harte visited them occasionally, but his appearances were likely to call forth violent outbursts of temper from Mrs. Harte. He made no complaints, and even to such an intimate friend as Pemberton had become, he never talked of his marital situation. Only once he seemed to speak dubiously under cover of an allegory. When walking, the two saw a donkey balk stubbornly and successfully; Harte burst out into a defense of the donkey's common-sense:

Now the horse is always described as a noble animal. Compare him with his humble friend the donkey, and he is an idiot. He has ten times his strength, and more than ten times the strength of a man, and yet he allows himself to be saddled and harnessed, bitted and spurred, ridden and driven, lashed and exhausted, until he becomes a mere bundle of trembling, sweating nerves....

If you come to think of it [he went on], my appreciation of the donkey race is not misplaced. Are they not like the enduring yet self-willed women of our creation, while we poor harassed men are like those imbecile neurotic horses? I wonder whether you and I are 'noble animals'? I wonder if the horse likes to think he's called that way? I wonder if the donkey plumes itself on the complete success of its alleged folly?

With most of the children taking care of themselves, his financial liabilities decreased somewhat. He sent his wife only one hundred and fifty dollars monthly instead of the previous two hundred and fifty dollars. But there were more extra expenses. His daughter Ethel was studying music in Paris, and her teacher's bills must be met. His own medical and dental charges mounted up until it seemed to him that his poor racked body was not worth the money. His income, too, decreased as his illnesses grew. In the last few years there were many titles, but most of the stories were short ones, and editors paid for space filled, not for quality. He seems to have kept out of debt, but he was again living almost from hand to mouth. He wrote to Frank in 1899:

As I cannot afford to take my own time in writing as I did formerly, I must work hard and continuously to meet my expenses week by week! Still, I do hope with some certainty to get a day off at the end of this week or the first of next....

I suppose all this is difficult to comprehend. But, alas! I no longer work with the readiness of youth — nor, I fear, even of middle age.

Again, he wrote: 'Everything lags with old age!' He was back at such petty expedients as dating checks a day ahead to give time for his own money to reach the bank.

Of all these troubles those who met him casually had no idea. He seemed entirely English even to his monocle and his accent. An occasional Britannicism, such as 'biscuit' for the American 'cracker,' even got into his writing. For all that, he remained wholly American in spirit, almost passionately patriotic. He was, for instance, absurdly gratified when a genealogist informed him that he could claim the (by no means rare) honor of being a 'Son of the Revolution.' When Cleveland's message suddenly threatened war between the two nations, Harte immediately declared his intention of returning to the United States in case of actual hostilities. In this he seems to have been acting on the principle, 'My country, right or wrong!' even though, as he noted sadly, 'much as I love my own country — it does not love *me* sufficiently to enable me to support myself there by my pen.'

But if he had ever revisited his country he might have

had a reception much pleasanter than he imagined. Although the press still attacked him at times, a friendlier spirit also was displaying itself. In California, more perhaps than in the East, his books began to receive better reviews. The reason was plain. In his absence a new generation had grown up to whom his faults as a man seemed petty in comparison with his achievements as the greatest of Californian writers. In 1897 the dramatic criticisms on *Sue* were as generous as those of *Sandy Bar* nineteen years before had been vindictive. The time was coming when schools, hotels, and streets would bear his name, and even a whole section of the State be known informally as the 'Bret Harte country.'

In the meantime people who saw him casually in London thought him merely a fine example of an elderly English dandy. One observer, sitting near him at a luncheon and ignorant of his identity, studied him with amusement to discover the secret of his perfect dandyism: 'Was it the glint of wax on the mustache, or the hair too artfully curled, or the extra height of the collar, or the five buttons on the sleeve, or the tricky cut of the coat, that no tailor would make on his own initiative?' There were his manicured finger-nails too, and the ring which set off his finger. Vanity, doubtless! Yet there was a touch of heroism, too. Harassed and tortured by disease, the old man still maintained his face to the world, still remained true to the ideal already set for himself when, a boy of fifteen in his first morning-coat, he had gone out in the pleasant consciousness of a perfect costume to pay his New Year's calls.

A more penetrating observer pierced beneath this exterior. Once a young American writer from the West,

Bret Harte

Hamlin Garland, came to London. He met Harte first at a tea, and was disappointed, almost disgusted. Later he called at Lancaster Gate. Alone with another American, Harte thawed; his speech became American, even Western. Suddenly Garland sensed the bitterness of exile beneath the fine English clothes. He suggested to Harte his return to America, but the idea only threw him into a deeper melancholy. When his caller finally left, Harte accompanied him to the door, even into the street. Garland walked away, but when he had gone some distance, turned and looked back; he saw Harte still standing on the steps — his white head bowed in thought.

CHAPTER XXXVIII

SORE THROAT

By the opening of the new century the end was at hand. His friends did not yet realize it, but perhaps Harte did. Otherwise, one can hardly explain the many curious evidences in his writings that his mind was casting back to the early days, as if he felt his circle almost rounded. He became reminiscent, and broke his habitual reticence in several sketches which, however elaborated the details, were essentially autobiographical. He returned to the work which had first won him fame by writing a second series of *Condensed Novels*. His story, *Liberty Jones's Discovery*, repeated the idea of a poem which he had written along with the *Luck of Roaring Camp* for the second number of the *Overland*. Even more strange — *A Vision of the Fountain*, appearing the year before his death, was only a reworking of his earliest published short story, *My Metamorphosis*, his first contribution to the *Golden Era* after his return to San Francisco. Another interesting echo was his sentence in *Three Vagabonds of Trinidad* written in 1900: 'It was only the ordinary request of an agricultural subscriber — one Johnson — that the Editor would 'notice' a giant radish grown by the subscriber.' That old 'raddish' of the *Northern Californian*!

Besides showing the completion of the circle, the second series of *Condensed Novels* is interesting as further evidence of how Harte had become out of touch. The first series had been remarkable in that a young man in a provincial city had been able to choose for

(321)

parody novelists who with few exceptions were the leaders of their time; in the second series nearly all the novelists were mere nobodies. This is not surprising in face of the fact, displayed in his letters, that for many years Harte had read only to escape from the tedium of his own daily writing, and so had seldom sat down with anything except the lightest current fiction. So in the second series appeared no Hardy, no Meredith, no James, no Stevenson, none of the great Russians or Frenchmen. Since Harte, however, had some acquaintance with the work of most of these, and since he had a real appreciation for at least Hardy and Stevenson, part of the blame for the omissions may rest upon the editors who wanted parodies of only the most popular writers. Even so, the contrast between the youthful and the elderly Harte is depressing. In the sixties he was leading his public; in the nineteen-hundreds he was following it. In other ways, the second series was a triumph. The humor was often brilliant. Although Harte wrote the parodies in sickness and even in actual bodily pain, no touch of bitterness or malice marred their good-spirited fun.

He was constantly becoming sicker. He complained more and more of a sore throat which was slow to heal. Neuralgia plagued him, but he stuck to his pen. On March 1, 1900, he wrote to his wife from Madame Van de Velde's at Camberley where he had gone to recruit: 'I have, thank Heaven! not yet been kept from my work — the neuralgia only affecting my lower limbs (like sciatica), and I have been writing ever since I left London.' Browning's grammarian has achieved immortality for working while 'dead from the waist down'; Harte worked while the same portion was aflame

d partial paralysis would have been a happiness. ... much, as another modern poet has pointed
out, does the heroism of men going quietly about their
... make pale the heroics of fiction.

... under the hand of pain, he wrote
some of his most delightfully funny stories. _The
Heathen Chinee_ alone excepted, a case can be made for
Colonel Starbottle for the Plaintiff as Harte's finest
humorous piece. Not far behind it are two or three
other stories of these last years. _A Ward of Colonel
Starbottle's_ showed also a remarkable return of his old
power of dramatic intensity and quick revelation of
character. In fact, explain it as one will, during these
last two tortured years he in some strange way did better work than he had at any time since leaving the
Overland.

He even maintained his old-time boyish eagerness
for experiment. When drama had failed him, he tried
his hand at operettas. In 1882 he had once sketched a
Californian light opera (God save the mark!) in collaboration with his friend Sir Arthur Sullivan, but the
plans had fallen through. Now just at the end he wrote
many lyrics for a musical production of _At the Mission
of San Carmel_. In 1901 — a year when pain was constantly gnawing harder at his throat — he wrote with
youthful hope lyrics and libretto for _The Lord of Fonte-
nelle_, based upon his story _The Strange Experience of
Alkali Dick_. At the same time, the Hungarian com-
poser, Emanuel Moór, prepared the musical score.
Harte worked eagerly; almost daily in the presence of
friends and his collaborator he read aloud what he had
written. Then he usually asked to hear what new
music had been composed since the day before; leaning

(323)

back in his chair, cigar between lips, an earnest look in his eyes, he listened with pleasure, smiling now and then as some happy strain caught his fancy. He desired greatly to hear the opera performed.

Through this year of 1901, although sometimes a paroxysm of illness incapacitated him, he remained steadily at work. Among his writings for these last months of weakness and agony were *Rupert the Resembler*, that gayest of condensed novels, and *The Convalescence of Jack Hamlin* and *Prosper's 'Old Mother,'* two of his best humorous stories. Late in the year he suffered an additional blow in the death of his elder son, Griswold. By November his efforts to keep on writing had become a daily physical struggle; in December, he collapsed. Still he managed to get off a few Christmas presents. 'I hope you won't mind the sentimentalism of the legend!' he wrote to Watt on sending an envelope-opener; 'I think our chance for being remembered in the future is the luck we have had in keeping the affections of our friends.'

After the beginning of the new year, he could write no more, although Watt still had contracts ahead. He was sixty-five, but he was a worn-out old man. The doctor, puzzled by the sluggish ulcerated sore throat, sent him off to Southsea to nurse himself into some sort of health; then, unimproved, he went to Madame Van de Velde at Camberley. He was still engaged on a play with Pemberton, and wrote some letters about it. In March the surgeons worked upon his throat; later he wrote to Pemberton: 'the operation and the instrument were so fascinating that they delighted even the victim!' By this time the doctors must have discovered that his sore throat was a cancer. He failed to improve, and

after his custom of thirty years, he blamed the weather.
As he wrote again to his collaborator:

I am still very poorly; everything is against me — even
this smileless, joyless, 'sere and yellow' spring! I get no
stimulus from it. I can scarcely write a letter. The grass-
hopper is indeed a burden!
Nevertheless — Yours always.

On April 17, saying he felt better, he began a story.
His recent *Ward of Colonel Starbottle's* had received high
praise, and well pleased he decided that his next story
should be *A Friend of Colonel Starbottle's*. He boldly
wrote *I* at the top of the page. He wrote in shaky,
hardly legible script, the title and first sentence, rejected the latter, and after some scratching began
again:

'I said a friend of mine,' returned the Colonel, a little
loftily, 'and when I used that term I did not degrade its
sacred and er — responsible significance, with that levity
which I find, Sir, much too frequently in the er—present
day.'
The Colonel's manner was slightly exaggerated as he had
detected a cavalier turn in the stranger's first acceptance of
the statement.

He wrote no more. For the last time with the artist's
love of perfection he had scratched out the first sentence
and begun anew. After this he took up his pen only for
a few letters.

His last reading was Hardy's *Woodlanders*. It was a
strange book to die by — with Giles Winterborne
coughing out his life in the rain. Nevertheless, he was
often heard to say as he rested a moment from reading:
'That is fine — very fine.'

He never took to his bed, but on May 5, while he sat

Bret Harte

at his writing-table, he suffered a sudden hemorrhage. Everything possible was done, but toward evening, in the presence of Madame Van de Velde and her household, the end came. In spirit and almost literally, like a Western hero, 'he died with his boots on.'

THE BIOGRAPHER EPILOGIZES

THEY laid his ashes in Frimley churchyard, close to Camberley where he had died. Only a small group stood by the grave — his wife, his son and daughter-in-law, his younger daughter, Boyd, Colonel Collins, Madame Van de Velde, a few others.

The biographer hardly feels an apology necessary for carrying the record on a little further. Although the breath be out, the memory of a man, his reputation, and his work live on, and suffer vicissitudes; these are a part of biography as much as the vicissitudes of the body.

First of all came the 'morgue' columns of the newspapers. These observed generally the principle of *nil nisi bonum*; in San Francisco, however, several people who were interviewed as Harte's former friends showed that they were indeed *former* friends. Here and there much nonsense was spoken. The biographer believes that the palm goes to a certain author who, having admitted never meeting Harte, went on to talk from hearsay; this interview revealed the essential information that Harte was vain of his small feet, and that when first in London he rented rooms with an old German lady who took care of him when sick so that he lived there many years and was always grateful. One hopes Madame Van de Velde never saw this. How her Latin blood would have boiled at finding herself made in one breath old, German, the keeper of a lodging-house, and the recipient of patronizing gratitude!

After the musketry of the newspapers, the dead man's reputation had to withstand the heavy artillery

Bret Harte

of the reviews. It came off fairly well. The London correspondent of the *New York Times* declared that Harte had not been a snob, but a modest and unassuming gentleman, and doubted if he had an enemy in London. That rising young critic, G. K. Chesterton, in an unusually penetrating epigram stated that Harte had been admirable because, while both an American and a humorist, he had not been an American humorist. The *London Literary World* commented on the number of literary men who had died in the past year, and declared Harte the most loved among them. The *Academy*, less sentimental, pronounced him worn out long before his death. In the *Athenæum*, an article signed by the eminent name of Watts-Dunton gave him high praise as both author and man. An interesting contribution to *Gentleman's* was signed M. S. Van de Velde; *inter alia* it pointed out:

Bret Harte did not create a perfectly noble, superior, commanding woman: was it because such a model never offered itself to him, or because other memories clouded his perception of womanly excellence?

An article in the *Bookman* was one of those which relegated Harte to the past; on his death it felt:

Men seemed to be renewing an old emotion, a forgotten delight, a faded loyalty. There was a rustle in the newspapers as of old love-letters and ancient flowers.

The death made some old strings reëcho in America. Howells, in an article otherwise somewhat ungenerous, remarked significantly:

If his temperament was not adapted to the harsh conditions of the elder American world, it might well be said that his temperament was not altogether in the wrong.

The Biographer Epilogizes

When the news came to Mark Twain, he burst out, inexplicably it seemed, upon a long dissertation of nearly two hours upon someone called Frank Harte; only afterwards did the listeners realize that at news of the death Mark's brain had leapt back forty years.

Harte next got into the newspapers on the publication of his will. The world was surprised to find his estate was valued at only £360 6s. 9d. He could scarcely have died poorer, if thirty-two years earlier he had accepted a professorship at the University of California. His frequently expressed fears for his wife were only too well realized, for she was left almost destitute, and misfortune continued to dog the family.

Nearly a hundred years have passed since Bret Harte was born, more than sixty since he made his reputation, and almost thirty, a generation of men, since he died. Even from this vantage-point of time the biographer does not feel capable of dogmatizing about either the man or his work. To pass judgment on a human being is the part of Divinity; on his writings the part of that self-appointed demi-god, the critic. The biographer realizes that he has sometimes passed judgment upon particular actions or writings and that even the selection of materials postulates a judgment, but this is, he maintains, a very different matter from proclaiming a man or his work as a whole 'Very good!' or 'Very bad!' or even presenting the quantitative analysis into the two elements.

To trace in any detail what other people have thought about Harte and his work since his death would be too much for an epilogue. In general, opinion seems to have come to better agreement about the work than about the man. Although of course some have con-

(329)

Bret Harte

demned his writings almost *in toto* and others gone to the other extreme in praise, the literary world in general seems ready to accept the opinion of one of his own contemporaries, himself a master of the short story. In 1897 Ambrose Bierce wrote of Harte that his early stories

place him very close to the head of American authors, living or dead. They all have what the Latin critics called '*curiosa felicitas.*'... In those days, before the ubiquitous author's-agent was a power in Grub Street, Bret Harte illuminated everything he touched. Now in shilling-shockers contracted for, years in advance at so many pounds a hundred words, he slaughters cowboys to make cockneys 'sit up,' or hashes up a short story to serve as jam between commercial sandwiches in sloppy popular magazines.

Nevertheless, his later work has not been without apologists; what is needed is that it should be culled by a careful anthologist.

Harte has come to be known as the author of some half-dozen short stories and two or three poems. This is a narrow footing in the house of Fame, but it seems a secure one. His work is read almost universally throughout the United States in secondary and collegiate courses in literature. On both sides of the Atlantic his stories are constantly reprinted in cheap editions of modern 'classics.' *The Heathen Chinee* remains a universally known poem; one finds it quoted in even the unlikeliest places. Moreover, one following Harte's traces frequently discovers evidences of a surprising vitality in his work. Henry Adams, that John the Baptist of the moderns, declares him almost the only American writer who was not afraid of handling sex; H. L. Mencken grants Harte at least 'a sort of im-

(330)

mortality' on account of Mr. Jack Hamlin and Colonel Starbottle. In 1914, *Reveille*, written for the Civil War, was still found fresh enough to call for its printing upon thousands of broadsides to aid the British recruiting campaign.

As to Harte's character there has been much difference of opinion since his death. The first biography, by his friend Pemberton, naturally presented him in a very favorable light. But a few years later Boynton in his brief sketch never let pass an opportunity to interpret Harte's personality harshly, and Merwin, although offering little evidence on the subject, devoted a few pages to a fairly thorough vilification of the character of the man whom as an author he so highly admired. The opinion was well established that Harte was a snob and a scamp, when in 1926 the publication of his letters, edited by his grandson, showed that there was another side to the marital difficulties. The present biographer naturally has opinions upon the ethics of the life which he has studied. Anyone who reads the book carefully will probably discover them.

As to what may be called the æsthetic qualities of the life — this is an artistic matter and the biographer feels less diffidence in expressing himself. He has found many people, Mark Twain among them, declaring by implication or express word that Harte's life was a tragedy. The biographer has decided that he differs from these people except in so far as all human lives, chained by circumstance and ending in death, may be called tragedies. Harte's life is not a tragedy in the older style; in that case he would have died amid a flood of poetry about 1878. In a modern tragedy, he would have slunk off the stage at about the same date, con-

Bret Harte

demned to pass the rest of his life in poverty, obscurity, and bitterness. On the contrary, from 1878 until his health finally broke, his life was a constant progression upwards in almost every respect; his early years represented a greater literary triumph, his later years a greater triumph of character.

His life in comparison with lives in general was not even a tragedy in the loose sense of the word — a series of mournful events. He achieved a fame equaled by few in his generation. He knew the supreme joy of composing some works of art which have often been judged as close to perfection as man is likely to attain. He had the satisfaction of realizing throughout many years that all over the world thousands of people knew and loved his name and awaited his stories with pleasure. In spite of friends lost, he was successful in establishing a large number of unbroken, warm human relationships — to mention a few, in addition to those within his own family, Starr King, Ina Coolbrith, Hay, Froude, Gibson, Pemberton, and, most of all, Madame Van de Velde. In comparison with drab lives which attain domestic peace and a competence, if this be a tragedy, let us have more of them.

The ramifications of Harte's fame would alone make an interesting study. I have actual record of editions in German, Swedish, Danish, French, Spanish, Portuguese, Italian, Rumanian, Serbian, Russian, Hungarian, and Greek, besides Ido, Pitman's shorthand, and raised type for the blind. Ἡ καλὴ τύχη τοῦ Ῥώριν-Καμπ may well arrest the attention of the classical scholar. A few years ago the new style of book advertisements loosed the flaring headline SHE HAD CALLED HIM BEAST! — a slogan for the *Idyl of Red*

The Biographer Epilogizes

Gulch. Besides his own work several other dramas have been based on his writings. The lords of Hollywood have also turned him to their uses. How Tennessee's gentle partner would have been amazed to find himself heralded under the title *Flaming Forties*! My notes record some ten titles of moving pictures; Blanche Sweet has played as Cressy and Mary Pickford as M'liss.

But while friends and enemies, biographers friendly and otherwise, readers kind and unkind, went their ways, the ashes rested close by the wall of Frimley Churchyard, in the quietest of Surrey countrysides, far different from the shaggy, great, Sierran gorges. Covering the grave was a slab of red granite cut into a cross at the top. On the east was chiseled the name Bret Harte, the dates, and a line from *Reveille*,

Death shall reap the braver harvest

and on the south:

In faithful remembrance, M. S. Van de Velde.

Yearly until Madame Van de Velde's death a wreath came to decorate the grave.

Few people visit it. Once someone sent a wreath of Californian pine. Again a Californian lady came, saw, grew irate at the simple sufficiency of the monument, and went off home declaring that something would be done about it. Nothing was. Then in 1917 something stirred in the air. Groups of young men came wandering into the churchyard looking for the grave, lads in greenish-yellow clothes, speaking in keen hard voices, American soldiers from the aviation camp over the hill, Californians among them, doubtless. How the ashes below must have stirred to the sound of the voices and

(333)

the good old American wise-cracking! Most of them, you can be sure, knew little enough about him; they had heard that a famous American lay strangely buried in the country churchyard, and come curiously visiting or a little homesick. They read the inscription written for the fratricidal war of their grandfathers, equally ominous for them; they passed on.

Men famous in their day lie in Frimley Churchyard — an Admiral of the Fleet, high army officers, colonial officials, county folk — yet sometimes, the verger says, people come strolling idly among the graves and speak uncertainly: 'You have — er — there is — er — *some- one* — famous buried here —'; then the verger replies, 'Bret Harte.'

SOURCES AND NOTES

CHIEF SOURCES

THE purpose of this list is primarily to save space in the printing of the notes by furnishing abbreviations for the works more frequently cited. It is not offered as a bibliography on Harte's life or of his writings, although, in connection with the *Notes and References*, it is for the former a fuller list than any which has been previously published. For a bibliography of Harte's writings the best is Kozlay's (v.i. KozB). The *Cambridge History of American Literature* is useful, but lists only the principal editions. I expect to publish shortly a bibliography of Harte's writings for the Californian periodicals up to 1871. For first editions see *A Brief and a Bibliography of F. Bret Harte, Book-Lover*, July–Aug., 1902, and Merle Johnson, *American First Editions*, New York, 1929, pp. 83–86; neither of these is wholly complete or accurate.

When referring to Harte's own writings, I have cited the most available, not the original publication. Most of his work will be found in RE., Sue., Koz., and How., but some must still be hunted in the original periodicals or books in which it first appeared. Koz. now forms Volume XX of RE., but I have distinguished the two for convenience because Koz. represents work which Harte himself never apparently thought worthy of his collected works.

The notes which I have collected while preparing this biography I have deposited in the University of California Library, where they will be available for anyone wishing to check the accuracy of my work or to continue the investigation of Harte's career.

A.	*Argonaut* (San Francisco).
AC.	San Francisco *Alta California*.
Ald.	Lilian (Mrs. T. B.) Aldrich, *Crowding Memories*, Boston and New York, 1920.
AM.	*Atlantic Monthly* (Boston).
Bro.	Noah Brooks, *Bret Harte in California, Century Magazine*, July, 1899.

Chief Sources

Byers.	S. H. M. Byers, *Bret Harte in Switzerland, Overland Monthly*, Oct., Nov., 1903.
C.	*Californian* (San Francisco).
Cap.	*Capitol* (Washington).
ConLetC.	Consular Letters, Crefeld, Vol. 1, State Dept., Washington (MS.).
ConLetG.	Consular Letters, Glasgow, Vols. 8–9, State Dept., Washington (MS.).
Cum.	E. S. Cummins (Mighels), *The Story of the Files*, San Francisco, 1893.
Dam.	H. J. W. Dam, *A Morning with Bret Harte, McClure's Magazine*, Dec., 1894.
Diary.	Harte's MS. diary (Oct. 19, 1857 to Mar. 5, 1858) in possession of Mrs. F. W. Taylor of Berkeley, Cal.
EM.	*Eclectic Magazine of Foreign Literature* (New York and Boston).
ES.	*Every Saturday* (Boston).
Fields.	*Bret Harte and Mark Twain in the Seventies. Passages from the Diaries of Mrs. James T. Fields. Atlantic Monthly*, Sept., 1922.
Fre.	Mrs. J. B. Frémont, *Souvenirs of my Time*, Boston, 1887.
FWT.	Conversation with Mrs. Floy Wyman Taylor, of Berkeley, Cal., Harte's niece.
GE.	*Golden Era* (San Francisco, San Diego).
Good.	Mrs. L. G. (Belcher) Goodenow, *The Brett Genealogy*, New York, 1915.
H.	*Harper's Monthly Magazine* (New York).
HAC.	*Centennial Year Book of Alameda County*, Oakland, 1876.
HistGC.	Historical Sketch of the Glasgow Consulate (MS.) in the Glasgow Consulate.
How.	*Sketches of the Sixties* (items from the *Californian* by Harte and Twain, ed. J. Howell) San Francisco, 1926. Revised edition with omissions and additions, 1927.
Howells.	W. D. Howells, *Editor's Easy Chair, Harper's*, Dec., 1903.
HowLL.	*Life in Letters of William Dean Howells* (Ed. Mildred Howells), Garden City, New York, 1928.
Hut.	*Talks in a Library with Laurence Hutton* (Ed. Isabel Moore), New York and London, 1911.
JT.	Conversation with Mrs. James Todd of Arcata, Cal., one of Harte's pupils.

Chief Sources

Kemb.	Francis Kemble, *Further Records*, New York, 1891.
Koz.	*Stories and Poems and other Uncollected Writings of Bret Harte* (Ed. C. M. Kozlay), Boston and New York, 1914. Included as Vol. 20, of the *Riverside Edition* (RE.).
KozB.	C. M. Kozlay, bibliography of the writings of Bret Harte (MS.), in the Huntington Library.
KozL.	*The Lectures of Bret Harte* (Ed. C. M. Kozlay), Brooklyn, 1909.
KP.	Albany *Knickerbocker Press*, July 25, 1920.
Lat.	L. A. Lathrop, *Recollections of a Consul, Saturday Evening Post* (Philadelphia), Apr. 11, 1925.
LDN.	London *Daily News*.
Let.	*The Letters of Bret Harte* (Ed. Geoffrey Bret Harte), Boston and New York, 1926.
LT.	London *Times*.
McC.	J. C. McCrackin, *A Letter from a Friend, Overland Monthly*, Sept., 1902.
Mer.	H. C. Merwin, *The Life of Bret Harte*, Boston and New York, 1911.
MisRecG.	Miscellaneous Record Book (MS.), Glasgow Consulate.
MSV.	M. S. van de Velde, *Bret Harte, Gentleman's Magazine* (London), Dec., 1903.
MTL.	Conversation with Mrs. Mary Tingley Laurence of San Francisco, Cal. (See Index under Mary Tingley).
Murd.	C. A. Murdock, *A Backward Glance at Eighty*, San Francisco, 1921.
NC.	Arcata *Northern Californian*.
NL.	*San Francisco News Letter and California Advertiser* (San Francisco).
NYH.	*New York Herald*.
NYS.	*New York Sun*.
NYT.	*New York Times*.
OM.	*Overland Monthly* (San Francisco).
OMLet.	*Overland Monthly, Letters Received*. (MS.) In University of California Library.
Paine.	A. B. Paine, *Mark Twain, a Biography*. New York and London, 1912.
Pemb.	T. E. Pemberton, *The Life of Bret Harte*, London, 1903.
RE.	*Riverside Edition* of the writings of Bret Harte, Boston and New York, 1902.

Chief Sources

RecCCon.   Records of the Crefeld Consulate, now in the Cologne
            Consulate.
Scrap-book. Harte's Scrap-book containing clippings of his writ-
            ings and of reviews of the books and magazines with
            which he was associated up to 1871, in possession of
            Mrs. F. W. Taylor of Berkeley, Cal.
SDR.   Springfield *Daily Republican.*
SFB.   San Francisco *Daily Evening Bulletin.*
SFC.   San Francisco *Call.*
SFCh.   San Francisco *Chronicle.*
SFE.   San Francisco *Examiner.*
Stod.   C. W. Stoddard, *Early Recollections of Bret Harte* (in
            Exits and Entrances, Boston, 1903).
Sue.   Bret Harte and T. E. Pemberton, *Sue: A Play in
            three Acts,* London, 1902.
SWR.   Springfield *Weekly Republican.*
Twain.   *Unpublished Chapters from the Autobiography of Mark
            Twain, Harper's,* March, 1922.
TwainL.   *Mark Twain's Letters* (Ed. A. B. Paine), New York
            and London, 1917.
ZABT.   Bret Harte, *Zum Andenken Bayard Taylors, Berliner
            Tageblatt,* Dec. 29, 1878.

NOTES AND REFERENCES

At the beginning of the section on each chapter, I list the general authorities, if any. I give additional reference (1) for direct quotations not located explicitly in the text, (2) upon doubtful or controversial points, (3) for material not contained in the general authorities. To avoid the annoyance always caused the reader by index-figures occurring in the text, I have located my notes by reference to page and keywords. This will, I believe, make for easier reading without adding materially to the labor of the few who may wish to use the book as a work of reference.

For background material, the careers of Harte's friends, etc. (i.e., anything not immediately a part of Harte's life), I give no references except in the case of direct quotations.

PART I

CHAPTER I

General authorities: Mer., Chap. I; Good., pp. 376, 378, 389, 403.

PAGE

3 August 25, 1836. The birth-year is often given as 1839 (see p. 303 and note.) That the earlier date is correct is shown (1) by the San Francisco *Great Register* of 1866, which shows that in 1866 Harte stated *under oath* that he was thirty years old, (2) by the Albany and Hudson directories (see KP.), which show that after 1836 the Harte family was not living in Albany. I have also much other evidence which confirms the date 1836 (see, e.g., my note, *The Year of Bret Harte's Birth, American Literature*, Apr., 1929). The year 1837 is also sometimes given, and appears on Harte's tombstone, but has no evidence to support it. See also How., facsimile of *Lines by an Ex-Schoolmaster*.

3 15 Columbia Street. See KP. This was Henry Hart's only address in the directory for 1835–36, and so was presumably both his school and his residence and Bret Harte's birthplace.

6 Bernard Hart. See also art. in *Jewish Encyclopedia*, and H. I. Davis, *Bret Harte and his Jewish Ancestor, Pub. Amer. Jewish Hist. Soc.*, 1931.

Notes and References

PAGE

7 'left behind...,' Mer., p. 4.

8 In 1817. I am indebted to a letter from D. R. Weeks, Asst. Sec'y, Graduate Council, Union College, for confirmation of Mer., and for some additional information.

9 Frequently visited. See Good., p. 403.

Chapter II

General authority: Mer., Chap. II.

10 Principal. KP.

11 First recorded memory. Harte, SWR., Oct. 6, 1866.

12 'Tubbs.' Koz., *Ran Away*.

12 Seaside village. Koz., *Ships*.

12 Another incident. Koz., *Ran Away*.

14 'my Puritan training.' RE., *Bohemian Days in San Francisco*.

14 'Always make it...' RE., *Colonel Starbottle for the Plaintiff*.

15 *Conversation*, etc., Koz., *The Angelus*.

15 'Did I dislike...' *Ibid*.

15 Yellow-Dutch-brick church. Harte, *Town and Table Talk*, GE., Aug. 12, 1860.

18 'All that...' E. J. Edwards, *New News of Yesterday*, *New York Mail*, Feb. 5, 1912.

Chapter III

General authority: Mer., Chap II.

20 'a dreamy...' Pemb., p. 2.

20 'a slight...' RE., *How Reuben Allen saw Life in San Francisco*. On autobiographic value of this story see p. 60.

21 On early reading see Koz., *Ships* and *Ran Away*; Pemb., p. 5; Dam.; Harte, GE., Oct. 21, Dec. 30, 1860 and Feb. 10, Mar. 17, Apr. 14, 1861; Fields.

21 'very much...' See Pemb., p. 330.

23 *Autumn Musings*. Information and quotations from Dam. I have been unable to find a file of the *Sunday Morning Atlas* for the period desired.

24 'It was...' Dam.

25 Pitted for life. See, e.g., Kemb., p. 122.

25 Attended lectures. See Harte, ZABT.

25 'a living...' *Ibid*. 'Ein leibhafter Robinson Crusoë, ein lebendig gewordener Sinbad.'

Notes and References

PAGE

25 'peerless creature...' RE., *Neighborhoods I have Moved from.*

25 January 1, 1852. Harte, *The Bohemian's New Year's Retrospect*, GE., Dec. 30, 1860.

CHAPTER IV

27 Songs quoted from *Put's Golden Songster*, San Francisco, 1858.

29 Henry. Mer., p. 15. He died *ca.* 1860 (*ibid.*). I have been unable to discover anything about his life in California.

29 Eliza. Mer., p. 13.

29 Andrew Williams. FWT.

29 February 20, 1854. On voyages see AC., Mar. 27, 1854. C. W. Stoddard, *In the Footsteps of the Padres*, supplies the description of the crossing of Nicaragua.

32 'Yellow and...' RE., *Crusade of the Excelsior.*

33 Sensitive-faced. See portrait at age of seventeen, Pemb., p. 32.

PART II
CHAPTER V

37 Cabin passengers. AC., Mar. 27, 1854.

38 Colonel Williams. HAC., pp. 499, 507, 508, 620.'

38 'Another incubus...' HAC., p. 565.

39 Mary Tingley, MTL.

39 Regular work. According to Mer., p. 18, he taught school.

39 Mr. Sanford. FWT.

39 'votes then...' HAC., p. 451.

42 Priest. Pemb., p. 58. No definite place is mentioned.

42 'Schwappelfurt...' RE., *Ruins of San Francisco.*

CHAPTER VI

43 Legendists and counter-legendists. I have discussed some of these accounts in *The Bret Harte Legend, Univ. of Cal. Chronicle*, July, 1928. Since gaining access to Harte's diary I have changed my ideas slightly on the expressman incident, but not otherwise. Other experiences attributed to Harte in this period are tax-collecting and stage-driving; these stories rest entirely upon unsupported statements of writers who cannot be accepted as original authorities. Some of the more interesting references in this connection are: Bailey Millard, *When they*

Notes and References

43 *were Twenty-One, Bookman*, May, 1913; H. C. Merwin, *Bret Harte*, AM., Aug., 1902 (Merwin tacitly omitted much of this in his later biography); Stod. (Stoddard did not meet Harte until 1863, and his account of Harte's earlier life lacks any special authority); C. L. Canfield, *In Bret Harte Land, Sunset*, May, 1907; H. J. Logan, Jr., A., Feb. 5, 1894; J. R. Colter, *Bret Harte as a Wells-Fargo Express Gun Guard*, OM., Dec., 1916; *Bret Harte as a Stage-Driver, New York Herald*, June 15, 1902. On the other hand, for highly skeptical articles on Harte's early experiences see G. P. West, SFC., May 24, 1924; R. L. Fulton, *Bret Harte and Truthful James*, OM., Aug., 1915.

A Morning with Bret Harte (Dam.) undoubtedly contains much truth, but has also too many inaccuracies to allow one to trust it implicitly. For instance: 'Went by way of Panama, and was at work in San Francisco for a few months in the spring of 1853, but felt no satisfaction until I reached the gold country, my particular choice being Sonora in Calaveras County.' This contains three demonstrable errors, viz., Harte went by Nicaragua, and arrived in 1854; Sonora is not, and never was, in Calaveras County.

43 First occupation. See, e.g., *The Author of 'That Heathen Chinee,'* EM., June, 1871.

44 Harte himself. E.g., Dam.

44 'near Sonora.' Dam.

45 La Grange. Mentioned in, e.g., RE., *Four Guardians of La Grange, In the Carquinez Woods*, and *Who was my Quiet Friend?* The last may have an autobiographic germ (see Kemb., p. 123). Mr. H. N. Pratt, former editor of the *Overland*, informs me that Miss Ethel Harte remembers her father telling of once arriving in Sonora afoot, hot, dusty, and exhausted. Mr. Pratt and Miss Harte searched the school records of Tuolumne County unsuccessfully for any record of Harte. In spite of great efforts, I have been unable to find the early records of Stanislaus County, in which La Grange is located.

47 'abandonment of...' RE., *How I went to the Mines*.

48 'Then we...' *Ibid*.

49 From Fiddletown. See RE., *An Episode of Fiddletown*.

50 Place-names. See, e.g., RE., *Jinny, Mrs. Skaggs's Husbands, Jeff Briggs's Love Story*.

51 'the log-built...' Harte, *Town and Table Talk*. GE., Aug. 12, 1860.

Notes and References

PAGE

51 Enterprising clothes-dealer. See RE., *Intro., Tales of the Argonauts*, p. xxii; Dam; Let., p. 352.

52 William Gillis. Stockton (Cal.) *Independent*, Apr. 13, 1924.

Since I wrote this chapter, Gillis's *Gold Rush Days with Mark Twain*, New York, 1930, has appeared. The account of Harte is on pp. 178–82, and is, I believe, considerably dressed up by a 'ghost-writer.' Still, the facts are the same on the whole. In conversation with me Gillis was not sure where Harte had come from; he mentioned Westpoint and Fourth Crossing, both vaguely.

CHAPTER VII

54 New house. FWT.

54 'A cozy...' Stod., p. 237.

54 Settled down. SFC., May 25, 1902.

54 Family tradition. FWT.

55 Sycamore Valley. Letter from Miss Ida S. Hall of Alamo. See also SFCh., Mar. 7, 1931. The name of Harte's employer is sometimes given as Bryant.

55 'A mere shanty...' Harte, letter to his sister Margaret in possession of Mrs. F. W. Taylor.

56 'wherein...' Murd., p. 72.

57 Out of work and in love. Diary, Dec. 31, 1857.

57 'Played the...' *Ibid.*

57 'It was...' Dam.

58 Other cases. See Chapter XXXVI.

CHAPTER VIII

General authorities: Murd., Diary.

64 'The thing...' Diary, Dec. 1, 1857.

65 'A Rose...' Quoted from C. A. Murdock, *Bret Harte in Humboldt*, OM., Sept., 1902.

66 'A matter...' Diary, Nov. 30, 1857.

66 'Mean to give up...' Diary, Nov. 23, 1857.

67 'Mrs. L....' Diary, Nov. 19, 1857.

67 'In the morning...' Diary, Oct. 22, 1857.

CHAPTER IX

General authorities: Murd., Diary.

71 Served in Indian campaigns. Byers quotes Harte as saying

Notes and References

71 that for a year he had helped protect California against the
Indians. See also Pemb., p. 37, and MSV. In his later years
Harte certainly allowed people to think of him as having been
a soldier either in Indian campaigns or in the Civil War or
both. He was sometimes addressed as Colonel (e.g., Let., p.
198) a title which he was said (Pemb., p. 66) to have won in
the Army of the Potomac! Neither the Adjutant-General of
the United States nor the Adjutant-General of California has
any record of Harte's having served.

71 Indians of his stories. E.g., in RE., *Princess Bob and her
Friends*, *Mermaid of Lighthouse Point*, *Drift from Redwood
Camp*, *Three Vagabonds of Trinidad*.

72 'He have...' Murd., p. 59.

72 'He was willing...' Murd., p. 73.

72 'He seemed...' Murd., p. 73.

72 Private school. JT.

73 Rougher part. Jacob Hartley, Sacramento *Bee*, Jan. 29, 1898.
See also C. A. Murdock, SFE., Feb. 24, 1889.

73 Comrades gathered. JT.

74 'That... must be...' Murd., p. 74.

74 'The Bailie...' Koz., *Bailie o' Perth*.

Chapter X

General authorities: Murd., NC.

76 Frank's work. C. A. Murdock, SFE., Feb. 24, 1889.

76 'We are...' NC., Apr. 27, 1859.

78 'The one half...' NC., Oct. 26, 1859.

79 *To Bary Add*. NC., Feb. 16, 1859.

79 *Why She Didn't Dance*. NC., Nov. 30, 1859.

80 'Large Raddish...' Quoted in NC., Dec. 14, 1859.

80 'If the...' NC., Dec. 14, 1859.

80 'On Sunday...' NC., Apr. 27, 1859.

81 'About twelve...' NC., May 25, 1859.

Chapter XI

General authority: NC.

83 Communication, SFB., June 1, 1860.

84 'Resolved...' *Humboldt Times*, Mar. 17, 1860.

85 'a short time...' SFB., Mar., 13, 1860.

88 Various traditions. E.g., ES., Jan. 14, 1871; Mer., p. 31.

Notes and References

PAGE

88 'He was...' Murd., p. 79.

90 *Humboldt Times* reprinted. Mar. 31, 1860.

PART III

CHAPTER XII

General authority: Harte's writings in GE.

93 F. Harte. SFB., Mar. 28, 1860, lists him as passenger on *Columbia*.

96 Restaurant. Probably the *Magnolia* under the superintendence of Edward A. Rigg. It had a reading-room attached, but seems to have been principally a saloon.

96 *Bohemian Days*. See RE. Reference to time 'three or four years' later when he was to be employed in Mint dates the reminiscence in 1860. Earlier memories, however, may have been mingled. Pemb. accepts as authentic, but dates 1856.

97 'the very pattern...' Stod., p. 243.

97 'P.D.D....' GE., Apr. 18, 1858.

98 'Not much...' Cum., p. 17.

98 'Learning to...' See R. L. Fulton, *Bret Harte and Truthful James*, OM., Aug., 1915.

98 'Nothing but...' John Mahoney quoted in Daggett Scrap-Book in California State Library.

98 'Wanted — a printer...' Koz., *Wanted — A Printer*.

98 'Occasionally...' Cum., p. 17.

99 Dollar a column. V.s. Mahoney, *loc. cit.*; Stod., p. 243.

99 Tradition of Harte's having set compositions directly in type may be found in various places, e.g., Brett Page (quoting Ina Coolbrith), *There were Giants in Those Days*, SFC., June 25, 1925.

100 *Lines by an Ex-Schoolmaster*. See facsimile in How.

100 148 Commercial Street. See *San Francisco Directory*, 1860.

100 Breakfast. SFC., May 25, 1902.

101 Whitman. *San Francisco, After Walt Whitman*. GE., July 22, 1860.

CHAPTER XIII

General authorities: Fre.; Harte's writings in GE.

102 A passage. I have never been able to locate in GE. anything of Harte's which fits this description. Her account may not be accurate in details.

Notes and References

PAGE

104 October 26. E. R. Kennedy, *Contest for California in 1861*, p. 158.

104 Elizabeth Frémont. See her *Recollections*, p. 119 f.

105 'One day...' Koz., *My Metamorphosis*.

106 On *M'liss*. See portrait in Dam., and note to p. 229.

108 'If I...' Fre., p. 205. Agua Mansa, *Bret Harte Recalled*, *Pasadena Star-News*, Jan. 24, 1931, gives the quotation in slightly different form.

CHAPTER XIV

General authority: Harte's writings in GE.

109 One of these flags. FWT.

110 Next to the last. See list in *San Francisco Directory*, 1861.

110 His work. There is a possibility that he may have had work in the field. *Notes by Flood and Field* and *The Reincarnation of Smith* (both RE.) contain vivid descriptions of the floods in the Sacramento Valley in 1861, and the former has also other suggestions of autobiography.

110 One hundred and fifty-five Spanish words. Carlos Vázquez-Arjona, *Spanish-American Influences on Bret Harte. Revue Hispaniqua*, 1929, pp. 573–621.

111 'F. B. Hart.' SFB., Aug. 13, 1861.

112 *Reveille*. Earliest appearance listed in KosB. is in *Poetical Pen Pictures of the War* (New York, 1863); in spite of careful search I have been able to find no earlier one. The tradition of the poem (see, e.g., Byers) is that stated in the text, and I see no reason to doubt it.

112 'Mr. Frank...' See C. W. Wendte, *Thomas Starr King*, p. 164.

113 Harte's family. FWT.

113 On her side. MTL.

113 Date of marriage. Pemb., p. 71.

113 524 Sutter. *San Francisco Directory*, 1862.

114 'Recited by...' GE., Nov. 9, 1862.

CHAPTER XV

General authority: Harte's writings in GE.

115 Harte's appointment. Limiting dates are May 2, 1863 (Swain's assumption of duties) and September, 1863 (the earliest pay-roll preserved at the Mint).

115 'He occupies...' *Inigoings*, C., Feb. 10, 1866.

Notes and References

PAGE

115 One hundred and eighty dollars. Pay-roll books in San Francisco Branch Mint.

116 Harte's illness. AC., July 6, 1863.

116 'Another patriotic...' SFB., July 5, 1863.

117 'The poem...' GE., July 5, 1863.

118 Another friend. McC.

118 Composite picture. There is no reason to doubt the autobiographic value of several of Harte's essays of this period, for the statements which can be checked from independent sources prove to be accurate. The essays utilized are: RE., *My Suburban Residence, Melons, Neighborhoods I have Moved from*; Koz., *Fixing up an Old House*; How., *Among the Books*; also Twain.

119 On Webb. See his humorous autobiography, *John Paul's Book*, Hartford and Chicago, 1874; the *Californian*; and C. W. Stoddard, *In Old Bohemia, Pacific Monthly*, March, 1908.

119 'For never...' *John Paul's Book* (by Webb), Hartford and Chicago, 1874, p. 22 f.

120 'Oh, Bret...' GE., Mar. 5, 1864.

123 'this splendid...' GE., Sept. 20, 1863.

123 'wound it...' Let., p. 23.

123 Farewell article. By Fitz-Hugh Ludlow, GE., Nov. 22, 1863.

CHAPTER XVI

General authority: Harte's writings in the *Californian*.

124 'Bret is...' GE., Nov. 8, 1863.

126 On Harte and Twain. See Paine, Vol. I, pp. 259–61; Twain; Dam. (The last is incorrect about publication of the *Jumping Frog*.)

127 'I quit...' TwainL., p. 100.

CHAPTER XVII

General authorities: *Outcroppings*; RE., *My First Book*; MTL., SFB., Jan. 6, 1866.

129 'A beautiful...' RE., *My First Book*.

130 On Roman. See OM., July, 1898, Sept., 1902; SFCh., June 22, 1903.

131 'Copies...' RE., *My First Book*.

133 'help thinking...' C., Dec. 9, 1865.

134 'Outcroppings is...' See SFB., Jan. 6, 1866.

Notes and References

PAGE

134 'I notice...' C., Dec. 16, 1865.

134 *Territorial Enterprise*, Dec. 17, 1865.

135 'purp-stuff.' See C., Dec. 23, 1865; NL., Dec. 16, 1865.

135 H.C.B. The poem in question is *The Omen*. It had appeared in C., June 25, 1864. Harte's name has been associated with it by the loose reading of a rather ambiguous passage on the editorial page of the same issue: 'an original story, (The Legend of Point Diablo [*sic*]) and an exquisite little poem written by a pen new to this coast, will be found on the first page.' The *Legend* was Harte's. The passage does not, however, ascribe the poem to him, but to 'a pen new to the coast'; Harte's pen could certainly not have been so described in 1864. H. C. B. also published *The Potomac* in C., Sept. 10, 1864.

135 'Rare good...' Unidentifiable newspaper clipping, Scrap-Book.

137 'I understand...' Let., p. 3.

CHAPTER XVIII

General authorities: RE., *My Suburban Residence*, Harte's writings in the *Californian*.

139 Too busy. See also TwainL., p. 102 (note by ed.), that in Jan., 1866, Harte left the *Californian* expecting to contribute to Eastern periodicals.

139 'By and by...' *Inigoings*, C., Feb. 10, 1866.

139 'Though I...' Paine, p. 280.

140 Two hundred and seventy dollars. Pay-roll book, San Francisco Branch Mint, Feb., 1869.

140 San Rafael. Letter from J. H. Wilkins of San Francisco, and OMLet.

140 *My Suburban Residence*. *San Francisco Directory* of 1866 gives Harte's address as 609 Folsom Street.

140 Playing funeral. SFC., May 25, 1902.

141 'The two...' *Inigoings*, C., Feb. 10, 1866.

141 'It is...' *Ibid*.

142 'It appears...' SWR., Sept. 1, 1866.

CHAPTER XIX

145 'On thin...' Richard Hooker, *The Story of an Independent Newspaper*, p. 125.

145 *Call*, Murd., p. 82.

145 *Alta California*. Bro.

Notes and References

PAGE

145 *Chronicle.* J. P. Young, *Journalism in California*, p. 66. I have located a few signed poems in the *Chronicle*, but they are all reprints.

146 Yosemite Valley. See RE., *On a Cone of the Big Trees.*

146 Sacramento. See SDR., July 18, 1866; Noah Brooks, NYT., May 24, 1902.

146 Virginia City. See RE., Intro. to *Tales of the Argonauts.*

146 *Californian. Podgerings*, July 28, 1866, *et seq.*

146 Sierras. Let., p. 151.

146 'The disused...' RE., *A Buckeye Hollow Inheritance.*

148 'Or so...' C., July 1, 1865.

148 *Territorial Enterprise.* See C., Nov. 23, 1867.

148 'Charming parodies...' AM, Jan., 1868.

148 'Its circus...' Letter, Harte to James R. Osgood and Company, May 30, 1870. (In *Concerning Condensed Novels*, Stanford University Press, 1929.) Note, however, that this letter dates from three years later, when Harte had established a reputation.

149 'An affectation...' C., Dec. 21, 1867.

149 *Daily Dramatic Chronicle.* Dec. 30, 1867.

151 'The less...' Boston *Christian Register, Sup.*, Oct. 13, 1866.

151 'Grand gold...' See C., Dec. 24, 1865.

151 Pooh-poohed. *Ibid.*

152 'Bill took...' How., Rev. ed.

153 *Life and Confessions*, etc. Published Napa, 1864.

153 *Sylvester Jayhawk*, Koz., *Popular Biographies.*

153 'We cannot...' C., June 29, 1867.

153 Sketches in the *News Letter*. The more interesting are *The California Homer*, Feb. 23; *St. Patrick's Day at Slumgullion Center*, March 23; *Our Foreign Correspondence*, June 22; *Our Traveling Correspondent*, July 13.

CHAPTER XX

General authorities: OM., July, 1868; Anton Roman, *Genesis of the Overland Monthly*, OM., Sept., 1902; Noah Brooks, *Early Days of the Overland Monthly*, OM., July, 1898; Anton Roman, *The Beginnings of the Overland*, OM., July, 1898.

159 'The prettiest...' TwainL., p. 183.

159 'As a bear...' TwainL., p. 183 f.

Notes and References

CHAPTER XXI

General authorities: Anton Roman, *The Beginnings of the Overland*, OM., July, 1898; Anton Roman (interview), AC., Aug. 4, 1879; Noah Brooks, *Early Days of the Overland Monthly*, OM., July, 1898; RE., Intro. to *Poetical Works*.

162 Yankee Jim's. See John Steele, *In Camp and Cabin*, Lodi (Wis.), 1901, p. 65 f.

163 At Santa Cruz. See Let., p. 152 f.

163 Proof-reader. Accounts of this incident vary in details; I have relied principally on Roman. The proof-reader has frequently been identified as Mrs. Sarah B. Cooper (see, e.g., McC., and portrait, OM., Sept., 1902, p. 206); according to her own statement, however (see Cum., p. 164), she did not arrive in California until 1869.

166 'The secular...' R.E., Intro. to *Poetical Works*.

166 'A capital...' Undated clipping in Scrap-book.

166 *Daily Dramatic Chronicle*. Aug., 4, 31, 1868.

167 'Newspapers and...' RE., Intro. to *Poetical Works*.

167 'A letter...' *Ibid*.

CHAPTER XXII

General authority: Harte's writings in OM.

169 Several have recorded. E.g., Stod., p. 248; McC.

169 'They were...' See H. N. Pratt, *The Man Bret Harte*, Step-Ladder, Apr., 1924; also C. W. Stoddard, *In Old Bohemia*, *Pacific Monthly*, March, 1908.

169 'Tell Ina...' SFC., June 25, 1924.

169 'There was...' C., Nov. 5, 1864; see also SFC., June 25, 1925, and NL., June 18, 1870.

170 Celebration. V.s., Pratt, *loc. cit.*

170 On Mrs. Harte. Cum., p. 126; McC.

171 'Bret Harte...' Twain.

171 For defenses of Harte's personality. See McC., Pratt, v.s., *loc. cit.*

171 Harte's snobbery and looseness in money matters. Conversations with the late William Gillis of Jackass Hill, and with C. W. Wells of Berkeley; Letter from P. B. Bekeart of San Francisco; SFC., May 25, 1902; W. A. Kendall, *Frank Bret Harte*, SFCh., Dec. 15, 1872. See also Chapter XXVIII. One story of this sort might be dismissed as gossip; so many cannot be.

Notes and References

PAGE

172 Pacing the floor. Stod., p. 248 f.

172 'It's no...' Bro.

172 Asked Brooks. Bro.

172 Letter from Fields, etc. See Let., p. 6.

173 Laurence Hutton, Hut., p. 407 ff.

173 Taliesin Evans, NYT, May 17, 1902.

173 Tom Hood. See Intro. to *Luck of Roaring Camp*, London, 1870.

173 Dickens. Pemb., p. 163 ff.; John Forster, *Life of Dickens*, p. 153.

173 'Rarely have...' Forster, v.s., *loc. cit.*

173 August 15, 1869. Pay-roll book, San Francisco Branch Mint.

174 Conditions. Let., p. 7 f.

174 Regular compensation. This amounted to fifteen dollars for each poem and between twenty and twenty-five dollars for each story. Soon, however, Harte received special prices. Beginning with March, 1870, he received one hundred dollars for a story and twenty-five for a poem. For his last two poems he received fifty dollars each. (See *Overland Monthly*, *Account of Moneys Paid Contributors*, MS., in University of California Library.)

174 *News Letter.* June 12, 1869.

174 By September. Letter, Harte to Fields, Osgood and Company, Sept. 8, 1869, in possession of W. S. Morse.

174 Thirty thousand dollars. Cum., p. 145.

175 'I will...' J. C. McCrackin.

175 Miller and Whitman. See Let., p. 8 f.; Horace Traubel, *With Walt Whitman in Camden*, I, p. 28.

176 *News Letter.* SFCh., Feb. 2, 1871. The story seems genuine; Bierce (SFE., Mar. 3, 1889) mentions the *Heathen Chinee* as the poem concerned. I accept, however, the contemporary account. There is too obviously a motive for the story-teller to transfer the incident from the less-known to the better-known poem.

CHAPTER XXIII

177 *News Letter.* Sept. 26, 1868.

177 Harte's satires on the Academy. See NL., Apr. 20, 27, May 4, 1867.

178 Truthful James. See *Phœnixiana*, p. 182, and Wm. Gillis, Stockton (Cal.) *Independent*, Apr. 13, 1924. Gillis denies, with

Notes and References

PAGE

178 reason I believe, the current story that his brother James was the original.

178 Minor satires. *Pleasant Games for California Children*, C., Sept. 9, 1865.

179 Manuscript. In Univ. of Cal. Library.

179 Song versions, etc. See KosB.

180 *Every Saturday*, Jan. 14, 1871.

181 'Perhaps you...' Mrs. M. E. W. Sherwood, NYT., May 10, 1902.

181 'The worst...' S. R. Elliott, *Glimpses of Bret Harte*, *The Reader*, July, 1907.

Chapter XXIV

183 University of California. Minutes of Univ. of Cal. Regents; AC., Aug. 17, 1870.

184 Carmany. Cum., p. 145.

184 October. Minutes of Univ. of Cal. Regents.

184 January 10. See SFC., same date.

185 'Presently while...' Bro.

186 'None save...' SFCh., Feb. 2, 1871.

186 'During a...' AC., Feb. 2, 1871.

PART IV
Chapter XXV

General authorities: Howells; Ald.

189 On the Chicago incidents. See Mer., p. 221; Noah Brooks, NYT., May 24, 1902 (for Harte's version); McC. This last quotes a letter from Harte.

191 Stopped a few days. Mer., p. 222. Harte left Chicago, Feb. 11, arrived New York, Feb. 20; arrived Boston, Feb. 25.

193 'Why,' cried Harte... Howells.

193 'Never was...' *Ibid.* Howells's judgments on Harte's character seem to me to indicate that he completely failed to understand his guest.

194 With Ralph Keeler. Howells, *My Mark Twain*, p. 6 f.

194 'Why, fellows...' *Ibid.*

195 'At ease...' Fields.

195 Holmes. Noah Brooks, NYT., May 24, 1902.

195 Whittier. Letter, Harte to Whittier, Feb. 26, 1871, in Huntington Library.

Notes and References

PAGE

196 Longfellow. Koz., *Longfellow.*

197 'Till now...' HowLL., p. 159.

197 'I accept...' Let., p. 12.

198 'that progress...' W. D. Howells, *Literary Friends*, p. 114 f.

198 'This young...' ES., Mar., 11, 1871.

CHAPTER XXVI

199 Bowles's luncheon. G. S. Merriam, *Life and Times of Samuel Bowles*, II, p. 170.

200 'Bret Harte...' *Ibid.*

200 'He and I...' Noah Brooks, NYT., May 24, 1902.

200 'Too much...' A. Roman, *Genesis of the Overland Monthly*, OM., Sept., 1902.

200 'I think...' A. Roman, quoted in clipping in Daggett Scrap-Book in California State Library.

200 First affair. *Letter from Boston*, Cap., July 9, 1871.

201 Phi Betta Kappa poem. *Ibid.* See also Ald., p. 142; Howells.

201 'Plainly indifferent...' Cap., v.s., *loc. cit.*

202 'His personal...' *Ibid.*

202 'a Mrs. Cabot...' Let., p. 15.

202 Emerson. Howells.

204 In demand. See, e.g., letter to Whitelaw Reid, May 9, 1871, in Library of Congress.

204 Harte chafed. See, e.g., p. 220.

204 Mrs. Harte. The conclusion is obvious from the course which events took. For the family tradition confirming this I have a letter from Harte's grandson, Geoffrey Bret Harte (Sept. 6, 1930). This letter also states strongly Harte's own lack of the Bohemian quality.

204 'In the...' Let., p. 71. This letter should be dated as of 1872, not 1877–78. The poem accompanying it was probably *Half-an-Hour before Supper* which appeared in AM., Sept., 1872; Harte had no connection with AM., as late as 1877.

205 They met. Mrs. M. E. W. Sherwood, NYT., May 10, 1902.

205 Conversationalist. Hut., p. 409. Comparatively little of Harte's conversation has been preserved, but we have much testimony as to its brilliancy. See, e.g., pp. 269, 285.

205 'Cultivated foppishness...' C. Barrus, *Whitman and Burroughs, Comrades*, p. 64.

205 *Condensed Novels.* Compare reviews in AM., Jan., 1868, and Aug., 1871.

Notes and References

PAGE

206 'Ho, Starbuck...' RE., *A Greyport Legend.*
206 Howells. Howells.
207 Harte's answer. Let., p. 13.

Chapter XXVII

General authorities: Let., pp. 17–49; KozB.

209 His books. He told Howells that in its first six months the *Luck* sold only 3500 copies (see Howells).
210 Lecture. See KozL. The text has been reconstructed from newspaper excerpts, and is probably not complete.
210 Officer of the law. Howells; Ald., p. 137.
210 'Well, Harte...' Howells.
212 On night at Aldrich's. Ald., p. 136.
212 Letter from Fields. Pemb., p. 134 f.
212 *Times.* Dec. 17, 1872, p. 5.
213 Later advertisement. *Brighton (Eng.) Gazette*, Apr. 5, 1879.
213 One hundred and twenty-five dollars. Let. p. 36. This letter is incorrectly dated 1874 instead of 1873. Cf. allusions in letters on pp. 25–31.
214 'Unless something...' Let., p. 49.
214 Teats and Throckmorton. See State Dept. (Washington), Miscellaneous Letters, May, Part II, 1884.
214 Met him. See e.g., A. D. Robinson, *Footprints on Piety Hill, Bookman*, June, 1920.
215 'I cannot...' Let., p. 40.
215 'You wonder...' Let., p. 40 f.
215 'You can...' Let., p. 27.
216 'The people...' Let., p. 32.
216 'Is this...' A., Oct. 11, 1884. The story may be apocryphal, but is none the less illustrative. See also Fields.
216 'I have...' Let., p. 31.
217 The audience. Clipping from Kansas City *Journal of Commerce* (n.d.), in possession of Mrs. F. W. Taylor.
218 Actual handicaps. See H. P. Goddard, NYT., Book Review, June 7, 1902.
218 'I think...' Dam.
218 *American Humor.* KosL. Delivered in Chicago, Dec. 10, 1874; New York, Jan. 26, 1875.
219 Redpath. Let., p. 132.

Notes and References

Chapter XXVIII

PAGE

220 'Oh, Nan...' Let., p. 35 f.

220 Morristown. See J. K. Colles, *Authors and Writers Associated with Morristown*, p. 118.

220 'Bigoted, self-righteous...' Let., p. 181.

220 Friends. See Let., Index. In a letter of Sept. 27, 1875 (in Huntington Library), Harte mentions a breakfast with Houghton.

221 Moderate drinker. With the exception of the youthful confession on p. 69, all the references which I can give point to his having been a moderate drinker, although some of these allude to accusations charging the contrary. See Let., p. 59 f.; 176 f.; NYS., Nov. 8, 1888; Sacramento *Bee*, Jan. 29, 1898.

221 'Loose and...' W. A. Kendall, *Frank Bret Harte*, SFCh., Dec. 15, 1872. In spite of these attacks upon Harte, Carmany offered him the editorship of the *Overland* in 1875. (See OMLet., Harte to Carmany, Sept. 13, 1875.)

221 'I was...' W. R. Thayer, *Life and Letters of John Hay*, II, 402.

221 'On the authority of the butcher.' See, e.g., Noah Brooks, NYT., May 24, 1902.

222 'Damn his...' *Ibid.*

222 'You hear...' *Ibid.*

223 One thousand dollars. KosB.

223 Six hundred dollars. Excerpt from letter to wife in *Am. Art Assn. Catalogue*, MS. Room, New York Public Library.

224 'I want...' Letter of May 1, 1874, in possession of W. S. Morse.

224 July 17. See Koz., *What Bret Harte Saw*.

224 'Critics.' E.g., *Temple Bar*, Sept., 1873.

224 On the reception of Harte's work in Germany see Lewis Rosenthal, *Critic*, Feb. 21, 1885.

224 Translations. *Californische Novellen* (tr. W. Hertzberg), Leipzig, 1873; *Californische Erzählungen* (tr. W. Lange), Leipzig, 1874–80; *Die Argonauten-Geschichten*, Leipzig, 1873; *Scènes de la Vie Californienne* (tr. Pichot and others), Paris, 1873; *Récits Californiens* (tr. Th. Bentzon), Paris, 1873; *Kalifornii Besjelyei Angoból forditotta Benenyesi*, Budapest, 1875.

225 'Bret Harte...' Scribner's, Oct., 1875, p. 793.

226 June, 1874. Letter to Bliss, July 21, 1874, in possession of W. S. Morse.

226 'I have...' *Ibid.*

Notes and References

PAGE

226 Thousand words. Letter, Mar. 7, 1875, in Huntington Library; see also Let., 49 f.

227 Arrangements. On this and business matters in general see Let., pp. 49–53, and TwainL., p. 258 f. Twain gives price as $6500.

227 'The shorter...' Let., p. 50.

227 Highest price. Hut., p. 408.

227 Translations. By M. A. Goldschmidt, Stockholm, 1876; by O. Randolf, Leipzig, 1876; by U. Brachvogel, Stuttgart, 1876.

227 Fourteen versions. Rosenthal, v.s., *loc. cit.*

228 Favorite. Pemb., p. 268.

CHAPTER XXIX

229 *M'liss.* Printed versions exist by K. M. Widmer (San Francisco, 1878) and by L. P. Richardson (New York, 1878). For another version by C. M. Greene see AC., Aug. 7, 1877.

229 'Actor — whose...' Let., p. 51.

229 Financial difficulties. Let., p. 247.

230 Barrett. Pemb., p. 124.

230 On production of *Sandy Bar.* See Let., p. 432; NYT., Aug. 29, Sept. 29, 1876; Pemb., pp. 257–61.

231 'I've been...' Letter to Mrs. Gibson, Sept. 22, 1876, in New York Public Library.

231 'We are...' Pemb., p. 259.

232 'overweighted with...' AC., Sept. 29, 1878.

232 'Bret Harte...' TwainL., p. 287.

233 On the collaboration. See Paine, pp. 587–90; TwainL., p. 292. In fairness one must note that Harte's version of the disagreement and its causes is not preserved.

233 *Thankful Blossom.* Paine, v.s., *loc. cit.*, MS. in Huntington Library; letter to Osgood, Dec. 5, 1876, in Huntington Library.

234 *Ah Sin* in Washington. Washington *Evening Star*, May 8, 1877; Let., p. 432.

235 'The pleasure...' Washington *Evening Star*, May 8, 1877.

235 'I am not...' TwainL., p. 293.

235 Abandoned the play. Perhaps not entirely. A play-bill in the Columbia University Dramatic Museum announces that Harte will speak at one of the performances.

235 *Ah Sin* in New York. See New York papers, Aug. 1, Sept. 1, 1877. The *World*, Aug. 1, has a good synopsis.

Notes and References

PAGE

237 'trimmed and...' TwainL., p. 182.

237 Helped Harte. TwainL., p. 293.

237 Later mentions. Twain, *Autobiography*, I, p. 247; Twain, p. 459; Let., pp. 247, 249; speech at Royal Academy Dinner (see KosL.); Dam.

CHAPTER XXX

General authority: Let., pp. 54-70.

238 *North American Review.* E. S. Nadal, *Bret Harte*, Jan., 1877.

239 *On a Naughty Little Boy Sleeping.* C., Sept. 17, 1864; H., July, 1877.

239 'I think...' This and all the other quotations pp. 239-42 are ·from Let., pp. 54-62.

243 *A Sleeping-Car Experience.* This MS. and the others mentioned are in the Huntington Library.

243 '*That awful...*' Let., p. 115.

243 'I could...' Let., p. 308.

244 'Mr. Harte...' Let., p. 66.

245 Financial trust. See also Howells's very interesting reply to Pres. Hayes regarding Harte's fitness for a consulate (HowLL., I, p. 251).

245 May 11, 1878. ConLetC, no. 1.

PART V
CHAPTER XXXI

General authorities: Let., pp. 75-130; ConLetC.

249 Hoboken. NYT., June 28, 1878.

250 'A sluggish...' This and the three quotations following are from Let., p. 79.

252 *Figaro.* See an undated letter to Mrs. Harte quoted in catalogue of Amer. Art Assn., Nov. 24, 1925, no. 273, in MS. Room of New York Public Library.

253 Letters to the Consul-General. RecCCon.

253 Terrible loneliness. Pemb., p. 167.

254 'My dear...' Undated letter in possession of Frau Clara Heine (née Jentges), of Crefeld, through courtesy of Dr. Rembert. I date this 1878 instead of 1879 because for the latter year Harte planned to spend Christmas in England, and probably did so (Let., pp. 161, 163).

Notes and References

PAGE

255 Bayard Taylor. ZABT.
255 'Agony and misery.' Let., p. 111.

CHAPTER XXXII

General authorities: Let., pp. 131–78; ConLetC.
256 January 28. LDN., Jan. 29, 1879.
256 'The celebrated...' Advertisement, LDN., Jan. 27, 1879.
257 *News.* LDN., Jan. 30, 1879.
258 Birmingham. Birmingham *Daily Gazette*, Apr. 8, 1879.
258 Brighton. *Brighton Gazette*, Apr. 4, 1879; Let., p. 136.
258 'A very...' Let., p. 136.
259 Toast to Literature. Pemb., p. 204 ff.
261 'As full...' RecCCon., no. 3, letter dated Sept. 16, 1879.
261 'The table...' ConLetC., Harte no. 30.
261 'A prolific...' ConLetC., Harte no. 33.
262 'A reserve...' RE., *Unser Karl.*
262 'A race...' Let., p. 152.
263 'Frank, outspoken...' Let., p. 120.
263 First essay. A searcher whom I employed in Berlin could not find this. It was apparently the sketch known in English as *Views from a German Spion.*
263 'I grind...' Let., p. 154.
263 'I will...' Let., p. 106.
266 May 1, 1880. LT., LDN., May 3, 1880.
266 'In coupling...' LT., May 3, 1880.
267 'I presume...' *Ibid.*

CHAPTER XXXIII

General authorities. Let., pp. 178–206, ConLetG., HistGC., Lat., Misc. Record Book of the Glasgow Consulate.
268 'As to...' Let., p. 178.
268 June 18. ConLetC., Potter no 1.
268 *Kölnische Zeitung.* Mar. 31, 1880.
268 One observer. See *Personal Sketches, London Literary World*, Jan. 16, 1903.
269 William Black. W. Reid, *William Black*, pp. 243–45, 257, 282.
269 'If we...' *Ibid.*, p. 244.
269 'He is...' *Ibid.*, p. 245.
269 July 24. Let., p. 185; July 20 according to HistGC.
269 'One ray...' Let., p. 185.

Notes and References

PAGE

270 'I do...' Quoted, Let., p. 194.

270 Harte's letter. Let., p. 181 ff. Also Let., p. 185: 'Of course, this is only in case you do not think it best to come to Glasgow this year.'

270 'I have...' Let., p. 190.

271 Collection of letters. In possession of Mr. John McFadzean, the late Mr. Gibson's surviving law partner.

271 Harte's hand in the reports. A good example is a long letter of Sept. 15, 1883, criticizing kindly but keenly a report which Gibson had prepared on the credit system of Glasgow. This letter is in the possession of John McFadzean.

273 'Unseaworthiness...' ConLetG., Harte no. 9.

273 'The captain...' *Ibid.*

274 'I supplied...' ConLetG., Harte no. 24.

274 'Tell Mr...' Let., p. 191.

274 'Oh, I say...' Let., p. 189.

275 'My transfer...' Let., p. 188.

Chapter XXXIV

General authorities: Let., pp. 206–284, ConLetG.

276 J. L. Toole. Pemb., p. 276 f.

277 'The Webbs...' Let., p. 216.

278 'Intensely *un-English*.' Let., p. 215.

278 By 1880. See Pemb., p. 213–15.

279 'They have...' Let., p. 215.

279 'Happily renewed...' Pemb., p. 237.

280 'Amanuensis, translator...' See Pemb., p. 240.

280 *Found at Blazing Star.* MS. in the Huntington Library.

280 'A pretty...' Let., p. 201.

282 'Think of...' Let., p. 267.

282 'Do not...' Let., p. 211.

284 Consul of St. Kentigern. See RE., *Rose of Glenbogie, Young Robin Gray, Desborough Connections, Heir of the M'Hulishes.*

284 'The righteous...' RE., *Heir of the M'Hulishes.*

284 'I've unpacked...' *Personal Sketches, London Literary World,* Jan. 16, 1903.

285 'Why...' Donald Macleod, *Reminiscences of the late Mr. Bret Harte, Good Words,* Vol. 43, pp. 532 f.

285 'There is...' *Ibid.* See also RE., *Heir of the M'Hulishes.*

285 On lecture. Macleod, v.s., *loc. cit.*

Notes and References

PAGE

286 'And I...' For circumstances of the writing of the poem and for a complete text, see Lat. By courtesy of H. N. Leupp I have a photostat of a clipping from New York (?) *Times*, Aug. 22, 1894, which gives a slightly different text quoted apparently from memory. Because of errors in rhyme and meter neither versions seems exactly authentic, and in quoting I have to some extent combined the two.

286 'I suppose...' Letter, Harte to Gibson, Sept. 21, 1883, in possession of John McFadzean.

287 'What station...' Lat.

287 On correspondence with Department about absences. See Departmental Dispatch no. 35 to Harte, dated Nov. 15, 1882; ConLetG., Harte, no. 66; press copy of a telegram, Gibson to Harte, no. 108, in letter file of Glasgow Consulate.

287 'I'm rather...' Let., p. 205.

288 On Harte's removal. Mr. John McFadzean kindly informs me that in a letter to Gibson, Oct. 6, 1886, Harte 'expresses his belief that he was simply removed to make room for someone else.' See also Let., p. 284.

288 August 20. ConLetG., Underwood no. 1.

Chapter XXXV

General authority. Let., pp. 283–364.

289 On returning to America. Let., p. 182.

289 'I cannot...' Let., p. 236 f.

292 Liking for the motto. Pemb., p. 301.

294 *Knight-Errant, Young Robin Gray.* MSS. in the Huntington Library.

296 'The gentle muse...' Let., p. 299.

297 'I should...' Pemb., p. 264.

297 For Toole. Pemb., p. 275.

297 'Bread and butter.' Let., pp. 329, 350.

297 'You cannot...' Let., p. 354.

297 'Sick or...' Let., p. 349.

297 'A little...' Let., p. 315.

Chapter XXXVI

General authority: Let. pp. 365–415.

300 'It looks...' Let., p. 375 f.

301 109 Lancaster Gate. The Post Office London Directory (years 1894 and 1895) gives this as Mme. Van de Velde's address.

Notes and References

PAGE

301 Boucicault. Pemb., p. 261.

301 Yacht Club. Pemb., p. 334 f.

302 'They are...' Let., p. 404.

302 Interviews. See Dam., and G. B. Burgin, *Two Interviews, Idler*, Apr., 1892.

303 Colonel, Indians. See Pemb., p. 66; MSV., Let., p. 198.

303 Trigger. *Personal Sketches, London Literary World*, Jan. 16, 1903.

303 Rope about neck. John Hare, *Reminiscences and Reflections, Strand*, Aug., 1908.

303 Extant documents. See p. 3, note.

303 'An old...' Pemb., p. 282; see also SFCh., Aug. 31, 1919, and HowLL, I. p. 159.

304 Charles V. RE., *Secret of Sobriente's Well.*

304 Murrieta. RE., *Snow-Bound at Eagle's.*

304 Carquinez. RE., *In the Carquinez Woods.*

304 Bolinas. RE., *Judgment of Bolinas Plain.*

304 San Francisco Peninsula. RE., *Man at the Semaphore.*

304 'Crimson.' RE., *Susy*, Chapter XII. See also Chapter XI, and review of *On the Frontier*, OM., Oct., 1884.

304 'Which I wish...' C. S. Greene, OM., July, 1898.

305 'California was...' Let., p. 351.

307 Subtleties. Those interested in attempting, from the necessarily inadequate data supplied by biographical research, a 'psycho-analysis' of Harte will note in his letters and biographies the mention of an unusual number of friendships with women, especially older women. Except for letters to his son and to business associates the published letters of his last years are almost exclusively addressed to women. He also, however, maintained throughout his life a considerable number of friend-ships with men.

308 Music-halls. T. Watts-Dunton, *Bret Harte, Athenæum*, May 24, 1902.

308 At his desk. Pemb., pp. 296–98.

308 'Do you...' *Ibid.*

308 'I don't...' *Ibid.*

309 'Just like...' Let., p. 411.

310 'The dear...' Let., p. 412.

310 'East and...' Let., p. 10.

310 *My Favorite Novelist*, etc., Koz.

311 'How I...' Herbert Paul, *Life of Froude*, p. 195.

Notes and References

CHAPTER XXXVII

General authorities: Let., pp. 416–68; Pemb., pp. 269–75; Sue; a letter from **Mr. Geoffrey Bret Harte** (Sept. 6, 1930).

313 'Well received...' Pemb., p. 270.

314 Stories in dramatic form. See, e.g., RE., *Youngest Miss Piper*, *Lanty Foster's Mistake*.

315 *Three Vagabonds*, etc. **MS.** in Huntington Library.

315 Harte's stories of Europe. See, e.g., for England, *Ghosts of Stukeley Castle*, *Desborough Connections*, *Ancestors of Peter Atherley*, *Romance of the Line*; for Scotland, *Young Robin Gray*, *Rose of Gllenbogie*; for Germany, *Indiscretion of Elsbeth*, *Unser Karl*; for France, *Strange Experience of Alkali Dick*, *Two Americans*; for Switzerland, *The Man and the Mountain*.

315 'A promising...' W. C. Morrow, *An Estimate of Bret Harte*, *Sunset*, Aug., 1902.

316 'I can...' Let., p. 456.

317 'Now the...' Pemb., p. 335 f.

318 'As I...' Let., p. 461.

318 'Everything lags...' Let., p. 464.

318 'Biscuit.' RE., *Night on the Divide*.

318 'Much as...' Let., p. 419.

319 On *Sue*. See A., Oct. 11, 1897.

319 'Was it...' *A Bookman's Memories*, *Christian Science Monitor*, Sept. 30, 1919.

320 On Garland's visit. Hamlin Garland, *Roadside Meetings of a Literary Nomad*, *Bookman*, July, 1930.

CHAPTER XXXVIII

General authorities: Let., pp. 469–503; Pemb., pp. 338–45.

321 Autobiographica. RE., *How I went to the Mines* (1899), *Bohemian Days in San Francisco* (1900), *How Reuben Allen 'Saw Life' in San Francisco* (1900).

322 Hardy. See p. 325; on reading see also MSV.

322 Stevenson. See J. A. Steuart, *Robert Louis Stevenson*, Vol. II, p. 253.

322 'I have...' Let., p. 469.

323 On operettas. Pemb., p. 282 ff.

324 'I hope...' Let., p. 501.

324 'The operation...' Quoted, Pemb., p. 338.

325 'I am...' Quoted, Pemb., p. 96 f.

Notes and References

PAGE

325 'I said...' See facsimile of MS., Pemb., facing p. 340.

325 'That is...' MSV.

THE BIOGRAPHER EPILOGIZES

327 On burial. Pemb., p. 340.

327 Essential information. SFB., May 6, 1902.

328 *New York Times*. William L. Alden, in Book Review, May 31, 1902.

328 G. K. Chesterton. *Ways of the World, Pall Mall Magazine*, July, 1902.

328 *London Literary World. Table Talk*, Jan. 2, 1902.

328 *Academy*. Ed., May 10, 1902.

328 Watts-Dunton. *Bret Harte, Athenæum*, May 24, 1902.

328 'Bret Harte...' MSV.

328 'Men seemed...' James Douglas. *Bret Harte, Bookman*, July, 1902.

328 Howells. See Howells.

329 Mark Twain. Hut., p. 407.

329 Estate. E.g., SFCh., Jan. 3, 1903.

329 Misfortune. E.g., SFC., Aug. 29, 1905, Jan. 30, 1907.

330 Ambrose Bierce. *The Truth about Bret Harte, Anti-philistine*, Aug. 15, 1897.

331 Henry Adams. *Education of Henry Adams*, p. 385.

331 H. L. Mencken. *Characters not Plot live*. My clipping is from *Springfield Union*, Oct. 25, 1925.

331 *Reveille*. See edition of Harte's *Stories and Poems*, Oxford Univ. Press, 1915, *Intro.*, p. lxix; copies of the broadside are in the British Museum.

331 Boynton. H. W. Boynton, *Bret Harte*, London, 1905.

331 Merwin. Mer., pp. 284–87.

332 Translations. Since my notes on this subject are certainly far from complete, I refrain from publishing them. They are included in the notes which I have deposited in the University of California Library.

333 Frimley churchyard. Based on a visit to Frimley and a conversation with the verger.

INDEX

Index

Index

(369)

Index

Index

Index

France, Harte utilizes his experiences in, 315. *See also* Paris
Franco-Prussian War, 180
Franklin, Benjamin, his arrival compared to Harte's, 95
Freiligrath, Ferdinand, translates Harte's poems into German, 176, 224
Frémont, Elizabeth, quoted on Harte, 104
Frémont, Mrs. Jessie Benton, description of, 102; circumstances of her meeting Harte, 102, 103; her interest in Harte, 104, 107; obtains clerkship for Harte, 108; aids Harte, 114, 115
Frémont, Colonel John C., his house at Black Point, 103
Freneau, Philip, death of, 5
Friend of Colonel Starbottle's, A, quoted, 325
Frimley, 327, 334
Frohman, Daniel, negotiates for play based on *Luck of Roaring Camp,* 281; produces *Sue,* 313
Froissart, Jean, Harte reads *Chronicles* of, 22
Froude, J. A., Harte friend of, 220, 277, 332; Harte writes to, 250, 311; Harte receives invitation from, 251; Harte visits, 252, 307; speaks at Academy dinner, 260; at Academy dinner, 266

Gabriel Conroy, 110, 225–29, 237, 297.
Gadshill, 173
Garland, Hamlin, sees Harte in London, 319
Garrick Theatre, 314
'Gashwiler, Mr.,' 154
Gegenwart, 224
Genevieve, 66
Gentleman's Magazine, 328
George Eliot. *See* Evans, M. A.
Germaine, 281
Germany, Harte's popularity in, 224; Harte's first impressions of, 250, 251; Harte writes article on, 263; Harte leaves, 268; Harte considers living in, 291; Harte's writings published in, 293; Harte's opinion of, 309, 310; stories of, 315. *See also* under *Crefeld* and *Translations*
Ghosts of Stukeley Castle, The, 307

Gibson, William, vice-consul at Glasgow, 270, 271; Harte's letters to, 271; Harte's friendship for, 284, 286
Gilbert, John, plays *King John,* 13
Gilbert, W. S., Harte meets, 264
Gile, G. W., aided by Harte, 273, 274
'Giles Winterborne,' 325
Gillis, James, entertains Harte, 52, 53
Gillis, William, cited on Harte, 52, 53
Girl Who Ran Wild, The, 106
Gladstone, W. E., at Academy dinner, 266
Glasgow, Harte appointed consul at, 265; Harte visits, 268; Harte characterizes, 268; Harte takes over consulate at, 269; Harte's experiences as consul at, 270–74, 284–88; Harte considers bringing family to, 270; Harte's absences from, 271, 287, 288; Harte's reports from, 271, 272; Harte's relation to people of, 284, 285; poem written by Harte while consul at, 286; Harte leaves, 288
Goddess, The, 114
Gold Hill *News,* 135
Golden Era, Harte contributes to, 59, 63, 66, 74, 98, 99, 105, 106, 111, 112, 113, 114, 122; Harte ceases to contribute to, 77, 123, 124; history of, 97; Mrs. Frémont reads Harte's article in, 102; quoted, 117; Webb contributes to, 119; Stoddard contributes to, 120; Ina Coolbrith contributes to, 120; Adah Menken contributes to, 121; Mark Twain ceases to contribute to, 127; *Condensed Novels* published in, 148; policy of, 150; 'Lying Jim' employed by, 178
Good Words, 295
Grand Army of the Republic, 200
Grant, President, his message to Congress, 180
Graphic, The, 293
Grayson, A. J., Harte writes article on, 175
Greek, Harte's knowledge of, 20
Greenock, 272, 273
Greyport Legend, A, 206
Greytown, 30, 158
Griswold, Anna. *See* Harte, Anna Griswold

(372)

Index

Griswold, D. S., father of Anna Griswold, 112
Grub Street, 296
Gulliver's Travels, 21

H. C. B., pseudonym in *Outcroppings*, 135
Hamlin, Jack. *See* Jack Hamlin
Hampshire, 316
Hangtown (Placerville), 49
Hardy, Thomas, Harte meets, 264; Harte's appreciation of work of, 322, 325
Harper's Magazine, 239
Harper's Weekly, 292, 293
Harrogate, 275
Hart, Bernard, Harte's grandfather, 6, 7; marriages of, 7; career of, 7; supports Harte family, 19
Hart, Catherine Brett, Harte's grandmother, 6; marriage of, 7; sends Henry Hart to college, 8
Hart. *See also* under Harte
Harte, Anna Griswold (Mrs. Bret Harte), singer in King's Church, 112; ancestry of, 112; married to Bret Harte, 113; her difficulties after marriage, 113; domestic life of, 118; reads *Luck of Roaring Camp*, 163; dominant character of, 170; earns money by singing, 173; her part in the Chicago fiasco, 191; Howells quoted on, 197; character of, 204; consulted by Harte as to coming to Glasgow, 270; her relations to Harte, 282, 283, 290, 291, 306, 316; her improvidence, 299; comes to England, 316; at Harte's funeral, 327; her situation after Harte's death, 329
Harte, Eliza. *See* Knaufft, Eliza Harte
Harte, Elizabeth Ostrander, mother of Bret Harte, 5; character of, 6; married to Henry Hart, 9; in New York City, 19; her relation of, to Harte, 24; married to Colonel Williams, 29; in Oakland, 95; her opinion on Harte's marriage, 113; visits Harte, 220; death of, 220
Harte, Ethel, daughter of Bret Harte, birth of, 220; studies music, 317; at Harte's funeral, 327

Harte, Francis Brett (Bret Harte), birth of, 3; ancestry of, 5–7; name of, 10, 17; childhood of, 11–18; called 'Tubbs,' 12; reading of, 12, 21–23, 54, 66; runs away, 13; religious feelings of, 14–16, 66, 112; his relation to Roman Catholic Church, 16; his relation to Judaism, 16; his opinion of his father, 18; youth of, 22–29; education of, 20; his knowledge of Latin, 20; studies Greek, 20; influence of Dickens on, 22, 164; writes youthful verses, 23–24; writes *Autumn Musings*, 23; his feeling for children, 24, 45, 46, 316; has smallpox, 25; his interest in clothes, 25, 26, 61, 67, 201, 230; 319; makes New-Year's calls, 25, 26; his voyage to California, 29–33; his arrival in Oakland, 37; employed by Mr. Sanford, 39; his life in Oakland, 41, 42; his knowledge of Spanish, 42, 110; his opinion of Oakland, 42; teaches school, 44–46, 68, 72–73; his account of going to the mines, 46–48; his possible experiences in the mining country, 48–53; in Oakland, 54–55; employed as tutor, 55–57, 63, 67; employed as apothecary, 55, 60, 70; employed as expressman, 57–59, 68; contributes to *Golden Era*, 59, 63, 66, 74, 98, 99, 105, 106, 111–14, 122; uses pseudonym of *Bret*, 59; pseudonyms of, 59, 98, 100; in San Francisco, 37, 59, 60, 93–186; description of, 61, 93, 192, 249, 268–69, 319; in Union, 61–90; keeps diary, 63–69; his dislike of ministers, 66; his methods of writing, 67, 77, 172, 308, 311; touches of Byronism in, 23, 67; thinks himself in love, 68; consecrates 1858 to literature, 68; stories of his Indian fighting, 71, 303; characterized in 1858, 71; his social life in Union, 73, 74; works on *Northern Californian*, 75–90; contributes to *Northern Californian*, 76, 87; called 'The Junior,' 76, 79; in charge of *Northern Californian*, 76, 77; his reticence, 78; subscribes to Mount Vernon fund, 82; writes against Indian-killers, 87; leaves Union, 88, 89; his hatred of frontier brutality, 89; sympathy for weak creatures, 89, 316;

(373)

Index

Indians in stories of, 89; comes to San Francisco in 1860, 93; lodges on Commercial Street, 96; type-setter for *Golden Era*, 97; first uses signature *Bret Harte*, 98; his life in San Francisco in 1861, 100, 101; Mrs. Frémont's interest in, 104–07; his failure to enlist in 1861, 109, 110; employed in Surveyor-General's office, 110; serves on committee, 111; writes war poems, 112, 114; his youthful love-affairs, 112; attends Unitarian Church, 112; marries, 113; his difficulties after marriage, 113; employed in Branch Mint, 115, 140, 173, 281; poet-of-the-day, 115–17, 200–02; characterized in 1863, 117–19; becomes Secretary to Superintendent of Mint, 122; contributes to *Californian*, 125, 126, 127, 141; edits *Californian*, 126, 128; meets Mark Twain, 126, 127; edits *Outcroppings*, 130–39; plans book with Mark Twain, 139; his family life in 1866, 140, 141; writes *To the Pliocene Skull*, 142; contributes to *News Letter*, 149, 153, 176, 177; his attitude toward pioneers, 150–54; becomes editor of *Overland Monthly*, 155, 156; writes *Luck of Roaring Camp*, 163; as editor of *Overland*, 169, 174; friendship with Coolbrith and Stoddard, 169; his reputation in San Francisco, 170–72; his dialect poems, 175, 176; writes *Heathen Chinee*, 177–79; his situation in 1870, 183; offered professorship in University of California, 183, 184; leaves San Francisco, 185, 186; in Chicago, 189–91; his experiences in Boston and Cambridge, 192–97; his contract with Fields, Osgood and Company, 197; his mistakes in 1871, 199–202; visits Emerson, 202, 203; settles in New York City, 204; his relations with *Atlantic Monthly*, 206–08; his lectures, 209–19; his debts, 210, 214, 221, 222; spends night with the Aldriches, 212; lecturing tours of, 213; financial troubles of, 213; his trip into the South, 214, 215; his dislike for lecturing, 215–19; scandals about, 220–22; snobbery of, 221; writes *Gabriel Conroy*, 225–28; writes *Sandy Bar*, 229–30; collaborates on *Ah Sin*, 232–35; writes *Thankful Blossom*, 233–34; his friendship with Mark Twain, 236; his low condition in 1877–78, 238–45; appointed Commercial Agent at Crefeld, 245; leaves the United States, 249; his first impressions of England, 250; his experiences at Crefeld, 250–55; his lectures in England, 256–58, 265; asked to speak at Royal Academy dinner, 259, 260; his lack of confidence, 260; his reports to State Department, 261, 262, 272, 273; visits Switzerland, 262, 309; ill health of, 264, 274, 275, 281, 282, 299, 315, 316, 324–26; his relations to his family while in Europe, 264, 282, 283, 290, 291, 299, 306, 316, 317; appointed to Glasgow, 265; speaks at Academy dinner, 266, 267; leaves Germany, 268; characterized in 1880, 268, 269; takes over Glasgow Consulate, 269; as consul at Glasgow, 269–74, 283–88; his absences from Glasgow, 271, 287, 288; injury to, 274; his friendship with the Van de Veldes, 277–80; writes dramatizations, 280, 281, 297, 314; characterized in 1885, 283, 284; his life in Glasgow, 283, 284; his opinions of the Scotch, 283, 284; leaves Glasgow Consulate, 288; decides to remain in England, 289; goes to live with the Van de Veldes, 290; residence with the Van de Veldes, 291, 292; his association with A. P. Watt, 292–94; literary career of (1885–93), 292–98; Pettie's portrait of, 298, 299; characterized in 1893, 301–03; grants interviews, 302; his relations with Madame Van de Velde, 307, 316; later friendships of, 307, 308; takes trip to Continent, 309, 310; his romanticism, 310; collaborates on *Sue*, 312, 313; fallacies about, 315; characterized in 1895, 316; his Americanism, 289, 318–20; his work (1900–01), 321–24; writes operettas, 323; death of, 326; funeral of, 327; comments of newspapers on his death, 327; comments of reviews on his death, 327, 328; estate of, 329; opinions on his

Index

Index

Index

Index

Index

Index

Index

Index

Index

(383)

Index

Index